21 LAYERS of the SOUL

HEALING THE KARMIC TIES WITH FRIENDS, LOVERS, FAMILY AND ENEMIES

ANNEMIEK DOUW, MSc

SouLink Publishers, The Netherlands

ISBN 978-90-820891-0-3

Translation: Jörgen van Drunen, www.vertaalenzo.nl
Cover: Renee Duran, www.duranwd.com
Interior Design: Lynn Serafinn, www.spiritauthors.com
Editing and Proofing: Vrinda Pendred, www.vrindapendred.com
Author Photo: Peter Nugteren, www.prents-and-more.nl

This book is also available in electronic format.
Please visit www.annemiekdouw.com for details.

This book contains case studies from actual clients. However, all the names are fictitious and their situations have been altered so they cannot be recognized.

On the LAST page of this book you'll find a link to download a FREE poster of the 21 Aura Layers, suitable for framing.

Praise for 21 Layers of the Soul

"In 21 Layers of the Soul, Annemiek Douw writes from years of experience working with her rare gift. This book helped me understand our soul's journey better. It's a must-read for anyone interested in discovering more about their soul."

~ DR ROY MARTINA

Holistic doctor, bestselling author of *Emotional Balance*
www.christallin.com

"Reading The 21 Layers of the Soul was like discovering a trove of unexpected gifts within a gift. It opened up new self-insights and expanded my mind, heart and spirit. I'm eager for this book to get out there and reach the public. It will change people's lives."

~ BRENDA MACINTYRE

The Success Shaman
www.successshaman.com

"Annemiek Douw provides answers to the deeper questions we have about why we are living now, and how we encounter situations and people according the soul's journey. What are we supposed to learn? Her impressive presentation of over 100 cases of healing provide guidance for your journey, and you can have the same personal joy of completion. Enjoy!"

~ DR. CARON B. GOODE, ED.D., NCC

Author of *Raising Intuitive Children* and *Kids Who See Ghosts*
www.academyforcoachingparents.com

"Annemiek's statement 'Light is contagious' explains it all. She leads you through 21 Layers of the Soul with new discoveries of self and the journey within. This is a must-read for anyone on a spiritual growth path!"

~ VIVIAN BAXTER

Feminine Magic, Creator of "The Phenomenal Love Process"
www.extremesuccessnow.com

"For those seeking deep healing or answers about their soul's journey, 21 Layers of the Soul reveals enlightening insights regarding the human experience. This is a must-read for healers of all modalities and people pursuing wellness and joy."

~ **DANA TAYLOR**

Reiki Master, author of *Ever-Flowing Streams: Tapping into Healing Energy*

www.SupernalLiving.com

"If you are at all interested in metaphysical explanations to why your life unfolds as it does, Annemiek Douw has written a very easy-to-read and thorough book to enlighten and answer such unanswered questions from a spiritual perspective. I found her words to be comforting when it comes to explaining the harsh and painful events we all experience at one time or another."

~ **ROCHELLE GORDON**

Spiritual empowerment coach, author of *Body Talk: Why We Get Sick and Why It Need Never Happen Again!*

www.CoachRochelleGordon.com

"In 21 Layers of the Soul, author Annemiek Douw demystifies the esoteric of the soul and karmic ties and helps the reader understand these topics in very practical ways. Through stories, channeled information and a series of exercises, Douw presents the information in such a way that the reader feels both comfortable and empowered to explore and better understand their own soul's journey. This book is a definite tool in opening the door to self-knowledge for readers. I REALLY like this book!"

~ **JANET ROPER**

Animal communicator, host of talk2theanimalsradio

www.talk2theanimals.net

"21 Layers of the Soul is a must have for those searching for a deeper understanding of healing within the Soul level."

~ **ANGELA JEFFREYS**

Shamanic Teacher and Healer

www.bluecrowinspirations.com

"Truly impressive, Annemiek Douw provides her readers with a raw and conversational understanding of the soul and auras—all in the context of healing—using her own work and direct experience. The subsequent experience for the reader feels quite real and practical, as 21 Layers of the Soul effectively brings a framework for what many might consider overly elevated concepts to even attempt to understand ... well within reach."

~ **PAMELA MALINIAK**

Editor of *Breaking Free from Critical Addiction, 12 Weeks to Self-Healing: Transforming Pain through Energy Medicine* and others

"Annemiek Douw! This lady knows her own soul and understands how to help those in need with past life and auric problems. Her own story resonates with anybody who is close to spirit and has discovered their true path. She has a wonderful way of bringing you into her story."

~ **DENISE ROBERTS HART**

Spiritual medium, guidance counselor, spiritual coach, writer
www.deesinspirations.com

"In 21 Layers of the Soul, I discovered new tools to eliminate life-long back pain: I call on my guides to help remove past-life trauma! Thank you, Annemiek."

~ **ROBERT GLUCKSON**

Good Cause Marketing
www.goodcausemarketing.com

"21 Layers of the Soul by Annemiek Douw was written to give insight to the willing to awaken the giant--the soul--and assign our angel to work on our behalf. It's the vehicle of healing, control, influence and inner peace. If you desire inner progress, favor and help from higher and lower quarters, then you need to read this book. I recommend it to everyone."

~ **ISAAC AYODELE ADELEKE**

Media Consultant, Author and Life Coach
PFM Organisation & PFM Media, Nigeria

"As soon as I began to read 21 Layers of the Soul, I knew I had found what I'd been looking for. With depth and clarity Annemiek Douw shares her experience and wisdom. Anyone who is searching for answers and a deeper understanding of the soul's journey and how it's guiding you all the way, this book is for you. Annemiek Douw writes from her soul to yours."

~ **MAEVE CRAWFORD**

The Soul Mate Catalyst

www.becomingyourownsoulmate.com

"21 Layers of the Soul, is Annemiek Douw's personal story of her awakening to her full potential while giving a unique look into the many layers of the aura and how it directly relates to issues we all have in our lives. Through this understanding, she relates how she developed a powerful means of healing others so they too can live their full potential."

~**SUZANNE O'BRIEN**

Energy Healer, Pet Psychic, author of *A Heavenly Presence*

www.reikichicktraining.com

"Annemiek Douw, is a truly gifted healer and medium. In her amazing book, 21 Layers of the Soul, she shares how reading and working with auras will help you heal the traumas of past lives. Through this approach, she brings us personal a much-needed insight into the way we function in today's world."

~ **FLEUR HOLS**

Author of upcoming book *Without a Goodbye*

www.fleurhols.org

Table of Contents

Notes from the Author

Words marked with an asterisk (*) are explained in the Glossary.

Exercises marked with double asterisk (**) are in the Appendices.

All drawings are taken from my client notes, to show in which parts of the aura I worked or how the blockages looked.

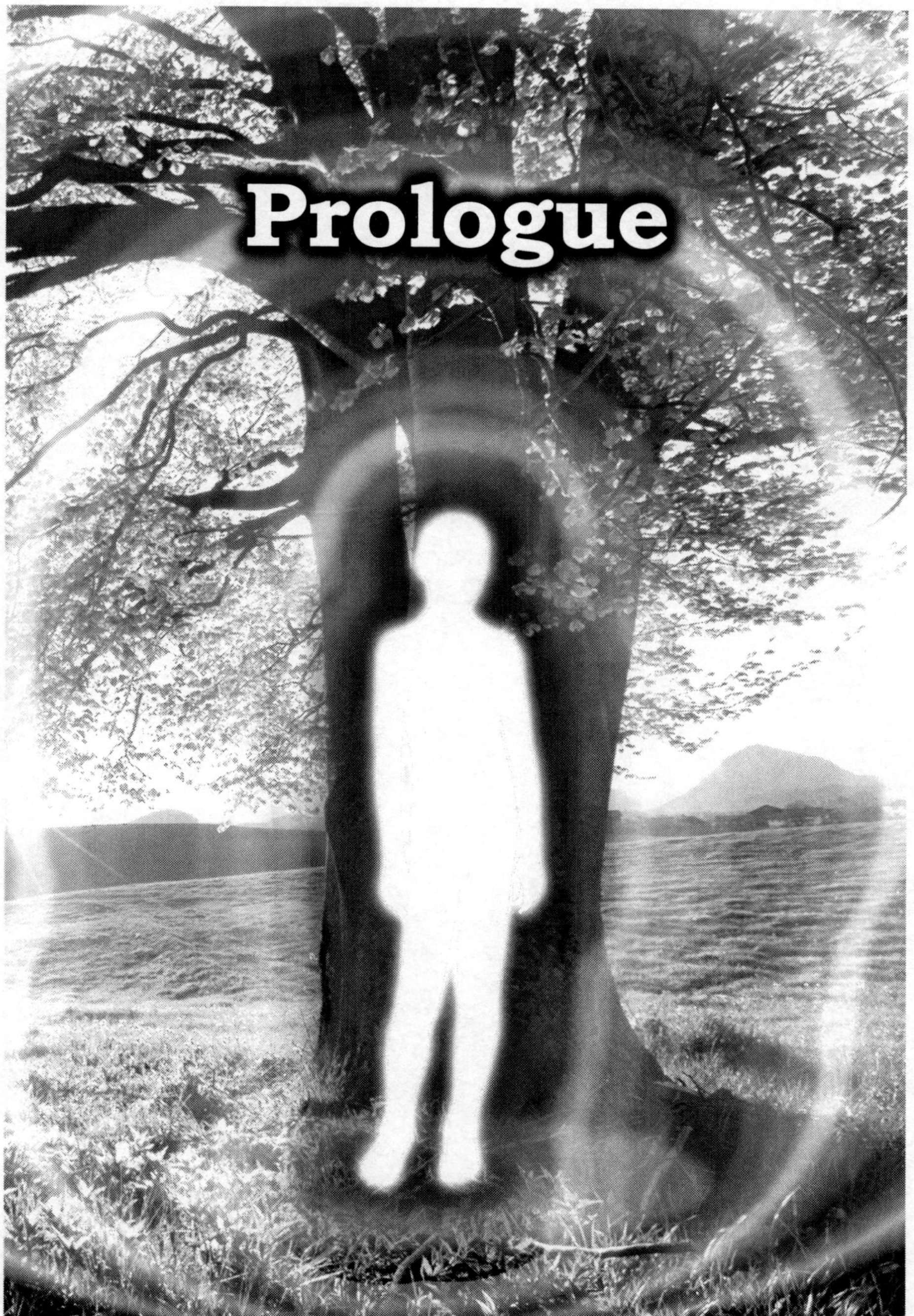
Prologue

Prologue

New information about the twenty-one layers of the aura, countless true cases from a medium's practice, a part of the writer's life story, a lot of 'technical terms' and esotericism – combined with angels, guides, the deceased, chakras, traumas and past lives. At first sight, they do not seem to have much in common, and yet they have: together, they are the basis of this book.

In this book, I will demonstrate how you – as a human and a soul – can grow and develop by living through the experiences you encounter, and by dissolving blockages if living turns out not to be so successful.

All these experiences can be found in the layers of your aura – of which there are no less than twenty-one. Because I come across the most beautiful things there every day, it was my dream to publish this book. I wanted to share my experiences.

The book is made up of three parts. In part one, I outline all the basic terms you will encounter, using examples from my own life. I originally worked in the business world, as an engineer. Then I discovered there is more between heaven and earth than what you can lay your hands on – a process that finally resulted in my retraining to become a paranormal therapist and practicing medium.

During this quest to find my own place in our society, I came across such terms as aura, chakras, karma, entities, soul agreements, Pleiadian Light Worker, medium and extra-sensory perception. And although I had previously been averse to 'jargon', in this case I have no option but to use them. Unfortunately, technical terms are not always univocal. Sometimes, different meanings are attributed to one term. Therefore, I explain these in part one, giving the generic meaning of each term and my personal interpretation. In addition, I give an outline of the background and creation of this book, why it was so important for me to write it and why I find these twenty-one layers of the aura so interesting.

If you are familiar with the terminology and not so interested in the background, you may want to skip ahead to part two. Part two starts by describing how a blockage develops in the layers of your aura. Subsequently, the twenty-one layers of the aura are unfolded, each in a separate chapter. For each layer I point out the meaning of the energy in that layer, and what the result could be if you know how to address and dissolve your blockages. I also give a number of examples for each layer of the aura, to illustrate how this theory works in practice, and I describe the way in which I work, what I perceive and what can happen in the practice of a healing medium.

The case studies presented in this book are all true. In respect of the eight most complicated cases, I have obtained explicit permission from my clients to publish their stories. In all cases, I have changed my clients' names to protect their privacy. One client said he considered it a gift to read his story again so many years later and stated, 'I am sufficiently disguised and I do not think someone will address me by Charles, [the fictitious name assigned to him].'

All other information detailed in these case studies – the method of treatment and the corresponding energy – is very real. Everything is based on experiences I have documented in my files. At the end of each chapter I have added, where necessary, remarks or overall conclusions I have drawn and comments to convert the individual practice to a more general perspective.

Part three contains the appendices. There you will again find, in alphabetical order, all technical terms and 'strange' words, including their meanings. In addition, this section contains the background information to which I refer in this book: the exercises, an illustration of the chakras (including their location and function), and a list of recommended reading and websites. A list of issues is also included. You may use this list to find a certain chapter in which the complaint is described by clients who consulted me.

I have designed this book to be read in whatever way you feel most comfortable with. You can follow my logic and start on page one; if you are already familiar with the subject, or you are not really interested in my personal story, you may want to start with chapter two; or, once you have read the entire book and know what you are looking for, reread parts about certain layers or cases based on the table of contents or the index. What I sometimes prefer is just to open the book and see what hits the eye and consider what it means. Let the Law of Synchronicity do what it has to do. Have faith that coincidence does not exist and see what that page will bring you.

No matter what you choose to do, I wish you a positive experience and thank you for reading this book.

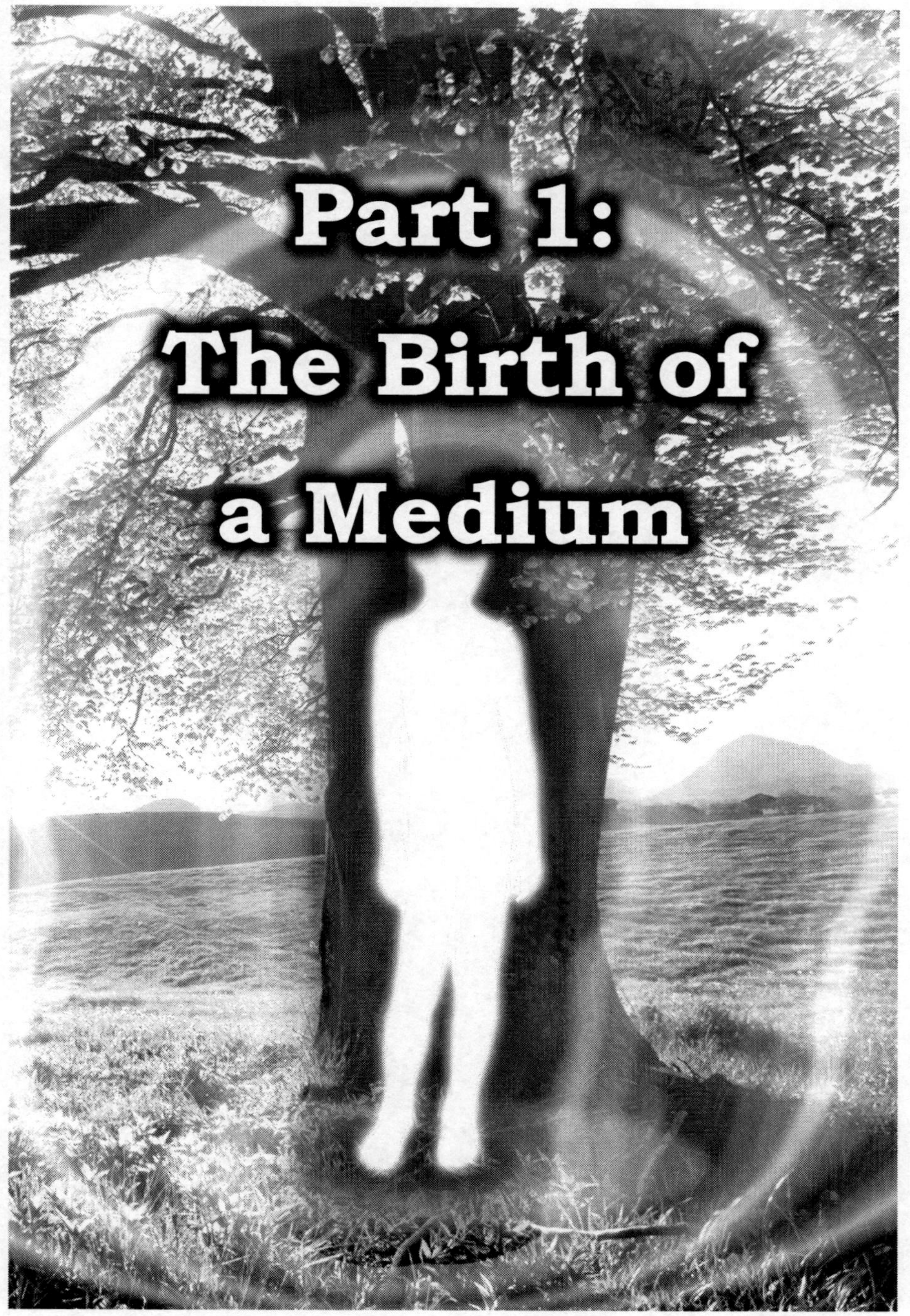
Part 1:
The Birth of
a Medium

The Beginning

With a supreme effort, I bend my right knee as deeply as possible and stretch my arm out as far as I can. I hit the ball with the very top of my squash racket and, for the first time in my life, score the winning point. Almost at the same time, I hear an ominous crack. I fall to the ground with a piercing pain in my ankle. Even as my 'winner' is blasted off the court, I'm brought down from the clouds.

Moments later, someone comes and puts an ice pack on my ankle to combat the swelling. Clearly, there's something wrong. Although I've become a master at ignoring the pain signals in my body, even I can't ignore this one. I can no longer stand on my foot and I must recover. My body has finally given up.

When my ankle ligaments tear, I am twenty-nine. I'm living with my boyfriend Serge and, after completing my studies in Training and Development at the Eindhoven University of Technology three years ago, I have already been making a nice career for myself. I'm working hard, taking a lot of pleasure in my job, and doing the 'right things'. The result is that I have moved in the right direction very quickly. In no time at all, I have received promotions and the world looks bright.

If this sounds like a well-structured and well-executed career plan, the reality is different. In fact, I simply follow the dictates of my heart and do what feels right to me. From a business perspective, my life has been exploding like a bomb. I first started working in government for the Ministry of Agriculture, Nature Management and Fisheries as a Training and Development Policy Adviser. Then I changed over to a job in the private sector as Training Adviser for the commercial divisions of the telecommunications company Ericsson. After that, I became an executive: the Competence Manager for the mobile phone division. Coaching, counselling, and supporting people all day long, in order to bring out the best in them, feels fantastic. Now I work more hours than the day is long, and I get a lot of pleasure out of it. For me, it has always been so important to treat the people I supervise and work with in a pure way, and I love to spend a lot of time on them.

At twenty-nine, I am very busy. In addition to the demands of my workload, my family members need my attention. One after another, they have turned seriously ill. Since I am a naturally caring person, I spend a lot of time with them as well.

But they're not the only ones with physical issues. I have been facing some physical challenges myself. Altogether, I have suffered seven concussions, one of which I got by tumbling down the stairs, an accident that also resulted in whiplash. I still have some lingering symptoms in my neck, but I've learned to live with them – or at least, I thought I had. There's too much to do for me to let pain derail me.

I try hard to work my way around the pain and stiffness, because it is not convenient for me to be bed-ridden; I need to keep going. But my range of motion is limited and complicates even the simplest of tasks. For instance, I can't raise my arm anymore when I want to blow dry my hair, so I bend my head forward. Such adaptive tricks help me ignore my discomfort for a long time. I don't want it to occupy my mind. My work and the way I am caring for my family keep me busy. I want to be there for others, not to have needs of my own.

Outside these obligations, I just want to spend time with Serge and my friends. I know I should practice a sport, because that is supposed to be healthy. So Serge and I started playing squash together, hoping to receive optimum results in minimum time – within half an hour, you can get pretty tired. This gives me the illusion that I am getting sufficient exercise.

In other words: I'm always busy and on the road. In fact, I have been rushing through life. Yet, I thought I was doing the 'right thing'.

My ankle thought differently.

The weeks after I injure my ankle are a reality check. For a whole month, I am dependent on others. I can't do anything by myself and need help for everything. I can't walk, others need to drive me, and everyone at work has to come to my office to have our meetings. I feel pitiful and frustrated and I don't understand why this should have happened to me. All day long I dutifully sit with my leg up, yet still there's no sign of progress. It seems as if my ankle doesn't *want* to heal.

I now visit the physiotherapist three times a week – outside office hours, of course – who finally gives me the biggest eye-opener of my life. After a month, I impatiently ask, 'When will my ankle start working again? I am scheduled to go on holiday in Tuscany in three weeks' time and I want to go hiking.'

His reply is, 'That will be a no-go.'

Feeling

John, the physiotherapist, looks at me and says, 'Annemiek, if you go on like this, your ankle will never function again. You act as if your injury doesn't exist. You have not accepted that there's something wrong. You're completely ignoring the signals your body gives you.'

I object to his assessment, because for days I have been obediently sitting with my leg up all day long and I consider this quite an achievement. But John continues unrelentingly.

'Your body is trying to make something clear to you,' he says, 'but you don't want to feel it. You've essentially amputated your leg below your knee by pretending there's nothing wrong.' My eyes fill with tears. Even though I'm trying so hard to understand what he is saying, I seem to miss the essence of the message.

I wallow in my miserable state for a few moments and then reply that I feel he's right, but I have no idea what I should do. John explains that although I do not want to feel the pain (in my opinion, that's only logical, but I swallow my words and try to listen anyhow), I should *go into* the pain.

Hearing this is more than I can bear. I don't see the point and think it makes no sense at all. 'To go into the pain' turns out to be a fancy phrase among physiotherapists meaning experiencing and feeling what you feel, while being totally focused on those sensations. And if that's painful, you will feel the pain.

Apparently, I'm a champion of the opposite style of coping. Sometimes I feel pain and I quickly focus on something else, to distract me – for instance, on thinking. I do that a lot, and often. And I'm very good at quickly thinking of something else, so that's a fantastic distraction from the things I prefer not to feel. In this way, both physical pain and emotional issues are easier for me to handle (read: easier to suppress and ignore). I can just pretend that pain and emotions aren't there. As far as I know, if I keep that up consistently and long enough, the problem seems to work itself out.

This has seemed to work for me – until my ankle, as the representative of my body, decided to confront me with the fact that I was turning myself into a complete wreck. Unfortunately, when I listen to John's theory, I am quick to understand that he is absolutely right. This is not nice at all, because suddenly I feel like a clumsy five-year-old girl who can't deal with the things she is confronted with in her life. In the usual course of events, I would repress that feeling by focusing on something else; but now that I see this is not the right thing to do, I decide to take the bull by the horns and allow myself to continue feeling what I am feeling. It is one thing to do something wrong because you don't know any better, but it is quite another to know it and keep doing it consciously – so I do something else. I continue feeling what I am feeling. That turns out to be a wise decision. And while the tears are still rolling down my cheeks, I ask John what to do, because I have a problem that, in my view, is a considerable one; that much is clear to me.

Fortunately, apart from his confronting approach, John has a way of solving my problem. He explains to me that the human body has a memory of its own, which it uses to store everything you experience. I recognize this: a relaxed conversation or a sunny weekend recharges my battery, while a nasty remark can cause stomach aches and difficult conversations can get stuck in my shoulders.

John hands me a book, *Op Weg Naar de Energetische Mens* by Flemish doctor Yvo van Orshoven, who runs a center that has been the subject of both positive and negative headlines in the press. I don't know this yet and I start reading. I am touched by what I read, because the book is about me. Among other things, it describes ways to step outside of yourself, or withdrawing inside yourself as a survival mechanism. It also describes an approach that consists of bioenergetics-like physical exercises and Bodywork (a collective term for a number of therapeutic techniques that work with the physical body in order to release blockages in the functioning of a person, which are often related to having the courage to feel one's emotions) – all kinds of things you do in order to be able to feel your body again. The writer calls it 'being perceptive'.

I realize I am struggling with a number of physical complaints, when I don't necessarily have to. So far, I have assumed my problems are a logical consequence of the things I have experienced; but if I let go of this assumption, I might improve a lot more than I think possible – that is, if I'm willing to look at the true cause of my problems.

Facing One's Fears

I feel a strong urge emerge and, before I know what I'm doing, I register for a training week and I'm talking with the physician who wrote the book. Although later it turns out that I can't really get along with him and I gradually develop objections to the way he works, I somehow also feel how important it is to turn myself inside out. So I go for it.

The next few months are tough: at least two days a week, from seven in the morning until eleven at night, I have to do things I find scary and difficult. For instance, although I have whiplash and difficulty using my arms, I have to walk about while carrying adults on my shoulders and I have to perform martial arts exercises. 'Go ahead and feel your fear, go through how you feel afterwards....' It turns out fighting isn't really my cup of tea.

My fear of heights becomes a source for exercises and several meters above the ground I walk across a tree-trunk and experience my fears. I have to jump down and feel the difference. I do it all, faithfully. I crawl through dark, narrow spaces and try not to think, otherwise I would panic. I prefer to close my eyes; it makes it easier to navigate that dark, claustrophobic corner. I don't understand, but I experience and I feel.

One frigid afternoon, I plough neck-deep through a mud swamp for hours and I almost start to like it. For the first time in this course, I feel relaxed, because I have stopped offering resistance against the situation I'm in – up to my chin in dung – until I realize there are all kinds of small creatures in the mud and think of what other filth I might stumble across. When I need to pee and decently hold my water, I'm told, 'Just let it go. What do you think the others who were here before you did?' Suddenly, it's not so funny anymore.

So that's how it works: if you relax and go with the flow, you can learn to feel good, whereas if you resist, everything will be ten times heavier. I find I may not always be able to influence my situation, but I *can* decide how I will handle it – and this gives me all the freedom and strength I could wish for.

Inner Peace

I also learn to meditate, which has proven to be the key to myself. Every morning, from seven until nine, we have to be in the training area to meditate and perform stretching exercises that help you to feel your body.

The first few months, meditating isn't exactly a success, being compelled 'to empty your head and think of nothing'. If I have to sit still, cross-legged, I get cramps everywhere. But after some time, I know what to do: offer no resistance and 'go to the pain'. I can still hear John say it. I decide to do it the Annemiek way, and that means with a touch of humor. So, privately I conduct whole discussions with myself while sitting in the lotus position and trying to make my head calm.

But my head doesn't want to be calm. It's much too busy being present and talking nineteen to the dozen. All kinds of thoughts tumble through it and, again, I feel I am desperately failing while sitting there among a group of people who all seem to be meditating serenely. It occurs to me that just as I have surrendered to the cramps, I should not resist thinking either – that I should accept this is simply the way I am. I should not give up yet.

I give myself permission to think about everything I want to, during those peaceful hours in the morning, and after some time, I notice silence entering my head. Apparently, it has lacked attention and now wants to keep control for a while in the new situation. Then I carefully put a toe in the meditation pool and, for a few seconds, it's silent in my head, and thus in my body.

It's such an overwhelming relaxed feeling that I think, *Wow, it's silent!*

And just as quickly as it came over me, it leaves me.

I start thinking again and I have to laugh at me, for now I know I can do it. Not easily, but I, too, have it in me to stop my thoughts, even if just for three seconds. And if I'm able to do it for three seconds, then there is hope, even for my busy head full of thoughts.

I diligently continue practicing. That short experience is followed by longer ones and, after a few months, I can meditate without effort. More than that, in my usual daily routine I set an hour aside each morning and each night, during which I lay a pillow on the floor, light some candles, burn my favorite incense, perform my stretching exercises and meditate. Sometimes I focus on an issue that has been troubling me and needs clarity, and sometimes I just empty my head and enjoy the stillness.

Meditation becomes important to me, but sometimes there just aren't enough hours in the day for it. So I decide to sacrifice an hour of sleep each night, to give myself that much-needed time to clear my head. It's a good move, for me. I'm fitter and I feel structurally better if I meditate regularly, which removes all tension from my body.

The so-called pain exercises, however, are quite a different story. Their purpose is to discover where in our bodies there's a knot, a hardening or a sore spot. We are then encouraged to work on that spot in such a way that it will hurt even more. The underlying thought is that the knot is a *blockage* caused by an emotional issue, and by torturing that spot, we can remove the old emotion. My whole being resists, but because I'm afraid I am again on my way to ignoring something, I complete all the exercises, although with healthy dislike.

The Big, Dark Secret

While exercising, I sense something inside of me, something I can only describe as a big, dark secret. But I don't have the nerve to tell anybody, for I feel ashamed and I'm afraid of how others might react. Fortunately, one day I meet a therapist not put off by my standoffish look, who recognizes that I am awfully insecure. And amidst a room full of people doing pain exercises and screaming, thus expressing their emotions, he quietly sits next to me in my corner and asks what's wrong with me. His energy is so pleasant that I relax. The funny thing is: the moment I see him, I feel happy and think, *Oh, there you are, at last!*

There you are, at last? I'm certain this is the first time I have ever met Jan, and yet I have the feeling that I've known him for a very long time. I am overwhelmed with the surety that he is the reason I had to go to this institute – we were fated to meet each other, and now he's going to help me.

A sense of peace comes over me. And although I've never consciously thought about it, this makes me realize that, in fact, I believe in reincarnation. Reincarnation means you live several lives; as a soul, you incarnate, so you are born again into a new physical body. Sometimes you immediately recognize souls with whom, in previous lives, you have had positive experiences. They give you a love-at-first-sight feeling – or at least the idea that you just met a very pleasant person. It is an impression that, at first, might not be based on anything solid.

In my situation, it's like a shade has been pulled up and all of a sudden I have clarity. For the first time in months, I trust somebody. But I can't bring myself to put it into words yet, so I stammer that there is something, yes, but I'm afraid of feeling it and therefore cannot identify what it is. Jan accepts this response and stays with me for some time. I find myself thinking, *I don't have to face it all by myself* – and that's just what I need.

That experience proves to be the beginning of the end, for two important things happen to me. I begin to realize that all the pain and emotions surrounding me have been driving me nuts, since I feel them in my own body too. For instance, my head starts to ache above my left ear. Then someone tells me he too has a headache, right above his left ear. I get menstrual cramps, but I don't have my period. The next moment, my table companion tells me her belly aches, and I realize I am sensing her pain. Stomach ache, grief, fears – I feel them all and although I have never thought about it before, it hits me that I am clairsentient.

It explains a lot, for in my head I have always been inundated by images of situations that were unfamiliar, and yet made me feel such strange things; my inner moods changed so rapidly. Now I understand: I have been seeing glimpses of future and past experiences of others; I picked up their emotions and thought they were mine. One might expect this revelation to surprise me, but it makes sense to me. *I'm not an instable person; I'm just paranormal*, I think. No wonder I preferred not to feel anything as a child. I absorb so much and can't handle it, and the only way I've ever known how to cope has been to ignore and 'park' the feelings. Very effective.

The reason this all happens at once is that I have decided that from now on, I will allow myself to feel and experience everything again. And so I regain access to my paranormal abilities. But at the same time, the nightmares begin and my old memories surface. It soon becomes clear to me that it's impossible to feel one thing and ignore another. So you can't say: I feel the nice things and I let the misery pass me by. That's not how it works, for there is no middle course. You either accept it all or you accept nothing.

I accept it all and soon my memory returns, though I didn't know I had lost it to begin with. With the help of seven concussions, I have been able to block things out for years. But now all those repressed images, thoughts and feelings suddenly flood my mind, and I must be ready for them.

I remember the time when I was camping in France and went for a walk near the stables. I could see the hay, hear the horses snort, see the sunlight filtered through the leaves and smell the scents of the animals. I remember making the decision to never, never, never again think about this. I would just pretend it never happened to me. But now I can't do that anymore.

'It' is the fact that I was sexually abused. The first time it happened, I was a very young girl. The next time, I was seven, and the next, I was sixteen. That last time, the abuse came at the hands of a holiday 'lover' who wouldn't take no for an answer and who was physically stronger and simply forced me.

It's horrible. After my campsite memories, gradually all pictures resurface one by one, and with the pictures, the physical pain and corresponding emotions emerge, too. I know this time I just have to see them through, look at them and feel what I feel. And that's not easy. I feel terrible, as if the solid ground has been swept away from beneath my feet. I no longer recognize myself, although I've always thought I know myself pretty well, and I'm afraid I 'put away other important things'. I thought the only things I really struggled with were my parents' bad marriage and their subsequent divorce, the fact that my sisters and my mother have fallen ill and the ponderous relationship with my father. I've also never considered myself beautiful and, as a result, I've struggled with deep insecurity, but I thought that was about it. In fact, there turns out to be a lot more. For years, I have been dishonest with myself by blocking things. Now I am afraid that rather than being strong, I have been a coward.

I'm so ashamed of what happened that, at first, I don't dare talk about it. In fact, I think I should have been able to prevent it. *Stupid girl.* In other words: I pass a hard judgment on myself, which isn't really helpful for my process to cope with things. Thank God I get help from Jan, the therapist, who is of the same mind and lets me do things my way. He makes sure I know he's there. But during the hours when I'm by myself, the pictures and nightmares continue to assault and I struggle not to be swallowed by them. I try to feel and go through the grief and the pain, and at the same time try to realize that it's 'just' my past – that I am in the here and now, that *it* is over and, particularly, that I must keep my mind clear. I promise myself that from now on, I will accept everything I come across, and not park anything anymore. And I live up to my word.

Later, I learn that memory blocks following trauma are a positive protective mechanism of the body: it (temporarily) influences your memory so you can focus your energy on healing, rather than reliving the trauma. Compare it to a serious accident, when you can remember everything until the moment of the big bang, and the next thing you know, you're waking up in the hospital. It rarely happens that such a hole in your memory is a conscious choice of your conscious mind. Usually, the inner wisdom of your body knows how much you can take and which part is too much for you to cope with at that moment, and then it retains that information. So in fact, your body is your best friend. And in my case, I did not serve that friend well by judging her so hard.

The Soul and Its Seemingly Incomprehensible Path

The period that follows drains me of energy. I work full days and am forced to accept that I really was a victim – and that there's nothing wrong with that. At the same time, I learn to manage my paranormal gift. The victim part turns out to be my biggest handicap: I don't want to be a victim and I can't deal very well with the sympathy and compassion I receive upon sharing my story with others. While I know people mean well, their pity causes me to feel even better how hard I've been put to it, and that's difficult for me. And compassion makes me rebellious; I feel belittled and patronized, which causes me to become recalcitrant.

It takes a while before I realize there's a big difference between *victim behavior* (using or abusing your situation as a victim, as an excuse for your own misbehavior, or not taking responsibility for your own life) and *being a victim*. The latter is simply what you are. It's a fact and it says nothing about the way you deal with that.

My meetings with Jan make me realize that every person is in fact a soul in a human body. As a soul, you choose to incarnate as a human being, to gain experiences and, if possible, to learn or to grow. By really experiencing all kinds of situations (and not pretending they do not exist, like I once did) you extend your consciousness and the quality of your energy cloud changes, usually for the better. You also radiate that energy, and others can perceive that.

Every soul has certain qualities and a certain starting level at which it begins to live its live. Therefore, I do not believe in the notion that a child is born as a *blank slate*. However, I do think there are older and younger souls – that is, souls who have incarnated several times already and souls who are relatively new to life here on Earth.

Depending on what you would like to experience, before you start your path of life and inhabit a human body, you design a suitable life plan, a master plan. By doing so, you choose a life with certain life themes.

Life themes are different kinds of experiences that will be hard to take at first and, as a result, you will find them unpleasant. Time and time again, you will come across those themes, until you are able to deal with them differently and have learned your lesson. In this way, you grow steadily and get more and more balanced. And that balance is the aim, for if you are balanced, you have created awareness.

The moment I come to my personal conclusion that, at soul level, I apparently opted for the chain of being abused, I become very calm. My inner struggle comes to an end. I regain my power. I realize that, as a human being, I never would have chosen these events, but that it's different at soul level. While I have always shown compassion toward others and I hardly ever passed judgment, I never showed compassion to myself and I passed judgment whenever I could. If I really wanted to know what compassion is, apparently I had to experience bad things myself, denounce myself for it, live through it, and subsequently feel that compassion for myself – quite some lesson.

I also discover that I do not have to blame anyone. In fact, I never blamed anyone but myself, but now I can stop doing that. I realize the pain I was dealt was all written in my life plan, long before I even took this body. And if that's true, then my part of that plan was, too. To a certain extent, the abusers were like actors in a play we had agreed to see through. If they had not been there to hurt me, someone else would have taken on that task – for it had to come from somewhere – because it was an experience I chose to undergo at soul level and I needed to live through it, one way or another.

I should stress that I do not mean offenders do nothing wrong and nobody should be held responsible for grievous behavior. I only mean to say that, for me, besides the earthly way of looking at things, another way becomes visible, which enables me to cope better with all my memories and sorrows. And that's what gives me back my power. If I created that pain myself, at soul level, it stands to reason that I also have the tools to deal with it.

You start your journey fully equipped for your path and tasks. You do not start an impossible task, because in that case, as a soul, we would not agree to play this game. That's one of the rules. And so I start trusting myself more and more. I no longer doubt whether I will get through, but rather consider the best way to do it. When I reach that point, I'm certain I will fully recover.

My conclusion and anchor is: no matter how difficult life can sometimes seem, everyone is able to cope with the challenges his or her specific life offers. You are always sufficiently equipped and you are able to deal with everything life will offer you. Truly knowing that grants you access to your unique powerful force. It's a primal notion that makes every situation easier. Maybe you haven't got a clue yet how you will get through, but searching your path *is* your very path. It's not about the final result; it's about what you do while you're on your way there.

I do not believe that at the end of my life, I will have to give an account of what I have accomplished up to that point and that I will fail or pass. I have let go of that idea, for it no longer makes sense to me. Instead, I think the measure of my life is the consequences of the decisions I make, the way I treat other people, how I overcome my own difficulties and how much I love others.

That can be done; I can handle that. I can work on that every day, and if, unexpectedly, someday things do not turn out as well as I'd hope, there's nothing wrong with that. If I divide that big chunk that's called Life into smaller pieces, I can deal with everything that comes my way. I'm convinced of that. And if I can do it, everyone else can do it too, for why would there be different rules to the game for me and for others?

I have also found that deep inside, I know exactly what's right for me, and that my body is my best ally in this field. It tells me what suits me, it feels when something is good for me (my signal is that it's perfectly quiet inside of me), and once I dare to feel its signals and take them seriously, a new world opens up for me. Then I go with the flow, instead of fighting it. That saves a lot of energy and it feels so much better. And if I also realize that the entire universe pulls together to support my soul path as well as it can, it comes to mind that not only does it feel good, but it's also pretty clever to live in agreement with my soul, the purest part of me.

Things are coming my way, and what I used to call 'coincidence' no longer exists. Synchronicity enters my life. And like I said before (and this is confirmed by twelve years of practice), the same rules of the game are true for you and me, so *your* body is your best ally too, and the universe is helping you too, in following your soul's path.

Of course, I have also regularly exclaimed, *It may be true that I happened to create this myself at soul level, but as a human being, I don't agree at all! It does not make me happy.* But I've learned that's also true. I continue to be responsible for what I do with my life, especially how I prefer to deal with what I experience, and that's my trump card.

In addition to reclaiming my ability to create, I embrace another motto: if something seems to be meaningless, you can still *make* it meaningful. Even if later, it turns out that my model of how incarnations function isn't right, I still think: if it is supportive in a positive way, and it doesn't hurt anybody, it's fine for me to live by it.

Even if you have horrible experiences, you can surpass them; they can help you grow and you can move beyond them. And if later it turns out there was no greater purpose behind those experiences, I still think it's wise to get past them, learn from them and grow as a person. To me, what is most important is that we grow from, rather than being engulfed by, our challenges.

I am now at peace with my past. I'm able to look at it differently compared to when I started my therapy.

I take my mother into my confidence about two years later, and admit the reason for my trips to Belgium. I was never able to do that before, because I was still busy dealing with the trauma and grief. But now, I tell her about my memories, and she confirms their truth. But she had no idea just what had happened and my admissions shock her. I'm glad that, by this point, I'm able to be concerned about her. The fact that I am mostly healed enables me to understand her pain and sorrow, for it becomes clear to me that my mother would have rather experienced the abuse herself than learn it had happened to her child. She feels guilty for not interfering, but I understand it happened at a time when people did not realize something like that could really happen. I don't blame her.

She finds it hard to come to terms with my story, and I see that everybody must deal with what is his, but fortunately you can help somebody in that process. The very fact that I have never blamed anybody for anything allows me to try to talk my mother out of her guilt, and I share what I have discovered about the soul and its path. It helps, a little.

Although my mother and I love each other very much, we do not say 'I love you' very often. We use these words very carefully. Once, we agreed that we would live these words; we think that's more important. And seldom have I felt her love for me more strongly than through her sorrow for me during the moments we talk about the abuse afflicted upon her little girl.

A New Beginning

Back to the training area, while I perform pain exercises with other participants, I discover something else that is new to me: if I touch people, my hands start to flow. I, who have been so nicely detached, suddenly become quite a different person. I touch others and allow them to come closer to me. Under my hands, people fall asleep and if group members are hurt while exercising, I can remove the pain from their bodies with my hands.

Suddenly I understand why I took such a dislike to pain exercises. There is a much softer way. Most people have already been knocked senseless by the things they have experienced and the blows they have received. Do you really have to 'help' them by hurting them even more? Most people respond much better to softness. Really open up your heart to someone else and you will see him or her break up into a thousand pieces and all the sorrow will emerge. With this revelation in mind, I learn to touch people only where there is a blockage and I do not press anymore. I simply put in a little bit of energy and love and let the other person respond. My way of working has been born.

I register for a one-year course entitled 'Energetic Management', specifically designed for managers, aimed at locating blockages (things that settle themselves in your body) and their underlying causes. I register because I expect it will help me a great deal in my work. I also start a three-year training course in Paranormal Therapy at the Academie voor Natuurgeneeskunde Zuid-Nederland*.

This latter course is completely new to me. I focus all my attention on my intuitive development and gain more in-depth knowledge of the relationship between physical, emotional and mental complaints. I develop a sound medical basis for my work and want to acquire further skills in the field of extra-sensory perception, as well as how to perform an energetic diagnosis. After that, I go on to learn how to write treatment plans and how to heal people energetically, so that I can support people even better in cases of illness. I start to let my hands do their work.

By 1998, in addition to performing overdue self-maintenance, I want to learn how to handle everything I paranormally see, feel and sense in other people wisely, because sometimes it's like reading their personal diaries. And after all, I supervise quite a large group of people and I want to do that with integrity.

But I don't want to become a therapist. I just want to be able to handle all the information I pick up on. In fact, I'm afraid to admit to people that I am paranormally gifted. I am not even sure it's a 'gift'. A gift is something you are happy with. My paranormal abilities are qualities I know I need to develop. It's hard work and it costs a lot of my time, energy and endurance. So no, I don't consider it a gift.

And I worry I will be laughed at in the business world in which I live and I fear it may harm my reputation. So I don't say anything – and yet the very day I start my ANZN-training, I'm suddenly dismissed by Ericsson. I'm amazed at how calmly I take this news, and I say to my soul: *Things did not go as quickly as you wanted, did they? I was looking around and applying for jobs, wasn't I?* But my soul had another, better idea (as it usually does) and created a situation where I could leave with a nice compensation package. That's the advantage if you have to leave without a well-founded story.

I suddenly have the time and money to study. I can finally do everything I really want to do. That sounds more pleasant than it actually is. At first, the walls seem to close in on me, for I am still used to doing a lot in little time, but now there are hardly any appointments in my agenda and just vacuuming the room takes hours. It leaves me with plenty of time to deal with what is left of my abusive past, and that's just what I do.

I also find that I sell well on the job market. I'm surprised about that, because I wouldn't personally see being dismissed as a good thing. To this day, I still don't know the reason I was let go, and that's pretty hard to handle. Yet the people who interview me for jobs interpret what happened quite differently when they hear the whole story. 'In your profession, it's an advantage if you've been through a thing or two yourself and don't just have book knowledge.' So to them, dismissal has its advantages too. It makes me feel better, and I agree with them.

But at the same time, I realize none of these jobs will give shape to the integration between head and heart that I'm now seeking. They can't help me achieve my new goal to live (or start living) with heart and soul. And when I get a good job offer, I hear myself decline, saying I've just decided to do it my way from now on.

And so I start my own consultancy and coaching firm. My activities include supporting struggling management teams, coaching individual managers, supervising transformation processes in organizations and helping people cope with long-term illness, as well as helping them reintegrate following their recovery. As part of this process, I assist their managers in adopting a human-focused approach to high level absenteeism. In this way, I put into practice all that I have learned on my training courses.

Psychometrics and Extra-Sensory Perception

The academy taught me how psychometrics work and I use that frequently. Psychometrics is sensing, without saying a word, what's going on inside a person, physically, emotionally, mentally and spiritually. By doing so, you can make an energetic diagnosis. I discovered the various forms of extra-sensory perception: clairvoyance, clairaudience, clairsentience, clairsmellience and clairknowing. These forms are collectively known as extra-sensory perception.

I learn to develop my inner perception skills by consciously attuning to the auras of others around me. Your aura is the energy field within and around your body. You can liken it to those Russian nesting dolls, matryoshkas. Around the smallest one, there is a bigger one, followed by one that is even bigger, and so on.

My personal interpretation is that your physical, most visible body is the smallest doll (first layer), surrounded by a number of other 'dolls'. Each doll has the same contents as its smaller predecessor, but it also has an extra layer. The illustration above shows those layers.

For instance, the second layer contains your emotions and the third one, your thoughts. Each layer has its own color (the colors of the rainbow, red, orange, yellow, green, light blue, indigo, and purple – starting with red next to the body). Each layer has its own field, and each field has its own themes.

All day long, all kind of things are happening in your body. The same is true for the surrounding layers that consist of more subtle energies, for they reflect what is happening in your inner body. If you can perceive the layers of the aura, you are able to understand somebody at various levels and help that person from that perspective.

This concept forms the basis of this book. If the energy in a certain layer can't flow due to a blockage, it causes a lot of inconvenience for you as a person and it influences your functioning and your life. But this can be remedied. You could compare reading auras, and thus inner perception, to using a fiber optic cable: you can use the information sent through it to watch TV, for instance, or to surf the Net, to make a call or to Skype. The device, the medium you attach to it, determines what you can do with the available information. The same is true for the human being and his energy. It depends on who observes, reads and receives that energy and converts and translates it.

So, which 'device' processes the information from the aura? Not everyone is equally equipped or puts in the effort to develop his abilities, just like not everyone who kicks a ball now and then has the potential to become a top football player. I, however, set to work enthusiastically. At first, I'm mainly clairsentient. I feel every little ache, every tension and emotion, though I still have to learn where all organs and systems are located in the human body, and work out the meaning of the things I perceive. I notice I have a talent for the emotional, mental and spiritual problems of others. I easily sense emotions and I'm quick at observing when someone's thoughts are guiding him in the wrong direction. I also realize that, with respect to spirituality, I like helping people (re)discover their paths in life. At the academy, they did not teach that spiritual part; I taught myself, because I have a great liking for it. And if I help people in that field, it goes without saying that I do not decide anything myself. I do not tell them what their path is; I simply attune to and cooperate with their soul.

I am clairvoyant in the sense that I see probable scenarios and I am able to assess future developments. Or I see, for instance, images that make it clear to me what the problem is and where it originated. And of course when I treat people, I see the aura and the blockages it contains. It bears great resemblance to a translucent underwater world. It sometimes reminds me of sea anemones and other plants that sway with the current below the water surface.

I'm not clairsmellient, except when my deceased favorite grandmother comes to visit me. That's when I sometimes smell a very special kind of incense, but other than that, I hardly ever have smell experiences.

I am clairaudient, however, in the sense that when someone says something, I sometimes think, *Are you listening to what you're saying? You've already found the solution to your problem yourself.* In such a case, it's like I'm hearing in capitals and know exactly what is most relevant in their story, and sometimes I 'just know' certain things. That is called clairknowing; it's like a thought that suddenly pops up and, deep inside, you just know it's right. Of course, in the beginning I always check such 'clair-perceived' things numerous times before I have the nerve to say them out loud, for I'm afraid my imagination is perhaps a bit too vivid, but time and again it turns out that I'm right. It's a weird and wonderful experience.

I make it a habit to check what I perceive clairvoyantly by asking the person with whom I'm working questions. It looks like an ordinary, lively and interesting conversation between two people, with me being a good listener who is interested and keeps asking questions. In fact, that's what it is. It's just that I go on asking more quickly than I did before and usually I only ask questions about things that really matter.

On My Own

Right before the start of my last study year, Serge and I cut our ties. Things aren't working out anymore between us and our different views on life have started to pull us apart. It's an amicable separation, and as I go through the grieving process, it strikes me that love is timeless. We might not have worked romantically in the last couple of years, but I still love Serge. There is even a moment, eight months later, when I realize that now that we are no longer a couple, I love him even more than I did when we were together. I no longer expect anything from him; I just love him. It's a precious thing when you have known someone who will, in some way, always be a part of you, just because you love(d) each other so very much.

In the meantime, my life goes on and I graduate. I write a dissertation on the psychological impact of sexual abuse and I start to understand myself even better. I thought my experience was an abnormality and I blamed myself for it. But my research teaches me that if, as a child, you have been abused by several people, you usually blame yourself.

The logic behind this is that if it happens once, the abuser may be at fault; something horrid took place, but there are still so many grown-ups who are indeed friendly that the world is still a safe place to be. If it happens several times, however, or by people who should be looking after you, it's natural to convince yourself that it must be your own doing. You would rather blame yourself and hold onto the illusion that you live in a safe world, than have to acknowledge that some people are cruel and your safety is at stake. This is especially so when the abuse occurs at an age when you are unable to look after yourself and your safety depends upon the same grown-ups who did those things to you. When understood from that perspective, it seems you have no other choice than to blame yourself. And as I read this, another piece of the puzzle begins to fall into place. At last, I can stop feeling guilty *completely*.

After finishing my studies, there's a shift in my work toward energetic coaching and treating people. I continue reading, studying and searching, and I work mainly in aura layers 1 through 4, the physical, emotional, mental and spiritual layers. I also start working on the meridians and the chakras.

Meridians are energy channels that are also used in acupuncture. These are a kind of conveyor belt through which energy is transported to and from an organ. This comes from your aura layers, working its way through your nervous system and back again. Meridians work together and if one of them gets stuck somewhere, usually – after some time – the whole energy system gets jammed and you may suffer physical discomfort.

Chakras are your energy sources, a kind of distribution center that sends the energy to all parts of your body. If you imagine that the meridians are the highways your energy use to move on, then the chakras are the interchanges, and some of them are more sensitive to congestion than others.

So I continue developing myself and discovering new things, and I'm pleased with the way things are going, for it's quite a switch – from business yuppie to paranormal therapist.

My life is totally different from what it used to be: I mostly eat organic products and vegetarian meals, because that's what my body seems to want. I meditate often, I spend hours walking in the woods and getting in touch with the Earth and nature, and I feel great. My friendships become even more profound and my pace is more natural, no longer forced and stressed. I'm still sometimes boisterous, but the big difference is that I stay calm inside.

Despite my deep insecurity and tendency to stay on the safest side of life, I manage to let go of all my certainties and safety nets, such as a relationship, a permanent job and a regular life. I have chosen the path that, in my opinion, is the best one, but not the easiest one. I embody my sunny self. I feel good, stable. My head and heart are well-balanced and perfectly in sync with each other. Most of the time, I am happy, and I hope my vision of how life works will turn out to be true in practice. I am in joyful anticipation of things to come – but first I will be forced to face a major test.

The Big Change

It's November 2, 2004, and the whole world is startled. Theo van Gogh is murdered in Amsterdam, stabbed to death by someone who takes offence at his statements.

I hear it on the radio as I drive home after my visit to the family doctor. Later, that date acquires quite a different undertone for me. It starts with a lingering bladder infection, the reason for my visit to the family doctor on that second day of November. I turn out to be allergic to the prescribed medication and my body responds fiercely. I start to vomit, develop a high fever and experience pain in every muscle of my body, especially my neck – which has not given me trouble for years after the period I spent in Belgium, as long as I sufficiently relaxed and meditated regularly – and my head nearly explodes from the pain. I'm so tired that I can't keep on my feet any longer and I cancel all my appointments. It's the beginning of a period of illness that will last three-and-a-half years.

The first two years, my mental functioning worsens until I can't read anymore. Soon after that, I almost lose my power of speech. I can hardly maintain a conversation, because I no longer understand other people's words. My ears are still functioning alright – in fact, I'm oversensitive to acoustic stimuli – but I can no longer process the meaning of what I hear. Something in my head is not functioning properly anymore. It's horrible and scary and I'm confused because I didn't see it coming. Secretly, I think I must have done something wrong and overlooked certain signals. Later, that turns out not to be true, but during these early months, I torture myself with self-blame.

By putting myself under my own critical eye, I find that my (normally) rather non-judgmental view somehow got affected by my study at the academy and I fall into an old pitfall: blaming myself. For many years now, I have been looking beyond disorders and into the causes. If a person's ear is not functioning, what is it that he cannot or does not yet want to hear? If someone has a stomach ache, what is it that is difficult for him to digest? Thus, without noticing it, I start to assume that if someone has a disease, he must be doing something wrong. The body then gives a signal and he will fall ill.

For the first four layers of the aura, in which I have usually worked up until this time, this way of observing brings you a long way. But if I could fall so seriously ill myself, without any discernible cause, I realize there must be a greater reason than me simply overlooking something. There must be other reasons for illnesses in general.

I delve deeply into the subject and find that, as a soul, you sometimes choose to fall ill, as a way of developing yourself. Illness no longer has a stigma then, and it should never have had a stigma in the first place. Nothing is ever 'your own fault', you are never to blame for incest or whatever difficult situation you encounter in your life, you are not responsible as a human being and truly no one is to blame. At most, it's a way, a path your soul has chosen and created to gain certain experiences. When looked at from this perspective, I find myself unable to do anything other than treat people who have made such brave choices, at soul level, with the deepest respect.

The moment I become fully aware that my illness is a choice of my soul, I try to make contact with my soul and attune to it every day, to feel and to understand why things that happen do happen. It proves to be a great help.

What's painful is that the whole universe seems determined to make me get through it all alone. I live by myself, and because I'm ill, contact with other people is reduced to the bare minimum. If I were to slip and fall in the bathroom or something like that, it could take weeks for someone to find me. Therefore, my best friend and I agree that she will be my window to the world. We call each other every second or third day (sometimes the only thing I say is, 'I'm still alive, but I'm too miserable to talk, ok?') and that seems to work out fine. But after six months, she sends me a cool note in which she ends the friendship, without further explanation, and simultaneously gives me notice to leave the office space I have been renting from her. I have no idea why she is doing such a thing.

Unbelievably, my world collapses even further: my relatives also show very little support and understanding. Almost everyone I have ever trusted, even those for whom I have always been a tower of strength, appear not to notice that it's about me now. It's a tough wake-up call and it takes everything I have in me to guide myself through this process properly; to cope with this and not become bitter. Dr Phil would say, 'Don't invest more in a relationship than you can afford to lose.' Apparently, I've gone too far, time after time. One day, I will realize that being so lonely was the only way to explore myself so deeply, to grow on a soul level. In fact, it will turn out to be a blessing in disguise, but honesty will compel me to admit that as I lived through it, it didn't feel that way at all.

Meanwhile, nobody, regular or paranormal, can tell me what's wrong with me. The family doctor is slipping and misses the signals that are, in fact, so obvious – and the internist finally makes the diagnosis: Chronic Fatigue Syndrome. He wishes me good luck and says I must accept my condition for the rest of my life; I will crawl from my bed to the couch and back again. I'm indignant at this remark and don't agree with him at all, because I am well up to speed on this topic due to my work and I refuse to be pigeon-holed. As sick as I am, I still feel what's right.

Down in the Dumps

The turning point comes two years later, when I recall one of my mother's friends. My mother is at the art academy and one of the members of her group, Christophe, is a few years younger than me. When he was seventeen, he dived into shallow water and broke his neck. The result was a spinal cord lesion – paralyzed from his neck down. Now he is in a wheel chair and can't use his arms and legs, and he needs help with everything he does. Nevertheless, he is at the art academy and paints the most beautiful works of art with a brush in his mouth.

I can't bear to think about it, and yet I do. Christophe's spinal cord lesion is at the exact same spot where my whiplash was, vertebral joint C4-C5, and after my fall, I learn that cartilage is missing in my neck. Also, a few things in my neck have moved and I am allowed to see it all on x-rays. It's called demonstrable residual damage. C4-C5 is one of the lower vertebral joints of the neck, and since the whiplash, my neck is no longer able to perform part of its function properly: keeping my head upright. It has become instable. Of course, my body wants to keep my head in place and so it automatically starts to compensate. You can compare it with a stack of cups and saucers. If the penultimate cup is askew on its saucer, you must pile the dishes on top of it slightly in the opposite direction, so that the whole stack is well-balanced. Otherwise, the stack tumbles to pieces.

However, my neck does not want to let my head tumble, and it succeeds by tightening my neck muscles harder than usual. As a result, my other vertebrae are subjected to pressure too, and thus are no longer well organized and in place. Consequently, some nerves and other muscles get stuck, which can cause pain. I know residual damage in itself does not mean much, because I have lived quite some time without any problem or any pain, but it gives me food for thought.

I start to ponder the fact that both Christophe and I have a problem with the same vertebrae and that – in my opinion – he's obviously much worse off, for I am still technically able to move my entire body. Yet despite the fact that physically he is much more restricted than I am, I find it striking to notice that he handles it much better.

I keep struggling, even while I meditate, and try to find the solution deep within me, in my inner Self. I perform countless physical exercises every day to help my body get stronger and I feel what needs to be felt. Most of the time, it seems a matter of just surviving and waiting until the vomiting and pain subside, which happens very rarely. Once again, I decide I am failing badly, as if I'm supposed to make a clear round with a big smile on my face. I just can't manage to do this; it's too hard to bear.

Then I'm struck by a brilliant idea. Suppose that annoying internist was right (usually I avoid such negative thoughts, because I believe thoughts have creating power, so I find it scary to think this way and prefer to say, 'Suppose...,' and, 'Hypothetically speaking...'). Suppose I really won't be able to do anything anymore for the rest of my life, other than vegetate on the couch. Then what?

The first feeling of fear emerges: what should I live on? I've nearly run out of money and my disability insurance doesn't cover my condition. So I don't have an income and I've been eating into my savings for the past two years; there isn't much left. What should I do? I decide to let this thought pass by like a cloud. The only thing it does, is distract – and I'm onto something.

My second impulse is: but I DO NOT WANT THIS. I don't want to be like a house plant, just hanging around and unable to contribute anything anymore. There's so much I still want to do, so much to experience. But most of all, I want to put everything I've learned into practice.

I am here to bring the world something, am I not? I haven't experienced and dealt with everything for nothing. I just can't imagine this is it. That's not right. It really isn't! I enjoy my work too much, and I feel so good when I'm working, for I can now capture the essence of people. Nonetheless, I let this thought pass by as well. It just needed to be heard. Then I start to reach the core.

All of a sudden, I realize that when I was still able to do everything I wanted, I rarely thought I was good enough. I studied at the University of Technology and graduated as an engineer, but among all those brilliant people I often felt extremely stupid.

Among alpha students, I was a boffin and among the beta students, I was an open sandals and woolly socks type. I never had a sense of belonging and, in my book, things were never good enough. But which measuring rod do I use now? It all depends on whom you compare yourself with.

I've always been good at logical thinking, formulating and writing, and, fortunately, I enjoy that, although that too I took for granted. Only now that I'm no longer able to think and write do I understand the value of these things. I was once able to move my arms and legs and take care of myself and I didn't appreciate it. I sang all day long and enjoyed that thoroughly. Now I can't bear to hear music because sound hurts my ears too much. I thought I was too fat, but pictures show I wasn't. I had an average figure, not too slim and not too fat. I never noticed when I looked nice, and now that those days are over and I really am fat, I regret previously having such a distorted self-image; that I did not enjoy it more and wasn't satisfied with myself. Regret is a nasty feeling. And what a pity that, so often, I wished I was someone else.

I still did all kinds of things, and I felt good if I was able to do things for myself, but especially for others. So, in a way, I was still trying to prove my worth, albeit in a much more positive way than before, but nevertheless I was. Now I realize that I was convinced I had to do something in order for others to like me. I was a "human doing" instead of a "human being".

But what if I can't beat this, can no longer contribute or add something tangible to this world? Who will care?

Inside me, suddenly there is silence. Deep rest settles over me and fills me with inner peace. I'm there. I have finally reached the bottom of the pit. If that's how it must be, if I really won't recover, then I'm still happy that I'm me, and that I have reached this point myself – for if I could have chosen anyone in the whole world to spend this difficult period with, there would have been no one better than *me!*

I've become my own best friend. Quietly, without noticing it, something inside me changed. And it isn't because I *did something*. All I could do is 'be'. Exist. Nothing more. Yet that seems to have been enough – more than enough to let me feel at last what is most important for me. I will never abandon myself anymore and never again do I want to be someone else. I am who I am, with my quirks, talents, imperfections and strengths – the whole package is Annemiek and it makes me happy. I've come to terms with myself; finally I have peace and I can start loving me at last.

It sounds somewhat like a platitude, but that's really how it is; and from that moment on, there is progress. If you have really hit the bottom, the good news is that the only way out is up.

I soon discover that the dark pigmentation spots on my face indicate an adrenal gland disorder and, apart from my adrenal glands, my thyroid gland has some unattractive traits too. If you suffer from Chronic Fatigue Syndrome, your adrenal glands are already giving you trouble, but my internist formed his opinion too quickly and sent me off empty-handed. Further investigation shows that my adrenal glands and thyroid gland also caused the malfunctioning of my brain and other organs that have been having a tough time. Structurally, I produce too little cortisol, the adrenocorticotropic hormone. Cortisol is an important substance in your body that has a big impact. It helps control your blood sugar levels and it makes sure your brain gets sufficient energy, thus making it possible to concentrate. Cortisol also influences the impact of stress, so you can relax and heal.

I visit an orthomolecular therapist* and, together, we work out which orthomolecular medicines are able to support my body. Fortunately, by now I'm able to feel what daily dose I need. This is very practical because I am a woman and female hormone levels have their own cycles; not a single day is the same. It turns out that 'custom-made' is what I need, and every day I adjust my nutritional supplements.

I consult an NEI therapist* who helps me get rid of old emotions, and I visit a neuro*-foot reflexology therapist* because I have noticed that my frequent vomiting is caused by an over-stimulated nervous system.

And as soon as I'm able to read again – thanks to the

treatments and the medicines – I reach for my book about healing with angelic healers*. I'm touched by two little sentences about the hormone system: 'You can't fool the endocrine glands. To keep them healthy, you must be totally honest toward yourself and others.'

This is what I have been wanting to do anyhow, and I feel in my very bones how true it was, for me and for everyone else who suffers from a hormonal imbalance. I also realize that my hormonal system will always respond to dishonesty inside and around me, and that my body is becoming an increasingly sensitive instrument.

Entities, Angels, Guides and Master Energies

So I reach for my angel book and, in my own way, I set to work with the information it contains. Some methods do not work for me and that's fine. Every person is unique, different, so one single approach does not suit everybody. Usually, each person knows exactly what's right for him or her. I start to work with affirmations and sound healing for my hormonal and nervous system.

Affirmations are positive statements you tell yourself with the intention of programming your mind and body in the correct way. I should add that you must really believe in them, otherwise they will not work. For instance, I might say, 'Each day I feel a little better and I thank my body for all the work it does. My adrenal glands recover and produce the exact amount of cortisol my body needs. My thyroid gland responds adequately to the hormonal changes. Everything is good as it is, and yet, each day I'm feeling just a little bit better. My body dictates the pace and my recovery unfolds as it is meant to.'

I rely on the inner wisdom of my body, make an appeal to its self-healing power and trust the result. I let go of any notions I have of what the result *should be.* I do not assume I will become as strong as I was before, or as able. I live in *the now* and I'm completely satisfied with the way things are.

Well, I'm *mostly* satisfied with the way things are.

For the endocrine system, I also work with the A-EL-I-O sound exercises. Please refer to the book of LaUna Huffines* for a description of these exercises. Because I now know what I can do, I do it with renewed courage. And although nothing seems to change physically during the first few months, I feel the change is imminent.

Gradually I am able to communicate with my guides and the angels better and better. Angels are Light beings of the highest level, sometimes also called the heralds of God. In general, they do not incarnate as a human being. From The Other Side, they are always in stand-by mode to use their loving energy to assist people who need support. Not everyone can see them, but they are always there when you ask for their help. Unfortunately, they are not allowed to do anything without being asked first, because we all have Free Will. Therefore, it is practical to ask for specific help if you're having a rough time. Just ask if the most suitable angel of Light can help you with your problem – and by all means, do not forget to thank them (which I sometimes have, in the past). Then just see what happens.

Guides are also Light beings and your personal advisors on The Other Side. Most people have three guides who usually stay with you throughout your life. Unlike angels, they are souls who were once human beings themselves and, as such, they have gained a lot of experience and awareness. Based on that experience, and the overview they have because they know better what's written in your life plan than you can remember, they give you advice about the things you come across.

Before you incarnate, you agree on who will be your guides. Depending on what you want to experience, you select your personal group of guides. Each guide has its own task, role and qualities, and together they support you with devotion while you follow your path. When you learn to communicate with them, it's important that you always check whether you are speaking to your own guides or to frauds, also known as *entities*. Entities are also souls who have incarnated and passed away, but they linger on Earth. They are also called spirits, wandering souls or unwanted visitors.

Entities are not negative by definition, but they can cause you trouble if you are susceptible to it. They reinforce the emotions of their host, e.g. active children become more active, someone who is very emotional becomes a howler who quickly bursts into tears, and a rather cluttered person becomes a real scatterbrain. Some entities are teasers, to put it mildly. Others are actually tormentors. In the beginning they pretend to be loving and caring, so you start to trust them. As time goes by, they show their real faces and give you misleading information. The rule is simple: ask if you are talking to your own guide of the Light and tell everything that does not belong to the Light to go first into the Light so all personal issues will be removed, like a carwash, and so it is safe for you to communicate with them on a soul level. And if they don't want to go into the Light (which is their own choice, of course), that's fine too – then you can ask them to leave to some other place and never come back to you. Then consider whether their response is loving, and whether it places you under any kind of pressure. Your own guides will never tell you what to do – Free Will is too important and they acknowledge that.

A special group of Light beings are the Ascended Masters*. I first contacted them during my recovery and, since then, they have stood by me regularly, in my work and my day-to-day life. As the name indicates, they are souls who have reincarnated and achieved such a high level of awareness and enlightenment that they have a separate status.

If you want to put it into a hierarchic structure, the angels are closest to the Source, or God, or whatever you want to call it, followed by the Ascended Masters and then the guides. As far as I know, the Ascended Masters are not personal guides. However, you can call on them to assist you on your highest path, just like the angels, and they each have their own specific theme and qualities. The Ascended Master to whom I feel attracted is Master Kuthumi. He helps people increase their self-knowledge and find their purpose in life. He acts as a channel between the angels and the Earth, so that the Divine Master Plan can unfold itself.

Past Lives, Karma and Free Will

During my recovery, I'm intensively supported by a Pleiadian Light Worker. Although this sounds exotic, she is a woman of flesh and blood with a beautiful profession. She can read blockages in my aura and is supported by Pleiadian guides and Beings of Light. A Light Worker is a medium and a medium is a person who can communicate with souls who do not have a physical body, e.g. people who have passed over and guides, angels and beings of Light who come from elsewhere. A medium is able to read their energy and convert it to language. In that way, he or she can communicate with them.

A Light Worker is a special kind of medium who helps people in their process of developing consciousness during the energetic transition of the Earth and its inhabitants during the years around 2012 and beyond. In fact, what a medium does is comparable to what is described in this book. A Pleiadian Light Worker is assisted by guides from the Pleiades, a star system that is also called The Seven Sisters.

The Pleiadian Light Worker who helps me is named Ariel and she lives a long way off. Because I can't travel, and my brain is gradually able to absorb small pieces of information, we call each other now and again. Together, we continue the big, inner clean-up I have already been working on for years. Ariel is able to see and describe to me elements of the journeys my soul has previously taken, which I can't yet reach myself. All I can do is feel what's bothering me; usually, she can see the reason why. Often, it's about past lives.

Past lives fit in the picture of reincarnation. If you do not have a physical body but simply are 'Soul', you can choose to gain experiences in different ways and to incarnate several times in a row, to be born as a human. Often, you address certain issues more than once and in different ways, from various perspectives. Sometimes you do not fully address certain experiences. These you take with you to your next life in the form of fear, thought or grief.

It becomes clear to me that I've had plenty of these experiences. Ariel and I work through them like this: I describe what's bothering me and what makes my body hurt. For instance: the moment the disability insurance decided to exclude me and I would no longer receive even that small amount of money, I was struck with fear. I was so afraid I wouldn't be able to cope financially.

Ariel attunes, looks and describes a past life in which that fear came over me for the first time. It's about the moment a problem comes into existence, and it does not matter whether that happened earlier in this life, or in one or more past lives. It happened and became the stepping stone to the collection of painful experiences that now result in blockages in our energy systems. We look at mine and I learn to feel the emotions, to draw new conclusions. Then it fades away. The feeling softens. We cleanse it and I find I can go on.

I discover a lot about karma and how it influences my life path and experiences. Karma is the law of cause and effect, the law of action and reaction. Negatively put, it is sometimes explained as 'it's your own fault' or 'he that mischief hatches, mischief catches'. But in fact, karma is neutral. All it means is 'as you sow, so shall you reap' and it shows that every choice you make and everything you do will impact your life. Everything has an effect, some major, others minor. The only thing karma does not say is how quickly you will reap what you sow. Sometimes that will be one or more lives later, and in your current life, you can be confronted with the impact of now unknown choices, made during a previous life.

Karma is also a perfectly neutral solution of the universe for people who have committed horrible crimes. For sooner or later, they too will reap what they sow. If, from an earthly perspective, someone does not seem to be punished, it will be set right by karma in the course of time. That could take place sooner, i.e. the next day, or later, i.e. next week or in a future life. But it *will* happen, for that is one of the laws of nature: cause and effect.

To give a real-life example of karma: I met a very nice man and, for me, it was love at first sight. He felt familiar – I knew his soul, as experience taught me – and in the beginning, he responded positively. However, after we met twice, this changed and he became unfriendly.

I did not understand, because in my opinion I had not done anything wrong, but it was obvious he did not want to have anything to do with me. People around me noticed he had become extremely negative toward me. This confirmed that I was not imagining things, but it was no help. Then I was taken ill for a very long time and did not see him anymore. Two years later, Ariel and I start cleansing and gradually we come across my sadness over this situation. It turns out that indeed we have met before. In this case, the most important life was his as an Arabian, and mine as a young woman of fifteen: I was one of the women of his harem. Despite the fact that I was just one of his women, I loved him deeply. (I recognize the feeling of the now and I, too, see the pictures). Then I did something that did not suit him and, as punishment, I was whipped. Although it was not his intention, I died on the spot, right before his eyes.

In this life, we met to heal that piece and to let it continue in a different way. As souls, we agreed on that, but as a human being it was heavy-going for him to run into me. He probably did not understand why and simply thought it was unpleasant to look me in the eye. It was too confrontational for him. He was the cause of 'my' death in a previous life, and so he avoided me and chased me off with his words in this life. The moment Ariel and I resolve this piece, my initial wave of sadness is followed, as always, by overwhelming peace and acceptance. Finally, the hurting is gone.

What's more is that I learn one of my most important lessons so far about the human being, soul agreements and Free Will. As I said before, Free Will is about the most precious thing a human being possesses. And you can use it exactly the way you want to. Unfortunately, this sometimes results in someone choosing things that do not agree with his original soul agreements, which causes sorrow and misery for other people.

But, as a soul, you might find you choose situations that, in hindsight, once you have obtained a firm footing in the reality of them, act as a rude awakening. Usually there is an escape, an opportunity for something else, and you can choose a different path. Often this path is not quite as ideal as the original one, for in the first instance you obviously chose the best path possible in all aspects. But you have Free Will for a good reason, so you may use it as you please. And if it's about you, that is a nice thought.

Returning to my story, by looking at blockages from past lives, I discover why my father and I have always clashed so often. That, too, is karma and it involves soul agreements. That's why sometimes it is so painful and almost insoluble. From an earthly perspective, this is how it works: my father does not understand me, but because he is a smart man, he often thinks he knows what I think. Most of the time, I do understand him and I even understand what he thinks, because I used to think the same way. But now I no longer agree with him because my world view has broadened, so I react differently to how I did before. We both consider different things important and usually we have such disparate views of life that it interferes with our ability to communicate; he wants to have a discussion, while I prefer a dialogue. We don't speak the same language anymore.

And because I consistently live based on what I feel and believe, he thinks I'm obstinate. Of course I am, otherwise I never would have recovered from my illness. However, my father can't keep up with me anymore and I no longer want to adjust myself unjustly. That's why we have not succeeded in bridging the gap between us. Yet I do my best during the occasional contact I have with him. Meanwhile, I work hard on a soul level. I heal numerous of lives we lived together, which spawned the stepping stones for this life; and I heal lives we lived separately, but which for me contained the same themes. In this way, at least I have done my homework. I know that's all I can do, but unfortunately it does not solve the problems we have and it's painful for me to acknowledge that.

By looking at the family ties, among other things, I discover all kinds of connections between the soul plans of different souls. In this life, I recognize people I've known from 'all my lives'. Sometimes it's a group of people. That's why I have come to the conclusion that there are also future experiences you reach agreement about with a number of souls. There are so-called group aims, learning targets for which you need others and for which the agreement has already been established.

When you meet during the course of your lives, you will definitely trigger something in each other. The preconditions have been created and what you decide to do with that is your choice. Every human being is unique; nobody has the same life plan. Therefore, nobody has the same combination of qualities, circumstances and experiences. Those experiences are usually custom-made; they are perfect for learning the lessons you struggle with. But they are more than just a learning experience; life is about giving and taking.

Accept that you are here to get something, but you are also here to *bring* something. You've come to gain your life experiences and to fulfil your life goals. The latter is what you bring. Your unique combination of skills and qualities ensures that you are extremely well equipped to fulfil your unique role in the Big Whole. And because every person is unique, you take up your own place in the Big Whole, by determining your task in life and fulfilling it. In nature, everything has its reason. Therefore, every life is meaningful – even if we, from an earthly perspective, can't figure out the meaning at first sight.

Here, too, group agreements are in place. There are souls with whom you agreed to complete certain tasks because they are too big to handle by yourself. And that's a good thing, for it makes those tasks much easier and more enjoyable. Finally, at the end of your life, your soul takes all experiences and the ensuing consciousness to 'The Other Side'. Your soul has another quality now, will gain its breath and then is allowed, if it so desires, to incarnate again. For me, the picture becomes increasingly clear and I feel more peaceful than before. Most things happen for a reason and all I have to do is cooperate and allow my life to unfold.

With the patience of saints, Ariel and I work for months on end on all that pops up and it's a great help; I'm progressing well. Altogether, we delve thoroughly into fifty-five lives and, after some time, I start to see the images that Ariel sees. I'm learning to read myself. One day, I will derive great pleasure from this because I can also read other people – but that's something I do not yet know, now.

Angels and Neurology

Then one day, I have a light bulb moment: I suddenly realize it is coincidentally possible to be suffering from two different things at the same time. So I visit a neurologist, because I'm under the impression that hormones don't account for everything. I suspect there's also something wrong with my neck and nervous system.

An MRI scan is performed on my neck, several nervous system tests are carried out and an EEG is performed. I sit in a chair, my head donning a bathing cap covered with electrodes, and the EEG operators tells me to relax. *I can do that*, I think optimistically. Because I'm pretty nervous and my encounters with doctors so far have not been very positive, I call in the help of the angels.

I quietly ask, 'Angels of Light, will you please guide me through this? I let go of it and put it in your hands.' I take a deep breath and relax.

At that moment, the operator calls out, 'What are you *doing*?'

It turns out that his computer and all equipment attached have crashed. It makes me laugh and I tell the angels who are present, 'Okay, point taken. You really are here; I won't doubt you anymore.'

The only thing I tell the EEG operator is that I was meditating and had emptied my head. I can't summon the nerve to use the word 'angel' yet. He reboots the system and asks me again to relax.

This time, I let the angels be and empty my head myself. When the EEG is performed, the operator shows me the brainwaves and says it looks like I'm sleeping comfortably, because the image is so undisturbed. He tells me I have one of the most relaxed heads he has ever seen. I accept the compliment gratefully, for that head hasn't always been so peaceful.

Later, when the neurologist shows me the results of the MRI scan of my neck, it becomes clear that the whiplash has evolved into a neck hernia on vertebrae C4-C5. The exact same spot as Christophe. So it's not Chronic Fatigue Syndrome. At least that explains the awful pain attacks and the malfunctioning of my arms. Surgery doesn't seem such a good idea, because I feel the worst is over and, fortunately, the neurologist is of the same opinion. Carefully I ask if there is a link between my thyroid gland problems and other symptoms. It turns out this isn't a weird question and the neurologist explains how different parts of the body can influence each other. I tell him what kind of exercises I do already and I get the go-ahead: my approach is approved. In addition, I am referred to an osteopath* and I leave, much wiser and calmer than when I entered.

Light Worker and Medium

Yet, the way back, or rather ahead, is a long one and it takes more than a year-and-a-half before I have fully reintegrated and dare to pronounce myself truly recovered. Meanwhile, I cautiously return to work and find that I've grown.

Thanks to my illness and subsequent self-cleansing, my skills in perceiving and communicating with astral bodies have improved immensely. By now, I read auras effortlessly. I can communicate with entities and bring them to the Light. Moving on from this to talking to the deceased who have already entered the Light and now return to deliver messages to their living loved ones – that's not such a big step anymore. While I'm working, people who have passed over join me spontaneously, but only if that's important to the client.

They watch what I'm doing and give me faith and information, if the problems we're working on are rooted in family issues. Often they know things that are necessary to the healing, or hidden underlying issues are revealed. As long as the intentions of these people are pure, they are more than welcome. Without noticing it, I've become a medium – a healing medium, to be exact.

In addition, I sometimes energy-cleanse the homes of clients, if there are residual energy fields that make the residents' lives difficult, or if there are entities who do not want to leave of their own free will. I also immobilize or reroute the water veins* and earth rays*, so their energy can no longer disturb the aura of the residents and entities do not feel at home anymore. I only do this in special cases and in each case I assess the field, to check whether it is necessary to do it myself because the energy is of a certain type and I know *I* need to do this; or perhaps a colleague could do it just as well or even better. In that case, of course, I would recommend that colleague.

In addition to communicating with the deceased and the angels, I learn, with the greatest of ease, how to communicate with my clients' guides while I'm working. At first, I'm confused because I think I hear my own guides and sometimes receive contradictory messages. But I soon accustom myself to this and learn how to establish whom I'm talking to. I start by reading my client's aura, and give words to the energy and information, all in my head. Then, I check whether I have the full picture and, if necessary, the guides add something to that. Before I start working with a client, I reach agreement with their guides about the method to use, because some guides are so eager to help their protégée when they 'finally meet me' that their energy is a bit pushy and disturbs my reading process. With this working method, I can decide what to do with all the information myself. I am the one responsible for what I say out loud and I am the one reading and doing that by attuning to their soul. This way, it works for the client, the guides, and for me.

I find that, as a result of my contact with Ariel and all the practicing I have done, it becomes increasingly easy to hear what those guides say – although in the beginning, I frequently have my doubts, especially when the answer is different to what I expected. In that case, I ask a number of questions to check, or a closed question that can only be answered by 'yes' or 'no'. Those answers are the easiest to catch and once I've received an answer, I ask the question the other way around, by adding 'not' to it. Then I should get an opposite response and I know for sure that I've caught it right.

Apart from the guides, the angels come to help me more often while I'm working. They sometimes work collaboratively with me and then I create the basic 'surgical' energy field they can use to continue. I am the surgical nurse, so to speak, and I prepare the area that needs to be operated. Sometimes, the angels are right behind me and work through me and, by doing so, strengthen my power and teach me how to work with their energy. Other times, we just work together and each of us does his own thing.

I'm at a far greater distance from my clients when I treat them in my practice and I wonder why. The answer is simple, but quite new to me: I'm working in layers of the aura that were not discovered before.

I am familiar with the first seven layers of the aura and, before I fell ill, I used to work in layers 1-4. Sometimes I was able to see into layer 7, into someone's path of life, but I wasn't able to work in it yet. That's different now and I notice that frequently I'm some yards removed from my client. I count the layers: twenty-one. Astonished, I ask my guides whether I'm imagining things, but no: I hear that I work in layers 1-21 and that I have become a true Light Worker.

I ask what a Light Worker is exactly and I hear that they are the people who will help others during the big transition in consciousness around 2012. There are major shifts in the energy of the Earth and its inhabitants, everything is in the process aimed at a quantum leap in awareness and the human body must get used to those new energies. Moreover, most people still have to resolve some issues before they can increase their awareness. Light Workers assist them in doing so. Many people – both paranormal therapists and others related professionals – contribute to that process, but technically speaking, Light Workers work in aura layer 5 and higher, so I'm told.

So, I am a Light Worker and just the word makes me feel cheerful. It feels nice and something about it clicks for me; I'm on the right track. However, the twenty-one layers of the aura set me thinking, because I know the lower layers mean something. The idea enters my mind to put my findings on paper, for two main reasons. Just as with the first seven known layers of the aura, there is an underlying system to the remaining fourteen and I want to understand and describe that. The highest level a blockage can originate is the determining factor for the approach to address it. For instance, if there is a bump in layer 12 with bulges through layer 7, the best place to start is layer 12. Compare it to a splinter in your finger. The shallowest side is in layer 7, the deepest in layer 12. If you remove it from layer 7, it will still hurt and fester in layers 8-12. That's why I start in layer 12, to remove the core and, after that, everything attached to it. The result is a clean wound, which the client can further heal himself.

By describing the 'new' (i.e. previously unknown) layers of the aura, up to and including 21, it becomes clear why you cannot fully heal certain disorders in the lower layers, because there is still 'part of the splinter' remaining in the upper layers.

I hope I will be able to contribute to the further development of this discipline of natural medicine, by first gaining the knowledge and then publishing the information in this book. By doing so, I'm trying to do my part, so that people will be supported even better and, if possible, heal more easily and quickly.

The other reason is that, during my consultations, I thoroughly enjoy the special experiences I have during reading and helping to heal the numerous past lives of my clients, meeting the guides, angels and other Beings of Light that I connect with, the entities and the clients' deceased loved ones; the astounding connections that I discover between different lives of people; and other wonderful things I come across during my journey through the layers and dimensions. I enjoy it all so much that I want to share it. Some experiences are just too wonderful to keep to myself.

That's why I compile all my treatments of the past years, deducing and describing what is connected to aura layers 1-21 and which problems are linked to which layer. My approach is as follows: I make reports of my treatments and I conscientiously write down what I do in which layers of the aura. After having done that for three years, I feel the urge to convert all these consultations into the underlying system for the higher layers, just as I already knew existed for the lower layers. By now, my head is clearer than it used to be; I can see and comprehend more and I'm ready for it. Suddenly, I feel like time is pressing; I've found my goal in life and I need to rush forward.

For each client, I make an overview on the computer in a large spread sheet. Itemized per aura layer, I lay down the consultations. In this way, I can see exactly what I did for whom. And in just one glance, I am able to see underlying patterns. After months of typing, the overviews are completed. The results take my breath away, because there is a lot more material than I anticipated. Then I make another spread sheet in which I describe for each client how many examples I have for each layer of the aura, and I count up all these examples. When I start writing, I have around 40-70 examples for each layer of the aura, enough to draw plausible conclusions.

Of course, I can't prove anything scientifically, but that's not my intent. I just want to name and describe the layers and, by means of examples from my practice, show people what else is influencing their life and what can be done to resolve that. Then I plan to check the conclusions I have drawn with my guides and, if necessary, accentuate them. After that, I would like to create a book and share the information with those who are interested.

The book describes the layers of the aura, up to and including layer 21, with various examples per layer. In this way, you can co-experience which themes and problems are purely individual and in which cases transpersonal causes play a role, and you can discover the wider context of things. This will give you a more complete picture of the world and the way your life works.

Sometimes, the incomprehensible turns out to be comprehensible after all. And you will also see how we are all connected and that we all are one.

Critical Comment

Everything I write in this book is how I see and experience it today, the moment I write it. In good conscience, I put it into words the best I can. I vouch for what I say. However, I also know I'm still learning every day and tomorrow I will know just a little bit more than I do today; my views might be slightly different, then.

For I consider my world view no more than a model, a way to interpret what I see and what I experience. And although I fully stand for everything I say and write, of course I do not claim I know everything. I do not claim that everything I write is actually so; that this is The Truth (and that, as a consequence, somebody else might be wrong). I say none of that. I consider my model simply as a means to comprehend my world and make it manageable. And by advancing insight, I learn something new every day and adjust my opinions and ideas accordingly.

When I describe past lives in this book, for instance, these may have taken place exactly that way. It could be, and yet I do not dare claim it is so. It is not a scientifically based study and it's neither about proof nor is it my intention to convince people of something. With this book, the only thing I want to do is inform you, as a reader, and share my experiences and ideas.

And should I die and find out that past lives do not exist at all, and that their only aim now is to show me, in the form of a images, what a client's problem is, how it originated and, most importantly, they allow me to resolve the blockages after which a client can move on...that's fine with me. My only object is to help people heal – to inspire them to look for the truth behind the truth, for the so-called impossible possibilities, and to maintain their faith and trust in the self-healing resources every (human) being has. Every human being is able to handle everything that comes his way and is fully equipped for that.

Sometimes, the only thing necessary is that you remember or that you are supported, after which these self-healing resources can be re-employed and (re-)activated.

This book shows my way, and I hope it will increase people's understanding and compassion toward themselves and others. After all, we are all just souls who set out on a journey and we're all trying to do it the best we can, in our own way.

My wish is that this book will contribute to the quantum leap we, as individuals and as mankind, are about to make. I hope what you are about to read may have a positive impact on your path in life.

Part 2:
The 21 Layers
of the Aura

Creating and Dissolving Blockages

A blockage in your aura or body is usually the result of a longer process. Unless an acute trauma is involved, then it is formed in a twinkling of the eye. A blockage is created as follows.

You experience something that has an impact on you. You feel this impact in your physical body; that's why we call it *physical*. You get a certain feeling, which is called an emotion, and you have certain thoughts about it. You like or dislike it, or you form an opinion or draw a conclusion. That is called *mental*; it all takes place in your head, your mind. Most of these things happen unconsciously; you do not realize what you're doing and your body and aura store this information and retain it for another time. If it is a positive experience, you have a pleasant basis to move on. But if you label it as negative, it could be the basis for a future problem.

A brief example: you are a five-year-old child and the neighbor's dog bites you. Your leg shows the teeth imprint. The bite hurts (that's physical), you're scared out of your wits, which causes stomach cramps (that's emotional) and you think, *From now on, I will be very careful with dogs because they can't be trusted and they bite me whenever they get a chance* (the mental part).

The physical pain is stored in the first layer of your aura (the physical layer, your body), the fear in your second (emotional layer) and your conclusion about dogs in your third (the mental layer). When you grow up, you run into dogs more frequently and it's as if they smell you do not like them. They come up to you to sniff and lick, or they lie at your feet or want to play. In other words, they do exactly what you don't want them to do. Whether it's a big shepherd, a dachshund or a Chihuahua, it does not matter; you get frightened and agitated and prepare for the worst, because you know from experience that they can bite.

Now, you no longer see the situation for what it is: when a good-natured St Bernard puts its head in your lap and looks at you faithfully because it wants to be tickled, you freeze and all you want is for him to leave. So next time, you'd rather walk around the block if you see a St Bernard coming your way.

Unfortunately, the world is filled with dogs and you can't always make a detour. That's why it's clever to address your problem, for it affects your life in an unpleasant way. Sometimes you can resolve such things by talking about them. The feelings of fear will decrease and you will be able to guide yourself through such situations. Other times, it might be helpful to come face-to-face with the things that frighten you. For instance, you could start petting dogs, while you're being supported by someone else.

And sometimes, it's more convenient to take yet another route, because just talking about it may not help if you have stored the experience and the resulting tension in your body and aura, for instance in your stomach and belly. That's what I will call a blockage, from now on.

And if that tension is stored this way, confronting your fear is not the most efficient way to get rid of it. In that case, you would ignore your own feeling of being scared and, in the long run, you won't be able to make an appeal to it in other situations. That's not very clever. Fear is a signal that can save your life, so that you make a move and start acting in case of an emergency. So if your body gives you a warning, you must be sure it is a genuine hint. In such a case, or if you simply don't know why your life isn't running smoothly, or if you are unable to change the situation yourself, it might be wise to resolve that blockage, that tightened energy knot. After all, it will save you a lot of stress (and miles of walking).

For, in addition to the old stress that emerges when you run into a dog, you have to deal with all the tension you built up in the course of time caused by the dogs that came uncomfortably close to you. If you add the tension of your current encounter with a dog, you will understand that your body and your aura are under a lot of pressure as a result of an unpleasant encounter and being unable to let go of the stress it caused. You could compare it to a snowball that is growing bigger and bigger.

Suppose this old feeling can be removed so that the breeding ground for your fear of dogs disappears. Maybe then you're no longer afraid of dogs at all, because you are a grown-up now and no longer a child. Only, because of that, you're physically much bigger and stronger than a dog and you are now able to respond differently to when you were a child.

In this example, I would start working with you on analyzing and understanding what happened. That's the mental part. While we're talking about it, you will automatically feel the corresponding feelings again. Only this time, we will make sure you just feel them, experience them for a short moment. After that, they can leave. Most of the time, they will more or less disappear of their own accord, because emotions are only there to make it clear to you whether you like or dislike something. Once felt, their warning function is fulfilled. That is the emotional clear-out.

Meanwhile, I start working on your aura, because the blockages are activated in the corresponding layers as soon as we start talking about it. I see them lighten. That even happens without a conversation, for instance in the case of memories that are too painful to talk about but may be neutralized by now; or if the complaint the client wants to discuss is not the only important issue that may be addressed that day. The path of the soul can be read through the aura and I follow your soul conscientiously. I attune to those specific spots and start reading and cleansing for you.

For this part of the treatment, you lie on my examination table, on your back and fully dressed. You can compare that table with the one a physiotherapist uses. I wrap you up in a blanket because the energetic clear-out usually makes you feel a bit chilly, and then I wait and see what happens. Then I'm working in the air – or so it seems. I move my hands and feel and see the blockages. Sometimes it looks like I'm washing lettuce, and I'm fishing seemingly in the air as long as is necessary to fish all parts 'from the sink'. Other times, it is a granular substance that I level. Then again, it looks like I'm picking sea anemones underwater, and sometimes you can see me make the same stroking movements at the same spot in your aura dozens of times to smooth out the bump of energy, the blockage in your aura.

There are many different ways to do this, but no matter which way you see me work on your aura, I will inevitably yawn quite a bit to release the energy I took over from you. For an outsider, it may look rather comical, and especially children think it's amazing, because I do exceptional things and keep yawning like a hippo.

By removing the blockages from the highest layer of the aura that they are located, I make sure your energy can start flowing again so your body can handle it by itself, from that moment on. The field of a higher layer of the aura also contains all smaller matryoshka dolls, which is why a blockage in a higher aura influences all layers beneath. If you remove the main blockage, the blockages at a lower level that resulted from the main one will also disappear.

You can compare this process with a masseur who massages a knot out of your muscles. After that, your body can take over and your self-healing power will take care of the rest. You are less likely to get caught in old behavior and standard responses. This makes every experience unique; each can be treated individually, rather than as just one more in a chain of repeated experiences. It is the difference between the 'here and now' and the 'now it's happening again...it's always the same'.

While I'm working, I tell you everything I'm doing in your aura and what I'm finding in the various layers. That makes it easier for you to handle similar future situations more consciously, so that fewer knots will develop. This way, you can live your own life as comfortably as possible, which is a pleasant prospect.

By now, you should have a rough impression of the basic principles I use for my work. In the following chapters, I will describe what exactly is going on in those twenty-one layers of the aura.

Aura Layer 1: The Physical Layer

Of all the aura layers, layer 1 is the most tangible and concrete. It is the physical layer. It contains the structure of your physical body, as well as your organs and all the other bodily tissues. Furthermore, it determines how your body is constructed and how it can function mechanically. This layer is an individual one. It is yours alone and it is different in every human being. This is only logical, because every human being has a unique physical body.

I do not have a lot of practical examples related to this layer, because I mostly work in the higher aura layers. Nevertheless, everybody is familiar with the minor accidents children have, such as tripping over something, bumping their heads against something, bruising their knees, crying their eyes out to get Mum or Dad – whoever is nearby – to come and rub over the sore spot. A small kiss where it hurts – all better now? That is what working in the physical layer is about.

Animals also have this layer and you can often do very helpful things with it. For example, my very exuberant black Labrador Senna and I go to the seaside for a few days. We stay at a hotel that is built into a dune, with a small patch of grass outside our front door on the first floor. On the second day of our stay, Sen meets the dog from next door and I allow them to play for a while. When I call her back to me, she decides to ignore me and jumps over a small hedge. Unfortunately, she doesn't realize the hedge is also the fence of the patch of grass on the first floor....

She makes the jump and lands three yards further down on the concrete parking space. All I hear is a dull thud. The result is a gaping wound in her jaw. They have to anaesthetize her and stitch her up, her legs and muscles are stiff and sore and she has a heavy concussion. Later it turns out she is almost deaf in her left ear. After our visit to the vet for the stitches and the regular check-up to find out if anything is broken or ruptured – after all, I am not a vet myself and I'm too emotionally involved and shocked from the whole experience to be able to look at things neutrally – I treat her physical body, which feels bruised all over. I feel the pain and distress of her physical injuries and remove them from the first layer. Two days of sleep do the rest.

Aura Layer 2: The Emotional Layer

Fortunately, my dog has no memory of hedges and she did not sustain any emotional damage. If she had, I would have undoubtedly stumbled upon it in her second aura layer, because this is the emotional layer. It is also an individual and therefore personal layer. This means your personal emotions are stored in it and can be found there. It is a flowing layer in which you can see or feel the change in the movement of your emotions. Sadness, happiness, anger, irritation – they can all be found in this layer. A few examples of clients with blockages in their second aura layer show how it works.

Chantal, a sturdy woman in her early seventies, lives alone and has problems with relationships. She doesn't think much of herself and believes other people have the same impression of her. She has never been married or had any children, which she experiences as a great loss. She does have a sweetheart of sorts, her ex-lover, whom she cannot live with or without. It has been a while since Chantal found life worth living and she is struggling with an alcohol addiction. She decides to make an appointment with me.

I clear up layer 2 at a time when her boyfriend/ex-lover has gone abroad for a long period. She feels very lonely. She doesn't want to commit, but she doesn't want to be alone either, and she thinks it's too late for new relationships and friendships. The clearing up of the unhelpful feelings of loneliness in her second aura layer helps her find some inner peace and feel at home within herself.

Francis is struggling with something else. A large strong man in his mid-forties, he is confronted with severe illness. That is why he asks me to help him. During the first session, a large lump of emotions is released in the second aura layer. His emotions are very much related to the situation he is in. They are about his fear of not getting better anymore, about suddenly being dependent on his partner and about grief over the fact that his body no longer does what he wants it to do. The clearing up of this layer gives him the ability to accept the situation he is in and allows him to continue his healing process with renewed courage.

Josh, a therapist who wants to live a spiritual life, is a little too dependent on getting validation from the opposite sex, which is preventing him from putting his spiritual ambitions into practice. Fortunately, he is aware of this and can laugh about it most of the time. However, sometimes his need for attention causes him to make the wrong choices. He comes to me because of a relationship crisis.

The problem that announces itself in layer 2 is jealousy. Ever since he was five years old, he has felt unworthy of existence, and he is jealous of people who succeed in connecting to their soul. He is unable to get rid of this problem on his own, because he has denied his soul since he was a child and doesn't know how to do things any differently; his patterns of behavior have become too habitual.

His jealousy appears to have an attachment point on his right shoulder and it is very persistent. Fortunately, I get help from two angels: Rachmiel* comes to help me with medicinal herbs and Archangel Uriel* helps restore the connection between Josh's soul and his cerebellum, which is positioned at the back of his head. This happens in an extraordinary way, a way I have never heard of before, let alone had any experience with.

Uriel and I build a new piece of Light Body for Josh. We simply create a new part of his aura; just as the whalebones in a corset give structure to the dress, this supports the aura field. I am used to doing that kind of thing in the affected area of the person in question. With a spinning motion, we usually make a new light cocoon to replace the old one.

This time, something else happens. First, Uriel heals the connection. He simply removes the affected part on his shoulder and together we make the donor connection – but to my surprise, this takes place in the abdominal area of my body. Next, the energetic donor organ is 'transplanted' in Josh. It is a fantastic thing to witness: it looks like a whitish, cobweb-like, transparent, stretched stomach that forms a bridge from the back of his head, through his head and his fontanel, sticking out a little more than an inch above his crown chakra.

His way of thinking and living are reconnected to his soul, which means that from that moment on, he will be able to feel from his heart and make choices that are attuned to his life path. The cause of the jealousy has been tackled and I can do the rest of the clearing up of accompanying emotions in the second layer myself.

Of course, there is nothing inherently wrong with emotions and they do not always need to be cleared up. Being able to go through them and feel them usually does the trick.

However, in my line of work, I deal with emotions that have somehow become a problem or become overwhelming over the course of time, which causes people to get stuck. Or I deal with emotions that cause people to isolate themselves from others because they are disconnected from their emotions. Emotions can also cause people to overreact to those they interact with, which does not lead to anything good either. In such cases, 'vacuuming' the second aura layer is a soft way to enable people to get on with their lives in a more relaxed way.

Aura Layer 3: The Mental Layer

In the third aura layer, things are totally different. This layer is where your thoughts reside. It shows what your mental side is like, what and how you think, how much you think, how your ideas are structured, what your habitual thoughts are and what limiting beliefs you have.

Limiting beliefs are opinions you have – often on a subconscious level – that cause you to respond to situations habitually and automatically, without looking at what's really going on. For example, if you fail your driving test three times in a row, you might come to the conclusion that you will never get your driving license. 'I can't do it, I'll never get it.' By thinking this way, you will indeed never get your driving license and you will fail every exam you take – not because you're incapable of passing the exam, but because you *think* you are. This, in its turn, stops you from making any real effort.

This third layer also shows the thought patterns you cling to and how much you worry. Again, layer 3 is an individual and, therefore, personal layer.

Of course, the people you interact with and your life experiences can affect what you think: your family, your upbringing, your friends or your partner or colleagues. If someone is negatively affected in his way of thinking, and if it is relevant to do something about it, I encounter these outside influences in the higher aura layers. The third layer shows how these external influences affect your own thinking. It shows what you do with them.

Jude, an exceptionally friendly and obliging man in his early forties, works in services and has visited my practice regularly because of his ADD and concentration problems. In addition, it is difficult for him to attune his own perception of the world around him to that of his wife. They are literally living in two separate worlds because his way of thinking is completely different from hers. We worked on that on an earlier occasion and this went so well that we did not have to schedule another appointment. Now he has come back to me with a 'very busy head'.

It turns out that his wife has been ill for several weeks and the things she usually takes care of are now his responsibility. This causes problems. Due to his ADD, his wife has always made the important decisions. They do discuss everything together, but she is the one who makes the final decision. After all, she always knows best. They have an unequal relationship because Jude is supposedly unable to take stock of situations and often misjudges the consequences of the choices he makes. This has made him very insecure about his own capabilities and he finds it hard to develop his own opinions, which makes life very difficult for him when he is suddenly faced with the responsibility of looking after his family, including two adolescent sons.

Jude is mentally stressed out and tends to think too much in situations in which other people would trust and go with their feelings. He gets endlessly stuck in details and worries about doing things the wrong way or overlooking things. In short, he worries himself sick. In this particular session, I work together with a large Light Being. We work on Jude's mental aura layer and on his pelvic area, which is at the root of how he goes about living his life. This problem extends to his throat chakra, which stands for communication and expressing yourself. It is clear that the things he says are not taken very seriously at home. His family hardly listens to what he has to say, which hurts him deeply.

All of this is related to his third aura layer. The field extends through his head, where it also has an attachment point. It affects his mental capacities because it overstimulates and upsets his brain. The energy radiating from his brain surprises me. It's different to what I normally pick up from people; it's a different pattern. During the session, the overstimulation is removed and neutralized and left and right are balanced. In this way, Jude's rational and emotional sides are in balance again.

At the end of the session his mind has calmed down, he is able to stay relaxed when he is thinking about something and he is his old self again. Now he can continue taking care of his family in his own way.

Martin's is quite a different story. He is a tall, charismatic man and managing director of a multinational company. Martin is in his late thirties, has a way with words and can be extremely rational, but he is really quite an emotional man. He has a thyroid problem (hyperthyroidism) that has left him without a thyroid gland. He takes medication that partly takes over the thyroid gland function, but it also causes mood swings. Ever since he started taking the medication, he has undergone a personality change he is not happy with. He is grumpy, distant, sharp and cynical in his comments and both he and his family suffer from the fact that he is no longer his likeable self.

He comes to me with an emotional problem: he has been taken in by several of his clients and, as a result, has lost some of his trust in people. He suffers from negative emotions and does not know how to get rid of them. This turns out to be related to his thinking, which is affected by his thyroid medication. It also turns out that this seemingly emotional problem must be tackled in the mental layer first.

When I work with people who have problems in their third aura layer, I usually start by extensively grounding them. Grounding means that clients really make contact with the ground beneath them, not only literally but also energetically. This allows any accumulated excess tension to leave the body through the feet. This is similar to the grounding wire of a socket: if the tension gets too high, it runs safely through the wire into the ground, which prevents the fuses from melting.

I scan Martin's energy field and feel his gallbladder stinging. Our liver excretes bile, which is then collected in the gallbladder and used for food digestion. The expression 'to vent one's gall' has its origin in this process. People vent their gall when they are angry about something and want to release their anger. This usually concerns something that is indigestible and has to be addressed. Martin is more than a little angry. His anger is also connected to his lack of trust in others.

On top of that, his mucous membranes are hypersensitive. Mucus membranes play a part in our contact with the outside world and our defense against it, so I can imagine that in this particular situation, Martin's have gone through some rough times. Fortunately, his heart feels very strong and he has a well-functioning liver, which surprises me as his daily intake of alcohol is quite considerable.

Then I discover the cause of his imbalance: it is an energetic-hormonal problem. On a physical level, his medication solves all his problems. He takes in the substances that his thyroid gland normally produces. There is only one big difference: in healthy people, the proper functioning of the thyroid gland depends on substances produced by the pituitary gland, which is situated in the center of our head and produces hormones. On an energetic level, the pituitary gland passes information to the thyroid gland about what a person is doing on this planet and what his or her life mission is. So apart from the chemical substances produced to let the body function properly, these substances carry another message, which allows people to know what to do with their lives.

Every organ also has a spiritual function in the body and in people's lives, and the pituitary gland has the function described above. The thyroid gland allows us to deal with grief and other types of suffering. It passes on the message that comes from the pituitary gland to the pancreas and adrenal glands, which also produce hormones that pass on information to the ovaries (in females) and epididymis (in males). The ovaries and epididymis are where our creational energy is stored. We create children and we create possibilities. Eventually, people create new things and shape their lives at the end of the chain directed by the soul (in other words, with the help of the ovary or epididymis energy). If all goes according to plan, the creational process is prompted by the soul. In Martin's case, however, something has got stuck there.

Martin's creations are directed by his thyroid medication, which does not carry the soul message. This makes him feel lost and causes him to trust his reasoning, his thinking power, more because the alternative path – feeling and experiencing what is right and in attunement with his soul – is blocked off for him. He simply cannot get there anymore. Therefore, I reconnect his body to his thyroid gland. I make a conscious choice to do this from bottom to top, because there is an overkill of tension and negative thoughts in his head. If I worked from top to bottom, I would first spread this negativity throughout his entire body, which of course I don't want to do. So I steadily work from bottom to top and release the tension in his head through his crown.

Next, I work on the connection between the thyroid gland and the pituitary and pineal glands. The latter are also collectively called the epiphysis. The pituitary gland has information about what you have come to do in your current life and what you would like to experience. Your pineal gland is the gateway to your soul, your divinity, your most accurate compass. So through the pineal gland, your soul directs the pituitary gland, which is the storehouse of action plans for this life. This in turn affects the functioning of your thyroid gland, which sends information to the rest of your body. Since Martin does not have a thyroid gland anymore, I make an energetic one to replace it. In this way, the soul information sent from the pineal gland to the pituitary gland – the interaction with the Higher Self – can be spread throughout his body.

After that, I rebalance his left and right hemispheres so that his rational and emotional sides are in balance again and attuned to each other. Meanwhile, Martin is so relaxed that he lies snoring on my treatment table. About a month later, he tells me he is no longer suffering from mood swings and he is much happier, which his wife confirms.

During the following months, I give Martin three follow-up treatments. All three are focused on the thyroid gland and functioning of the pineal gland. Both his wife and Martin himself are very enthusiastic about the treatments. He feels relaxed again and is back to his warm, engaged and exuberant old self. However, there is a small problem: his wife tells me she likes him best right after he has had a session with me and she asks me politely if I would be so kind as to pay him a visit on a daily basis.

Aura Layer 4:
The Astral Layer

The fourth layer is a special case. It is the transitional layer between the first and last three (layers 5, 6 and 7) of your personal layers. Your astral contacts take place in this astral layer. This means your non-physical contact with others, for example, in your dreams when you meet other people during your sleep. Your light body travels half the globe to different places, while your physical body is comfortably resting in bed. We also make astral contacts by means of cords. Cords are energetic connections between people. They are lines of communication that allow you to exchange energy with others, even from a distance. In this way, love can flow from one heart chakra to the other.

If you have a lot of these lines and you are not aware of them, other people can use them to drain energy from you when they are in need of a little bit extra. This is not very helpful because it can create an energy shortage as a result of you unknowingly giving away too much.

For the first example from my practice, we look again at Chantal, the woman who does not think much of herself and is therefore afraid to enter into relationships. I come across a problem in layer 4 preventing her from developing friendships and opening herself up to others. In other words, she does not create positive and friendly energetic lines between herself and other people.

The problem is linked to her solar plexus (stomach chakra, linked with perception and being open to connections with the energies of others), her third eye (brow chakra, being open on an intuitive level) and to her first chakra, which represents her foundation in life. The moment I start working on the problem, her deceased father comes to help me and tells me about their past in the Second World War. He describes how, as a little girl living in a war zone, she experienced certain things while she and her father were travelling around looking for food for their family. Her father tells me that during wartime no one could be trusted, because anyone could betray you to the Germans. It was all about surviving and finding food. Nobody knew anymore what was good and pure. Being a toddler, Chantal felt all the fear and worry on a very deep level and this period in her life made a great impression on her.

As a result, from a very young age she learnt to distrust other people and keep them at a distance. And because she kept doing that, she has seen evidence supporting her attitude all her life. When her trust is betrayed, she thinks, *Told you so*, not realizing that 'action = reaction' is also valid in her case. Her environment keeps mirroring the problem until she has healed it within herself. As long as she is distrusting, she will attract people who respond to that and enjoy breaking down her trust even further. In Chantal's case, her distrust has also affected her thinking in layer 3 and her emotions in layer 2. One of her basic beliefs is that 'people can't be trusted' and 'if something bad happens to me, I can't deal with it'. These patterns are removed and replaced by something more constructive: 'I know exactly who I can trust' and 'I can deal with anything I am faced with'. Next, we work on the underlying fear and loneliness in layer 2. This allows her to start making new connections with other people.

Connecting to other people is not exactly a problem for Hank; he has a very busy social life. Hank is seventy-four years old and is engaged in development projects and enjoys what he has achieved in his life. The reason for his visit is what he calls an 'old man's problem': he has trouble urinating and has to use a catheter every day. This is a limiting belief, which can be found in his third layer, the mental layer.

His nervous system is in disarray and over-stimulated and his urethra is not responding properly when he decides he wants to urinate. As a result, he is unable to relax fully and empty his bladder, which causes bladder infections. Apart from that, he has had several kidney stone operations and it's clear that he finds it difficult to deal with his emotions. This is not very surprising when you know your kidneys help with clearing your emotions.

Hank is the eldest boy from a family of eight children. He too was a child of the Second World War. He was living in the Randstad (an urban agglomeration of Western Holland). Hank is several years older than Chantal, so he was more aware of what was going on than she was. His mother was probably psychotic. Today, she would be treated for this condition by good psychiatrists and she would be given medication to keep her life on track. In those days, people were not diagnosed as being psychotic, and so she raised her eight children herself as best she could. It was an aggressive and abusive family, which caused Hank to be overly assertive, unable to deal with his emotions, and to want to be right all the time under the pretext of justice. Unfortunately, this kind of behavior is not conducive to creating deeper social contacts.

After years of fighting injustice in the world, toward the end of his life his body indicates that it is time to start his inner process of learning how to deal with what is bothering him so much. Otherwise, he will miss out on things. He feels small and insignificant and if things are not going his way, this feeling becomes even worse. That is why he chooses to fight with someone. It makes him feel bigger. But what he would like most of all is to be able to relax, to turn off his overworked mind for a moment and just enjoy life and experience that he is okay the way he is, even if he isn't doing anything useful for the world. But he doesn't have enough courage to do this yet. It's not easy to break a seventy-year habit and I need to look very closely to determine where to start.

I start in layer 4, where the subtle energetic heart connections can be found. These are the connections Hank is struggling with and where other people can hit him the hardest and hurt him the most, which triggers his desire to be right all the time.

I perform a spiritual operation myself, which is a great thing to watch, because up until now I have only been allowed to assist at spiritual operations. In his light body, I restore the subtle energetic connection from his kidneys to his bladder, along his ureters; and I create a new energetic urethra so that the old settings can be relieved and the body can discharge its urine and emotions. After that, I cleanse the entire area.

Although I am working in layer 4 and there is no physical contact between Hank and myself, he feels his penis stinging during the treatment. The energy is starting to flow. Later, I work on his nervous system for more than an hour. The result of all this is that Hank has far less trouble urinating for days on end; his nervous system is recovering.

Despite the fact that for years Hank has kept track of the amount of fluid he consumes and discharges, and it is clear that since he was treated there has been a lot of improvement, he doesn't want to talk about his mental issues. He is unable to recognize that his way of looking at and dealing with things might be the source of his physical discomfort. As far as that is concerned, he is not open to any input from me. During our sixth session, he even denies the improvements he reported himself on previous occasions and he relapses into a very unpleasant habit of his: his need to be right. At that moment, my spirit guides indicate that under these circumstances this will be his last treatment, because he will not make any further improvements this way and it is starting to affect me negatively.

When I work with people, my energy system is open. It has to be; otherwise, I cannot perceive and work as sensitively as I need to. I create a temporarily energetic unity with the client and remove any disturbance that I am allowed to remove. So whatever troubles them, during a session I have to muster up the courage to connect with them fully, which leaves me unprotected. During sessions, I cannot connect to people and protect myself at the same time.

And of course, when I come across an intense energy that is new to me, my body might have difficulty getting rid of it. In that case, discharging the energy takes more time and effort than usual. This happens very sporadically, but when it does, it's like someone has thrown a new color on my palette and I have to figure out how to work with it.

So, although dealing with difficult energy and letting it slide off me is not usually a problem for me when I am working, it's different when the person I am fully connected to starts to hit out at me. If a client directs his aggression toward you when your heart is completely open, it is very toxic and painful. It literally hurts you physically in your heart and nervous system. And because there is no protective layer, it takes a while before you have rid your own energy system of the toxins. This happens to me during my session with Hank.

It is clear to me that Hank wants to get rid of this problem, but that he does not want to put in the effort that is (in my view) necessary – namely, taking a close look at himself and his motives. However, I am also told he needs two more sessions regarding this problem.

For a minute I'm confused, because I was given two contradictory pieces of information. Then I hit upon the idea to check my sources better. Up until I started working with Hank I only heard my own spirit guides, who proved to be very pure sources of information. But something has changed and now I can hear Hank's spirit guides as well. And because of the fact that *his* spirit guides put *his* interests first and will do anything to make sure he will be able to achieve his life goals, they make it clear to me that whatever I do, I should not discontinue treating Hank.

After consulting with my own team of spirit guides, and after listening to my own feelings and commonsense, I tell Hank that for the time being, this will be our last session; however, should he feel the need (i.e. if he is really ready to commit himself to working on his problem), he is more than welcome to come back after a month at the earliest, so his body has enough time to process everything.

Apparently, he does not feel the need, because I never see him back in my practice.

I think this is a shame, but I understand it as well. In general, the older someone is, the more difficult it is for them to let go of certain patterns, because these patterns have given the person in question something to hold onto for such a long time. And without being consciously aware of it, some people think that if they change something now, this means they are retroactively admitting they haven't handled it the right way their entire life. Of course this isn't true and it's simply a matter of progressive insight, but if you judge yourself in this way, it is very difficult to unlearn it.

Therefore, it's quite possible that when people are confronted with this at a later age, they will not learn how to deal with it in their present life and will instead carry the same themes over to their next life. There is nothing wrong with that; it's just a matter of choice. And sometimes someone chooses to do it in a different way. New round, new chances.

Aura Layer 5: The Blueprint of Your Body

In the next aura layer, the fifth, there are no emotions, thoughts or energetic connections. It contains the blueprint of your body. This fifth aura layer is also referred to by professionals as the etheric causal layer.

This layer is important because it contains the building plan in its perfect form, exactly as your soul has thought it out. In this case, perfect form means that the blueprint or master plan of your body is exactly how the wisest part of you – your soul, your Divine essence, your Higher Self or whatever you would like to call it – thinks it is necessary for you to live your life as intended and chosen by you at the soul level.

Unfortunately, this does not mean that everything in your body looks perfect or functions impeccably when looked at through our human eyes. What it does mean is that everything is working according to your personal master plan. And if your body is recovering from something, after a while it will align itself to that plan and will give it its exterior form. So the body expresses what is in the plan; it embodies the plan. If you have a crooked leg, this will be in your plan – otherwise, it would be straight (or bent)!

Differences in physical functioning between two people – even between apparently identical twins – are partly caused by the differences between their blueprints. Two people can have similar blueprints and look like each other on the outside, but your blueprint is in your fifth layer, which is an individual layer and therefore substantially different for everybody.

Illnesses and disorders, especially so-called chronic or genetic 'defects', can always be found in this layer. And although working in the first layer can result in temporary relief, which can be very pleasant for the person in question, it has no long-term effect. For example, if you temporarily take away the pain associated with a dislocated disc and the root of the problem lies in the fifth layer, the disc will always align itself to the blueprint and get dislocated and cause pain again. If, on the other hand, you are allowed to work in the blueprint, it is possible to achieve structural healing.

I am looking for such a structural solution when Mark walks into my practice.

Mark is a forty-year-old managing director of a food company. He works hard, travels a lot and spends a lot of time behind his PC. Apparently, there is something wrong with his sitting posture when he does this, because he suffers from neck and shoulder pains. I treat him in the fifth layer. Symptoms always manifest themselves in your weak spot. They are mostly linked to another afflicted layer, but this will never result in any symptoms if your blueprint does not contain a weak spot where you can experience the problem. This is the case with Mark.

I start by clearing up his entire aura to ensure that everything I will be putting in it will be able to flow and take effect. I notice his pelvic area is stiff and his lower back energy is not flowing the way it should. In addition, my stomach starts to turn. Mark notices this as well and gets slightly dizzy. I'm a bit dizzy myself and I notice there's something wrong with his vestibular system. Moreover, the bump in his neck is very tight, which causes stiffness in his neck, arms and shoulders.

In his third layer, I remove the persistent thought that he needs to be able to hold his ground in his busy job, and I notice this relaxes his lower back. Neck and upper back problems are usually rooted in a lower back problem or a problem in the pelvic area, or even in the abdominal area, so I am happy with the relaxation in the lower regions. Next, I clear up the fear-inducing thoughts in his third layer, which are stuck around his stomach. Now I can return to layer 5, where I settle down his field again. It feels a bit like stirring wallpaper paste. At first, it's a bit granular and contains several obstacles, so it needs some more stirring until it's a homogenous smooth mixture. Meanwhile, Mark has fallen asleep and lies snoring on my treatment table. When I finish, he wakes totally relaxed.

During the following session, the fifth layer needs a small adjustment, after which Mark's neck pains are gone – provided he pays attention to his sitting posture.

Finn is the thirty-five-year-old letter of the building where the company of an acquaintance of mine is established. Hoping I can help Finn, this acquaintance has invited me over. Finn has suffered from post-traumatic dystrophy fears. Post-traumatic dystrophy is an unpleasant and very painful illness in which the nervous system sends out strong pain signals when there seems no reason for it to do so. This can cause muscular paralysis and a lot of pain in the patient's extremities: their hands, arms, feet and legs. Eventually, the whole body can be affected.

While we are enjoying a cup of tea, I instantly pick up his dystrophy, which is quite remarkable, because a relative of mine has the same condition but until today I have never been able to be of any help to this person. In Finn's case, however, I can be of help. While I am drinking my tea, I can already feel the energy flowing in my hands.

We agree on a short session as a sort of test and, if he likes it, he will come to my practice thereafter. I do not touch him as I carefully feel my way around his fifth aura layer. I am extremely careful because I now have a deeper understanding of his condition and I have felt the severe pain before. I remove some blocking energy and notice that his energy field, which was very stagnant, is starting to flow again. Finn instantly starts complaining about the tingling and pain he feels, even though I haven't touched him at all. He is impressed and wants to know more about it.

When we start our first official session, he says he has been feeling different since the test session. Secretly, he has hope of improvement again, despite – or perhaps thanks to – the fact that since the test session, he has had severe pains in his arm.

This is his story: he developed the post-traumatic dystrophy symptoms after an accident when he was a teenager. It is an autoimmune disease and, as yet, there is no remedy for it. For no apparent reason, the body attacks its own cells; normally, the immune response is aimed at foreign cells. In Finn's case, it's his nervous system that is under attack. He spent the last three summers in a wheelchair because he could not walk anymore. When this happened, his lymph nodes and blood vessels were unable to remove his bodily fluids and he swelled up. This narrowed his veins and blood vessels, which in turn caused his failure symptoms. Finn also has a chronic infection in one of his fingers, caused by an animal bite. It has never completely healed and has affected his bones and periosteal.

Finn's finger turns out to be his canary in the coal mine, the messenger of news. Mine workers used to take along canaries into the coal mines. If the birds died, this was a warning to the miners that an invisible, odorless and life-threatening gas had escaped somewhere. Finn's finger is the bringer of *good* news. After the first set of treatments, his finger heals and thus tells him he is healing, even though he does not notice anything in the rest of his body yet.

Finn's job is quite physical. He works with animals and rents accommodations to third parties. He thinks money is important and he is sensitive to what others think of him. In his own words, he is 'not that good at relationships', but at the same time he judges other people pretty harshly. He has strong standards and values and he works seven days a week. He thinks people who have days off from work are 'wimps'. However, he gets tired of himself and of the world as he sees it.

He also thinks people cannot be trusted when it comes to money. Finn frequently has to deal with defaulters and even his parents have swindled money out of him in the past. So he expects the worst and, unfortunately for him, he gets it. Wanting to be in control, trust, judgment and fear of poverty are themes in Finn's life.

Apart from the sessions he has with me, he sees a chiropractor once every four weeks. I advise him to keep doing that and secretly hope that, in time, he will not need the chiropractor anymore.

Before we start the treatment, I consult an osteopath because I know that if I do things the wrong way, Finn will have a lot of needless pain. The osteopath tells me something very important: osteopaths are not allowed to treat body parts that have directly been affected by dystrophy, because it's no use putting more strain on an autonomic nervous system that is already overburdened. Nothing good can come out of that because the natural functioning of the autonomic nervous system is disturbed. The osteopath tells me that in cases like that, he always treats the surrounding body systems. First, he needs to make sure the healthy part of the client's body is working properly so it can actually process the treatment administered to the problem area.

I sense he is right and adjust my approach accordingly. Perhaps I would have also felt it without consulting the osteopath, because I always attune to the client's soul and to what I am allowed to do (I never decide this on my own), but the explanation my fellow therapist gives me is reassuring. My thinking mind gets it, which makes it easier to go along with. As it later turns out, it all happened for a reason because after the first two sessions, Finn notices no improvement whatsoever and it is difficult for me to maintain my belief in my approach. But Finn has his finger telling him he is improving – his finger is the only thing that is improving – so there we are.

Our goal will be to reduce his pain as far as possible and enable Finn to cope with the rest as best he can. I end up treating Finn eight times for two hours, at first once every two weeks, later on once every three weeks and eventually once a month. The results are remarkable.

I mainly work in layer 5, the blueprint of his body. Working on Finn's problems is quite painful for me. My own nervous system hurts during the sessions and most of the time I too have pains the day after treatment. Sometimes I stay in bed the whole day because my body has to learn to process the difficult energies. I do have some experience with learning to cope with new energies, but I'm not used to something of this caliber. It's not easy, but apparently it's the only way to go about it and it works, so it's absolutely worth it.

In short, it boils down to this: treatment of the autonomous nervous system (which after a while will cause the autonomic nervous system to join in), clearing it up and repairing it, getting the lymphatic system going again and building up a healthy immune system, stimulating his blood circulation and having it discharge all the energetic toxins together with the lymph nodes, instead of holding onto energetic charges; and finally, making a new plan in layer 5 that will be linked to the nervous system and will send out new impulses. So he gets a new operating system – and it works.

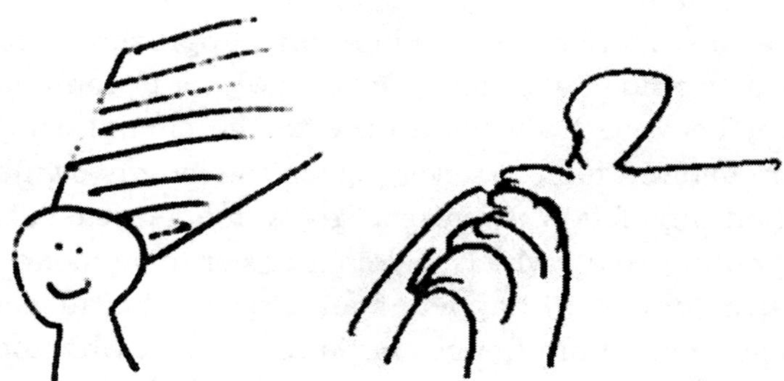

Figure 1: Blockages in Finn's body and aura that I worked on during treatment

In addition, I work on his hormonal system a number of times. The hypothalamus turns out to be the core of Finn's problem. The hypothalamus is the coordinating center in your brain, which forms the bridge between your hormonal system and your nervous system. It is where Finn receives the wrong stimuli from his nervous system, which causes his body to receive the wrong information.

Because he is in such bad shape, Finn is being treated by a neurologist. After looking at pictures taken after four sessions with me, the neurologist says Finn's legs have improved considerably. His arteries are less narrow and apparently his nervous system is letting go of its stranglehold. As a result, his veins are far more relaxed and the blood flow in his legs has demonstrably improved. This is good news because, otherwise, Finn would probably have to sit in a wheelchair for the rest of his life, with the prospect of an amputation.

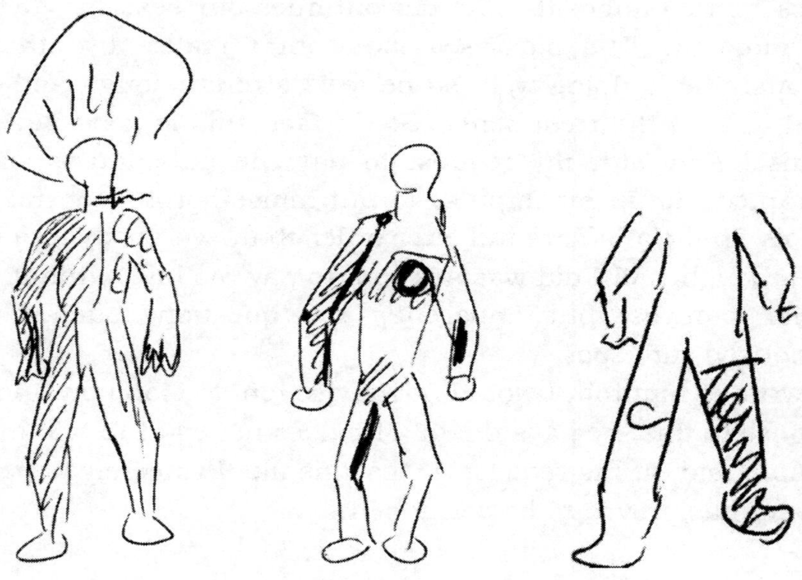

Figure 2: Blockages in Finn's body and aura that I worked on during treatment

Finn tells me the good news about the x-rays in such a stoic way that I burst out laughing, because personally I'm a bit surprised it is even possible. Up until now, I have rarely witnessed something like that. But he says, 'I know it works. I can feel it, can't I? Those x-rays are irrelevant.'

Meanwhile, he skips the occasional chiropractic session and, motivated by all of this, we continue our sessions. Finn is still improving very quickly. His long work days don't cause him any trouble, he does not suffer from physical setbacks, and in the final session we get down to his judging issue. He thinks he is the only person in the world who has his finances well-organized and that his way is the only right way. I suggest that many roads lead to Rome and that there are as many opinions as there are people. But what I hope are seeds of wisdom do not fall on fertile soil.

We have two more sessions remaining when he accidentally forgets to pay his bill. After a couple of weeks I remind him, which makes him so angry that he discontinues our sessions at that very moment. This surprises me until I realize two things. Obviously he is doing well, so he feels strong enough and can afford to stop the treatments. So, in fact, this is good news in disguise! And with my request to pay the outstanding bill, I confronted him in his impulse to put himself on a pedestal. He had his financial affairs in better order than everybody else – or so he thought. All I did was ask him to pay his bill, without any ulterior motives, but apparently my question touched the (previously) sore spot.

I write to him that I would not advise him to stop now and, in response to this, he pays the bill. He does not want to talk to me anymore and, at his request, I close his file. I sincerely hope his recovery has proved to be permanent.

Sandra's case is quite different. She's a thirty-five-year-old mother of three sons under the age of six and she's chronically tired. Her husband has a busy job that requires many trips abroad, while the responsibility of looking after the children weighs heavily and completely on her shoulders. Apart from that, she is very self-conscious and she often makes life difficult for herself. She has difficulty coping with what life has given her so far and she has doubts about her marriage.

In layer 5 I come across an energetically disturbed pituitary gland. As I said earlier, the pituitary gland sends out signals about what you have come to do and experience in your current life. Because Sandra's does not function properly, she finds it difficult to decide what she really wants to do; she receives contradictory signals. One moment she wants this and the next, she wants that. This disturbed function of the pituitary gland has also affected her physical hormonal regulation, probably because the problem has been present for years.

So during a series of sessions, I balance the hormonal axis in her fifth aura layer. In doing so, I adjust the blueprint and, consequently, the actual functioning of her body.

Mark, Finn and Sandra are three totally different clients with three totally different physical problems. Nevertheless, the solution for all of them is found in the fifth aura layer, in adjusting the blueprint of the body. This provides the body with new information, which allows it to continue its recovery and healing based on this revised building plan. This way, it becomes healthier.

Aura Layer 6: Individual Traumatic Experiences from Your Present and Past Lives

There are no signs of any blueprints when we look at aura layer 6. This is where the traumatic experiences from your present and past lives can be found, traumas on a personal level. This concerns things you have experienced earlier in your present life or further back in time in a past life. It is about experiences that are important only to you. These experiences left you with something negative, which is still troubling you in your present situation.

This is where 'illogical' emotions often spring from, sensations of déjà vu and fear, such as fear of heights, fear of water or being terrified of animals that do not live in your part of the world. You can like people the first time you see them (the positive variant) or you can instantly dislike them based on earlier unpleasant experiences, for example when a particular person's soul was wearing a different cloak.

The good thing about such previous experiences is that there is nothing you have to work out with this person right now. Initially, you still have old emotions, thoughts, fears or something else that the experience left you with, and the person you encounter triggers these in you. But by doing so, they present you with a gift. Without being aware of it, they hold a mirror in front of you. They make clear to you that there is work for you to do for yourself. They touch upon the old problem, which does not belong to your present life, in order for you to clear it out and let go of it so you can become more whole.

To put it another way, imagine three weeks ago you went for a swim and you are still carrying the bag with your swimming gear and bath towel in it. This is not very practical or even necessary. It has started to smell, because everything was wet, and you are needlessly dragging along a heavy burden. So when someone else somehow shows you that you're still carrying that swimming bag, it's a wonderful signal! And the nicest thing about it is that they do not have to tell you anything in words, because their energy is enough to trigger you.

John is suffering from a past life trauma without being aware of it. He is an independent salesman who is going on sixty. His marriage is fine, he works out a lot and he is passionate about what he eats and drinks. Physically, he is extremely fit. As far as his work is concerned, however, he has not been doing very well over the past few years, which has had its repercussions: he has no money left in his bank account and his wife has been paying the mortgage for several years, which puts a lot of pressure on her because of the financial responsibility resting on her shoulders. As a result, she is suffering from stress symptoms. John knows this, but he does not succeed in turning the financial tide. It's difficult for him to get going, because he doesn't know what to do anymore. He even gets a bit angry when we talk about his work, and I notice John is frustrated and feels he has been treated unfairly.

All the same, we start the session and in layer 6 I come across three relevant past lives. In the first one, he is a policeman in Italy. This life directly precedes his current life, so it is very recent. He is a policeman fighting injustice, in this case the Mafia, but he does not succeed in eradicating 'evil'. He is fighting a losing battle, which leaves him with a feeling of failure. This feeling is reinforced when his little boy is murdered in retaliation and he is unable to catch the killer.

This causes John to link 'effort' to 'results'. He believes his efforts were in vain because he didn't achieve any visible results soon enough. This thinking pattern is still bothering him in his current life. Sometimes we do the right thing, but the results don't come as quickly as we would like. This does not say anything negative about our actions; it only stands as evidence that on Earth there is a certain time span between cause and effect, action and reaction.

Next, I see a life in Ireland. Again, it is a life with a lot of aggression in it. He is a man, a Protestant, and his wife is killed while fighting for her faith. The message of this life is: 'fighting is not the way'. After his wife's passing, he is a gardener without work and he lives in poverty. The peculiar thing about reading this life as a fighting Irish gardener is that in his present life, in which he is having financial problems, he is a gardener on the side.

Then I see the life preceding the one in Ireland. He is a Belgian state policeman and leads a rather heartless life. In this life he does not have any real problems, but he does do some unpleasant things, creating karma that he is faced with in his subsequent lives. After all, the law of cause and effect works on the soul level and sometimes over a longer period of time than just one life.

As a result of this, John's themes are: 'What are the subtleties of good and evil? What do you believe in and what are you entitled to? What does justice mean? Do you trust life is treating you fairly?' For all these themes, I remove the obstacles and make sure things calm down again. Without being aware of it, John's past lives left him with a profound disbelief in happy endings, resulting in his getting stuck.

One week after this session, his wife tells me he is walking around cheerfully and that, thanks to his renewed energy and the trust he is able to feel again, he is working through a long 'to do' list. One month after his third and final session, he closes a fantastic business deal, which means he does not have to worry about money anymore and can earn his own money again.

Another enterprising type is Peter, a brisk sixty-eight-year-old man who is still working full-time. He runs his own business and spends a lot of time on his mobile phone and travelling across the country visiting clients on a daily basis. But these client contacts are increasingly difficult for him. Occasionally, he misses signals and shades of meaning because his ears are not functioning properly anymore: he has a punctured eardrum, he suffers from tinnitus, sometimes he hears a whistling sound and he is partly deaf in both of his ears, which is getting worse. In addition, he suffers from a balance disorder and during his first visit, the pressure on his breast indicates that he is very stressed by the present economic crisis.

While interviewing him on this first visit, his spirit guides tell me the tinnitus can be corrected in about five weeks. But this will not make his hearing better; unfortunately I cannot help him with that. However, his vestibular system is out of balance, which I *can* do something about, and I can certainly remove the stress and residual energies from his aura, which are creating all these problems. To keep his expectations realistic, I tell him what I expect the end result to be and we set to work.

In this case I start in aura layer 5, which is the blueprint of his body and therefore also of his ears. First I remove the excess tension because if I don't start here, his body will be unable to process the rest of the treatment. Next, I work on the cranial nerve of his right ear, which shows an under-voltage, and I work on his 'metabolism'. Here, metabolism means the exchange of stimuli and bodily tissues in his ear, such as the eardrum and the anvil, which have to be able to pass on the impulses. At the moment, they can't to do this because, energetically, they look sticky. This prevents them from vibrating properly, so first we increase their capability to pass on vibrations.

Next in line are the stomach and lungs, because the nervus vagus is overstimulated. The nervus vagus is the large nerve that provides all the organs in your abdomen with information from your brain. It also – as is the case here – reports back to the control center in your brain when stress levels in your body are too high. After that, I reset the voltage in the cranial nerve and I work on his left auditory nerve, after which I reset the corresponding cranial nerve. Then we go to layer 6.

In layer 6 I find an 'energetic wad'. You can compare this to a wad of earwax that you cannot remove yourself. The wad is made up of emotional stuff that Peter has blocked in the past, but which is important nevertheless. These are things that were painful and, at times, even traumatic for him to hear, so he managed to keep them outside his body (the outside of his eardrums). As it turns out, there is a link to his heart. The things Peter was told by his parents did not contribute to a pleasant inner balance. He was the black sheep of the family, career-wise he was the least successful and, because of that, his family made very unpleasant verbal attacks on him. So his parents' criticism had an effect on his inner balance. Balance is linked to the vestibular system and, consequently, the balance between Peter and his environment and the people in it.

I discover there was a serious fight during which Peter's brother shouted very hurtful things at him. These things were aggressive and hurtful to such an extent that he has put them safely away and cries when he talks to me about them for the first time in forty years. After this problem is cleared up and he can breathe more easily, two past lives pop up.

The first one is two lives ago. It takes place in Europe and ends around 1872. Peter is a twenty-two-year-old woman who is in love. This life is about aggression. Another woman grabs her by her throat, because she is jealous of her relation with a man. He is not even her husband. All parties involved are single and it is a sudden jealous fit of madness. 'Peter' did not see it coming and loses her balance both literally and figuratively, which she takes along with her when she dies and it is still with her in her current life. She drew from this an unhelpful conclusion that at the time was logical, but has now resulted in a limiting belief: 'loving somebody can cost you your life'. This unconscious thought is the reason why, in his current life, Peter only partly gives his heart to his wife; he never really opens up or has the courage to commit himself fully to the relationship. I neutralize this problem and rewrite the belief to 'it is safe to love somebody'.

We move on to the second past life. Chronologically, it seems to be the life after the first one, so the life between the one we have worked on and his present life. He is a boy who lives from 1931 to 1935. Because of his previous life, he quickly loses his balance and frequently suffers from inflammations of his middle ear.

That was his way of trying to resolve that aspect of his previous life, but unfortunately, he was unsuccessful. That is why he brought it with him to this life, aiming to solve the problem this time around – and he did! The accompanying theme is 'finding balance', not tipping the scale to one side out of safety, but being open to other people and connecting with them. In practical terms, this has to do with creating a balance between what you think and what the rest of the world and your family think; a balance between yourself and your wife, between working and living, and between rational and spiritual.

Already after the first session, Peter is a lot more relaxed. The whistling sound is gradually diminishing and his tinnitus is improving. He is also becoming more critical, because at this stage any little ringing sound is too much for him! His relationship with his wife is becoming warmer and they speak about each other in more positive terms.

After three sessions, I have done what I can and we round off our collaboration. For the most part, his symptoms have either gone or improved dramatically. The only thing that has not changed is his hearing problem, as anticipated before we started. In spite of that, Peter is satisfied and feels better than before. He plans on purchasing a trendy hearing aid. A new world will open up for him now that he is ready for what that world has to say to him.

Nate is a twenty-four-year-old creative graphic designer who has a number of food allergies. He thinks they are a nuisance and sometimes disregards them, which of course has repercussions. He is also a bit cross-grained in other ways. For example, he has difficulty complying with business conventions, the written and unwritten rules of business life. They make him obstinate and he doesn't intend on following them.

In addition, he is sensitive to the energy of entities (deceased people who do not go straight to the Light and are temporarily stuck on Earth). He can even see them, but this does not help his case. On the contrary, it makes him even more obstinate, because he doesn't want to see them. In short, Nate is paranormal, but he doesn't *want* to be paranormal. Furthermore, he has concentration problems. During four sessions I work on eleven problems in aura layer 6, among which are eight past lives, which is a considerable number.

It starts with Nate not really being here on Earth. He is not fully grounded and his energy sits half an inch higher than his physical body. As a result, energetically he does not touch the ground. I take over what is happening inside his body and notice that his eyesight is not what it should be. He doesn't focus with his eyes; they just wander around. It's clear that this is part of his concentration problem.

We start with two entities he is carrying along in layer 6. An entity can only stick to an energy it is familiar with. So, sad entities stick to a sad person, an angry entity seeks out a hot-headed person and a sarcastic entity looks for a place to stay in someone who is a real nuisance. By attaching themselves to the energy of people, they reinforce the energy fields of their hosts in a negative way. The sad person becomes even sadder, the angry person is full of rage and the person who is a nuisance takes out his frustration on others by tormenting them. This is not to say that you yourself are not responsible for your behavior when you have an uninvited guest, but it does mean that your behavior is worse than what it would normally be. So if you don't entirely recognize yourself in what you are doing, this could mean you are hosting an entity.

In Nate's case, entity 1 is a boy who died at the age of six. There is something wrong with his chest, with his heart chakra. He was living in Breda and during the Second World War he was selected to go to a concentration camp. He died there in the absence of his family and, in a way, he is still looking for them. During his search he met Nate and because they have a common problem related to their spleens – they both don't really know what to do with their lives – he has been able to nestle himself in Nate's aura. I remove their connection, I repair their spleen problem and I guide the first entity to the Light.

Then I meet entity number 2: a fourteen-year-old boy who has been dead for about eight years. He died in an accident. He was in a hurry, lost sight of the traffic and got hit by a car while crossing the road. Having a good overview of things is linked to Nate's left eye. I break this connection and explain the situation to entity 2 and how it can go to the Light. Then I help it make a safe crossing this time.

In the next session, two past lives come up. In the first, he is a woman who was born in 1912. She is thirty-two years old when she dies in 1944 in what is now called Indonesia. She is from the East, she is black, poor, already has four children and is twenty-seven weeks pregnant with her fifth child when she suddenly drowns. She just didn't pay attention while wading through the water to the other side and should have known better, because she knew the spot. The fact that she drowned is very frustrating for her because it means that she has left her children behind. The theme is 'having and keeping a good overview'.

It turns out that Nate also drowned in the life that comes up next. He was living in the central part of the United States of America, so I am told. I see a flood disaster and, even though he's a smart kid, the river sucks him down. He lives from 1873-1886. The theme is 'being smart does not help, nor does logical thinking'. But in his present life it does, so we rewrite that unhelpful final conclusion he drew in that past life.

One session later, there is a life involving the taking of hostages. Nate brought things up to discussion, endangering his own life. This ended in his death. This has caused him to keep his mouth shut most of the time in this life.

Then I see another past life – I see a building that keeps changing. It's symbolic. The building is very old; it is about something very old that has accumulated during an entire lifetime. It turns out to be about the anger of a five-year-old boy, who has a hard time watching anger in others. He suffers from aggression directed at him and he has accumulated this aggression throughout his life, taking it with him to his present life. Luckily, it can be released now.

Next, he is a female healer, a Shaman* in Central America, near Mexico. She's killed because she is accused of using black magic. There is also unjustified aggression and, as a result, an aversion to integrating and applying his paranormal qualities in his present life. After all, this has cost him his life before. This is followed by a life in which Nate poisons his wife and he is found out. The essence of this life is 'you are not supposed to do it and you know it is not right'. Purity and knowing what is right, and knowing who you are, are the issues that I clear up and reformulate.

In the life that announces itself next, he is a Canadian priest who is at the head of an orthodox religious community. He came to live there when he was seven years old and, at the time, he was brainwashed (my words) into judging other, non-religious people. When considered more closely, this judgment is unjustified. In this life, he learns you have to live according to the rules – or else. As a result, rules make Nate obstinate, which sometimes gets him into trouble. So we do something about it and remove the burden of that previous judgmental life.

During the next session, I come across a past life from very nearby, Belgium, just across the border in the Breda area. Nate lived there during the First World War. In this life, he has to defend his country, despite the fact that he does not want to and knows it is no use trying to fight or flee; he will not survive. He is killed by mustard gas and links this to the fact that he was supposed to obey. He wanted to do things differently himself. In his heart, he did not want to go to war. Following rules and obeying have not been very beneficial to him and, as a result, he has an obstinacy issue. I neutralize the 'mustard gas life' and he can continue with his life, on to the next experience.

In the next past life (which extends to layer 11), he is a woman with a weak heart, living about 350 years ago. She has a heart attack. A faith healer is called in, but to no avail; the man is a fraud. 'Nate' dies despite her devotion to her faith and deep trust in the church. This event causes her to lose trust in her religion, the church and the paranormal, because in her view they are unreliable. She is not aware of the fact that, in that life, it was simply her time to go. She drew a conclusion that is still affecting her: 'religion and the paranormal can't be trusted'. Consequently, she denies an important personal part of herself and leaves it unused. The result is clear: in his present life, Nate is incapable of using his paranormal qualities freely.

All in all, Nate proves to have had a lot of reasons for not wanting to see or experience certain things, and for becoming cross-grained when confronted with them. Fortunately, rewriting his limiting beliefs, freeing him of entities and clearing up other painful issues have a positive effect on his attitude toward life and work.

Joy is a twenty-seven-year-old nurse who suffers from neck pains and sometimes has difficulty coming to terms with the way she has to work. She doesn't know how to make this clear to her superiors. Part of Joy's work involves psychiatric patients. In layer 6, I come across a past life in which she was a slave in Madagascar 304 years ago. Counting back, this would be the year 1705. A friend of hers is about to be raped by her owner and 'Joy' tries to help her friend by stepping in. She has to pay for this with her life; he cleaves her neck with a big knife, cutting her head clean off her body.

Understandably, Joy takes away from this the following beliefs: 'I had better keep my mouth shut' and 'men with power can't be trusted'. The tension she feels in situations where she wants to tell people what's on her mind causes a blockage on the pain point of that past life: her neck. I heal the fracture in her neck and carefully replace her limiting beliefs with 'it is safe to say what I have to say' and 'I know exactly who I can trust'.

We agree that from now on, her heart chakra will be the determining factor when she has to make the choice of speaking up or not. Two years later, Joy tells me she has not had any neck pains since I treated her.

Layer 6 clearly shows that you can have a lot of strong qualities, but if you carry along experiences from the past that prevent you from deciding how to behave because they take away your free will, you will not accomplish as much as you would like. You become one of Pavlov's dogs*, automatically responding to a certain stimulus because you once had an unpleasant experience in a similar situation – even if you don't remember anything about it.

In Nate's case, there were a lot of past life experiences that made him cross-grained and prevented him from utilizing his paranormal abilities. Peter did not want to and so he could not hear anything, and John got stuck as a result of the supposed injustice he was confronted with at work. Joy preferred keeping her mouth shut to having her head cut off again. All of them exhibited behavior they preferred not to exhibit anymore. This behavior disappeared after the original sources of the trauma were healed.

Aura Layer 7: Your Life Plan

Your seventh aura layer contains your individual life plan and its corresponding themes. This blueprint of your life can sometimes be adjusted during treatments, when you want to make new life choices on the soul level and when you want to implement profound changes. In most of these cases, your soul has sufficiently undergone certain experiences it created for itself and it now chooses to enter a new phase.

As a human being, you can reach a stage where you are fed up with coming across the same themes over and over again and you can sense it's time for a big change. Unfortunately, in real life it doesn't work quite that way. The timing and changes and/or adjustments of your blueprint are prompted by your soul. Sometimes you are unable to make that turnaround or change on your own, but a Light Worker can support you in the process.

Please note that the Light Worker 'only' functions as an instrument and does not determine when it is time to move on to the next phase or what this should look like. But people who can help others at this level can translate and pass on your soul's intentions energetically. In this way, the Light Worker can clear up the layer and make adjustments to it in order for you to continue on your life path.

In my practice, I hardly ever work exclusively in layer 7. Usually there will be blockages in other aura layers, too. When I do work in layer 7, in two thirds of cases I start in layer 7 because I am allowed to write a new piece of the plan. Next, I go to the layers where the problems are that need to be solved.

The seventh aura layer has everything to do with entering new phases in your life. It is about making defining choices. I often notice this causes people to suffer from past life Issues when they reach the age at which the original trauma took place. Apparently, apart from the themes of your current life, you can find yourself faced with issues from past lives that require healing. If these are only traumatic for you personally, we come across them in your sixth aura layer. If they actually impact the course of your life and threaten to prevent you from going through important life experiences that are written in your life plan, these traumas can be found in aura layer 7.

An example from my practice: Sam is a four-year-old boy who refuses to eat fresh vegetables. He gets angry and throws tantrums in an effort to tyrannize the whole family. When I examine him, I see a past life in layer 7 in which he was a four-year-old girl who died from radiation. It is an Eastern Bloc country and I can see a nuclear reactor. I suspect we are dealing with the Chernobyl disaster. The girl lives near the reactor in the area where the radiation comes down. The radioactivity has accumulated in her body to such an extent that she dies from eating toxic vegetables.

As I wonder why I come across this in layer 7, I suddenly see that Sam has to make a choice. He is still carrying the memory of his previous blueprint and lives accordingly – but this time around he can choose to let this go and move on with his life. Therefore, I remove the old thought that fresh vegetables are life-threatening and I neutralize the memory. After that, things improve for him. The tantrums are a thing of the past and Sam occasionally eats vegetables, although I don't think he really fancies them.

Stefan's is quite a different story. He is an attractive manager in his early forties, the type that makes women's heads turn. But he is unaware of this, because Stefan is very insecure and sometimes feels he is still a boy. You see, he is an illegitimate child. His mother is married to what he calls his 'name giver'

when she gets pregnant by somebody else. When the secret is revealed, his parents instantly divorce. He only hears the real reason when he is a teenager and this causes him to lose his footing in life. He eventually grows up with 'father number three'.

In Stefan's case, 'having extramarital relationships' and 'having secrets' are relevant family themes. Throughout his lives, various men and women in his families have cheated on their spouses for generations, sometimes resulting in offspring. So, on the soul level he has chosen a family that forces him to deal with this theme. In fact, it fits perfectly, because in his life plan he has also written down the option to enter into an extramarital relationship himself.

He falls under the spell of a woman and starts an affair with her. His wife finds out and wants him to choose her and his children, but that is not so easy for him. He feels guilty and torn apart, which is not very surprising because he has a soul agreement with the person he's having the affair with. This agreement is written in aura layer 18.

I work with him in higher layers and Stefan finally chooses to break up with his mistress. They do not see or speak to each other for six months and her spell loses its hold on him. Stefan is actually doing quite well. He is putting his life in order and he and his wife work on their relationship. But his ex-girlfriend is not ready to let him go that easily and keeps approaching him with text messages and propositions. One day, he gets another of these invitations to have a drink together, which shakes him a bit. Eventually he decides to meet her one final time to make it clear that it really is over between them. He does this and it is a great relief to him. It makes him feel freer.

However, something is still not right: he has not told his wife about this final meeting. He doesn't have the courage to do so. When I hear that, I use my semi-strict voice to tell him this will be his homework for next time. I know this will stress him out and I am glad to see it actually does. It allows me to remove the stress so it will not bother him as much when he owns up to his wife later on. He laughs when I admit I triggered the stress on purpose.

The next thing I ask is why he is afraid to tell his wife. After all, nothing improper happened. He replies that they are going on holiday tomorrow and he is afraid his wife will cancel the trip, and his little boys will be the ones to suffer.

So I ask him, 'Why would she cancel the trip?'

'Because she might think I cheated on her again,' he replies.

'But you didn't, and there's nothing wrong with telling her that so she can feel you are telling the truth. You didn't kiss or touch each other, did you?' I ask.

'No, we didn't,' Stefan says.

I feel he is telling the truth, so I continue unrelentingly. 'And did you feel the urge to do so?'

'No, not for one second,' he says.

So in a cheerful voice I say to him, 'Tonight you are going to tell your wife that you met up with your ex-girlfriend and why you did so – and you're going to explain why you didn't tell her about it before. You can't undo the past, but you can prove to be reliable in the present. And you can build that kind of trust on moments like this. Talk about it with her so she can understand your point of view. She needs that because she also feels insecure. And she might think you should break off all contact with your ex, which is understandable, but you're a grown man and it's up to you to decide what's the wisest thing to do in a certain situation. And for you, it felt right to meet with your ex to close that chapter of your life.'

'But what about the holiday? We're leaving tomorrow.'

'Well,' I reply, 'if your wife blows her top and doesn't want to go, she's entitled to do so. It's her choice. You can still go on holiday with your children. Or you can stay at home. It wouldn't be the end of the world, you know – as long as you're aware of the fact that it is her choice and you don't have to feel guilty if your children are disappointed.' I can see he understands me, but that he still can't believe this might actually work.

Next, we work in layer 7, on his first chakra, the foundation of his life. It is about making new life choices and really standing up for what he believes and for himself. He leaves with his homework and, with a smile, I wish him a good holiday.

The next day Stefan rings me up. 'It all went well,' he says, somewhat surprised. He came home and told his wife that I had given him some homework. Then he told his wife what he had done. Initially, she didn't like it, but they did not fight or make a scene. They just discussed it calmly, which allowed her to notice that something had changed in him.

Stefan feels more relaxed and stronger now. He has had a positive experience with being the bringer of an awkward message. This is something he will build upon in the future. None of the things he was afraid might happen and therefore avoided discussing actually happened. He can conclude from this that he no longer has to keep his mouth shut in order to stay out of trouble.

With this lesson in mind, the whole family goes on holiday as planned.

Lobbyist Matt is also a frequent traveler because he has an international job requiring him to stay abroad at least three days a week. He is the father of three sons who are all under the age of seven and one of them has Down's syndrome. He manages to hold his own by having a rational approach to life. This is working fine, because he never really wavers and performs well professionally, but his wife is not very happy. She doesn't feel there is a real connection between them. Matt struggles with two things: his wife wants to have a fourth child and he has to dismiss a co-worker with whom he has worked for a long time.

The decision to have a fourth child is particularly difficult for him because during her previous pregnancy, his wife developed pelvic instability when it was still early days. This also caused a lot of pain and fuss after the pregnancy, with three children to take care of while he was abroad five out of seven days. So he is very worried about it. He gets particularly emotional when he thinks about the effect all this might have on his wife. This emotion is linked to his heart chakra; after all, Matt loves his wife.

He also spends a lot of time supervising the co-worker he has to dismiss. The meticulousness with which he does this is also linked to his heart – he is very involved – while the actual dismissal affects his bronchi. It literally makes him short of breath.

In both cases, it is about making choices on his life path. In practice, that means fearlessly choosing what he wants to do most and acting according to what he feels is pure and right. So in layer 7, I first remove his fear and other emotions that are unnecessary at this moment, thereby making room for the choices Matt is going to make. Two years later, I learn that the co-worker was dismissed in a respectable way and that Matt had himself sterilized. There will be no fourth child.

All the cases I described in this chapter might give you the idea that layer 7 issues are always related to sexuality, but this is not the case. However, sexuality does play a part in many cases, because it is a form of expression of our creative power. You can create something new in life or you can use the same energy to make love. If you do not succeed in creating your ideal life, a life which is aligned with who you are, in many cases this becomes manifest in certain problems and blockages related to sexuality. These are two variations on the same theme.

So despite the fact that examples from layer 7 are not necessarily linked to sexuality, here follows another one.

Charles is the forty-year-old owner of an advertising company in Rotterdam. He wants me to coach him in his interaction with his employees. Not long after the third session, he calls me for an emergency appointment. Somewhat bashfully, he tells me the reason for this: his life is falling apart because his wife has found out about his regular visits to prostitutes. For a moment, I am taken by surprise because I did not notice any of this during our previous sessions. This time, however, he opens up and I can see it. Charles has decided to share this issue with me and so I am allowed to see it.

I sense there is more and I ask him if this is all he has to say about it, because when you are 'owning up' to things, you might as well get it all out in the open. I turn out to be right and he tells me he has been a sex addict since the age of eighteen. His addiction causes him to download pornographic material from the Internet and to make daily visits to private clubs and streetwalkers. The problem is progressive; it gets worse and worse. Apart from that, the amount of alcohol he consumes on a daily basis could also be categorized as an addiction.

I tell him honestly that I am not an expert in this area and that I have to see if and how I can help him. I have to take a moment to check if I can see where the origin of the problem lies. I end up in layer 7, so I tell him I can assist him in his approach to his problem. The problem is related to what he does not want to feel, which he tries to avoid by drinking too much and giving in to his sex addiction. This is a soul issue that requires a lot of work.

Charles wonders if he should go to a rehabilitation center, but he prefers not to as it would take some explaining to his clients. He is in the middle of selling his company, so it might negatively affect the turnover and sales figures. He would rather put it off until after the sale. I understand this and we agree on four sessions within a two-week period. Cancelling an appointment means pulling out and ending our arrangement. If he does that, he can go straight to rehab if he wants to. I tell him I will contact an addiction expert for advice and if he agrees to my assessment and approach, that will be how we proceed. After the fourth session, we will have an evaluation and if my approach is working, we will continue and I will tell him when I think he is ready for the rehabilitation clinic. From then on, we can follow a two-track policy – mainstream and complementary – depending on what he needs.

This is my plan for Charles: I think his addiction is essentially related to fear and insecurity. Insecurity causes restlessness, resulting in compensatory behavior: doing things in order not to feel something, to avoid having to deal with it, as a means of distraction or as a way to release tension. The division between his feeling and thinking has become very serious. In Charles' case, emotion and physical security do not easily go hand in hand, because this would mean being vulnerable. This prevents him from relaxing with the person he shares his emotions with (his wife). But he does want to get rid of that physical tension once in a while, so he hires someone for that.

I can see energetic blockages in layer 5: they are physical blockages in his brain, so the predisposition is already there. In the second layer, I see emotional patterns and in the third layer, his mental blockages are emerging. In layer 7, I come across spiritual issues, as well as something that looks like an energetic malformation.

Apart from treating him and tracking down, clearing up and repairing blockages through his aura, I will teach Charles how to relax physically and what balance feels like. At the same time, he will have a close look at what he feels and does in any situation. He will write this down and we will analyze these things together, and he will show his wife what I do. Next, we will analyze and feel and really experience the things that disturb his balance between sessions, so he will notice that he can analyze, feel and experience these things, and that his world is not going to fall apart if he is faced with a problem. In this way, he will build his self-confidence and develop skills he can use to deal with situations that are new to him.

When I speak to addiction expert Tony, I am happy to see we are on the same page. He just describes it more elegantly when he says, 'When somebody does something he's not supposed to do and he's found out, this is an implicit call for help.' This is true. Some people want to be caught without being aware of it. And from the soul perspective, this is perfectly true. Now Charles is ready to work on this issue and he can get help with it. His soul has asked for it.

Tony also teaches me something else I did not know: addictions often run in families, so he thinks Charles, too, must have had a male example in his family. And he says, 'Breaking the addiction requires willpower, because his wife has (unknowingly) condoned his behavior for years.'

The first question I ask Charles at the beginning of a series of new sessions is: which of your relatives also visited prostitutes? The answer is: his father and his grandfather. Tony was right; it's a family theme.

Charles really looks up to his father and is so competitive because he wants his father's approval. Furthermore, he cried a lot as a baby and as a child he was overly anxious. Charles puts up a positive front and he likes to please other people. He avoids difficult situations and confrontations and hates arguing. However, he can also suddenly become very aggressive. Being an only child, he is quite spoilt; he often gets his way and his parents still almost cuddle him to death. Meanwhile, he has a lot of inner anger directed toward both himself and the world in general and he basically feels inferior and insecure. He is very sensitive to appearances; he has a good-looking wife, lovely children, a big house and a beautiful car. He also drinks a lot of alcohol, mostly wine and champagne. All of this is an attempt to restrain his dissatisfaction and anxiety. Luckily, he is aware of this, which makes him feel liberated. Putting his cards on the table has given him more energy and the willingness to work on his issues.

I also see a serious fear of failure in him and a number of other indefinable anxieties. As a child, he was attacked by some dogs and that fear is still present in his field. We work on that.

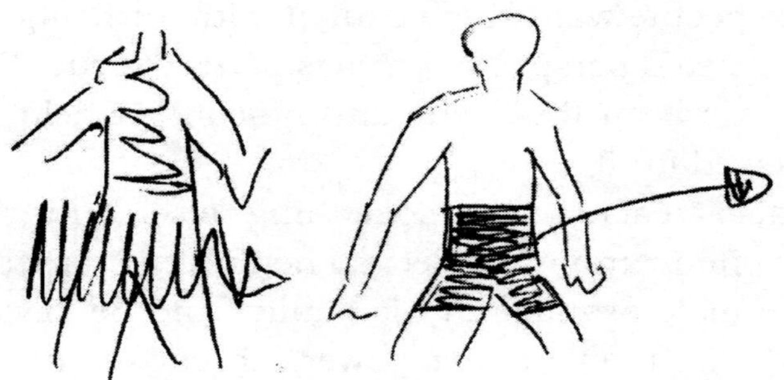

Figure 3: Areas of Charles' blockages during our sessions

During the following sessions, I do an exercise with him in which he learns first to contract his muscles and then relax them** In this way, he experiences his body a lot more, which allows him to release some of his tension. I advise him to perform this exercise in the morning and evening. The exercise works and the rest of the treatment also proves beneficial. Charles feels no urge to visit the red light district anymore.

The only negative thing at this stage is that he is too casual about it. He still thinks it's a matter of willpower and that he has enough of that. Unfortunately, this is not the case and, after two-and-a-half months of hard work, he experiences a setback. He is watching pornographic movies on TV again and he visits pornographic websites. This turns out to be linked to his head (his way of thinking) and to his second and third chakras. The second chakra is the energetic junction of sexual energy and the third is involved in receiving stimuli and emotions from other people.

Charles tells me he has witnessed a recent car accident and was the first to arrive at the scene. The car was folded around a tree. He called emergency services and stayed with the accident victims until the ambulance came. I can feel the stress this experience caused in him and I can also see how it works. Certain stimuli enter his solar plexus, his third chakra. Sometimes there are so many that he cannot handle them, in which case they go to his second chakra, where he finds relief through an orgasm. This seems to solve his tension problem, at least on a physical level.

There is a field attached to his head in which the time when he was bullied as a child emerges. When he had his first girlfriend, he ejaculated prematurely when they had sex for the first time, resulting in an inferiority complex and the first signs of the division between having a physical orgasm and connecting to someone emotionally. Now it gradually dawns upon him that willpower alone is not enough, and that it takes day-long effort; it's about time he accepts reality and lets go of his unrealistic expectations. However, this causes a severe headache and his negative self-image troubles him again.

During the next session, we come across a soul agreement between Charles and his wife, father and children in aura layer 9. As described in the chapter 'Aura layer 9', this is his main life theme, which he has chosen on the soul level. I support him in this by putting things back in order in his field and by cleansing it so Charles can move on.

After layer 9 has been cleansed, it's time for Charles to make an appointment with the addiction clinic and work on his addiction problem in a goal-oriented way. It will take a few months before they can admit him, but that doesn't mean he can't go into therapy in the meantime. I meet up with his therapist so we can attune our approaches and, after that, we start our parallel treatments.

During each of the treatments, I remove issues in layer 7 to enable him to put his life plan into practice, and in layer 5 I work on his blueprint, adjusting it a little bit every time I need to. I do this because, according to his blueprint and life plan, his brain is submerged in addiction mode. It always conforms to its blueprint. By gradually adjusting that blueprint, his brain is desensitized to the addiction. It's similar to getting braces. They slowly force your teeth into the right direction; they are not pushed into the right position all at once, because that would cause them to break. Every time you visit the orthodontist, your braces are adjusted, screwed more tightly, until the end result is good. This is similar to how the brain functions.

Among other things, I work on the dopamine level* and neutralize and balance the two hemispheres of the brain. Luckily, this works quite well. We have enough to do while the process of selling Charles' business is well underway and the takeover date is arranged.

Figure 4: Blockages in Charles' body: how he separated emotions from physical experiences

In the final two months of the six that I treat Charles, all I do is help him stay at a certain level and prevent setbacks, so he can get to the addiction clinic in one piece. I balance his brain hemispheres and remove excess stress. It goes well and he feels fine because he does not feel any urges anymore and there are no setbacks. At the same time, of course, he is not fully healed yet. If you need weekly clearing-up sessions in order to be able to maintain a certain level, there is still work to do.

The day after the contract is signed and his business is handed over to its new owner, Charles goes to Scotland and checks into a specialist clinic. A month later, he somewhat nervously returns home feeling like a new man and, in every aspect, starts his new life.

With Charles' case as a final example, you now have an idea of what the first seven aura layers are about. They only show issues that are important to you personally: your feelings and your thoughts; your connection with others and what this does to you; your body, with all its less pleasant and less attractive qualities, and the traumas that affect your daily life; and, finally, the course of your life.

However, you are not alone on this planet. You are part of humanity, a large group consisting of seven billion people who have all chosen to incarnate. And apart from being a human being, you are also black, white, yellow, red or brown – you belong to a certain race, which is another group of people.

Besides being a world citizen, you are also an Asian, European, African or American, which makes you part of yet another group. You also belong to a certain nation. For example, you are Dutch, German or English. And you are either a man or a woman.

You are born within your biological family (yet another group that you belong to) and sometimes you grow up elsewhere, for example, with the people who adopted you or in a children's home, where you meet members of other groups you are part of. If you are a woman and you fall pregnant, suddenly you're a member of the 'association of mothers'.

We all drift in and out of innumerable groups during the course of our lives. And all these collectives affect your life through your higher aura layers. In the following chapters, you can read how that works.

Aura Layer 8: Interpersonal Goals and Soul Agreements

Simply put, every life consists of coming to Earth to learn something in order for you to develop your soul (I call this 'getting something') and coming to Earth to do something (to bring something to the world). The learning part mostly involves being focused on yourself, because you are growing and becoming a better and more conscious person. During the course of your life, certain things get easier, which in the long run makes it easier to make the choices that reflect what you really want.

The bringing part involves you making the world a slightly better place to live for the larger whole of humanity. This may sound a bit heavy, but without becoming a Mother Teresa, you can still do something good for your circle of people through the positive things you bring to the world. So if you are a pastry cook, this may look like baking the most delicious and finest cakes every day for your customers to enjoy thoroughly, instead of producing average pastry on an assembly line.

If, on the other hand, you are an assembly line worker, this 'bringing' may look like doing your job with a smile and a cheerful heart in a pleasant atmosphere, thereby creating a pleasant working environment for your colleagues. Apart from that, you can do your best to make as few mistakes as possible and to connect to the product, which would give the end result a higher and more positive energetic charge than if you were to do the work on autopilot.

And if you were born to do something completely different, something you have not got round to doing yet, this means you are exploring the possibilities of growing toward what your heart says you would really like to do, and you are on your way to doing it. In this way, you can make the world a better place by starting with yourself.

So in every life, you experience things you can learn from, which helps you grow. Examples of these are written down in aura layers 1 to 7. Of course, this is not the only way you can learn and grow. Another way of doing this is together with other people.

When two souls decide to do so, they usually make agreements in order to work out soul issues. These agreements are called soul agreements. This often happens between relatives, parents and children, who prearrange a particular division of roles, which allows them to encounter the things that are difficult for them to cope with. For example, an arrogant father gets an insecure child who withdraws in order to protect himself, and this withdrawal is something the father has trouble coping with. In this way, both parties learn to deal with something they find difficult to handle.

There may also be a soul agreement between two lovers. This type of soul agreement can have many different faces. Sometimes the agreement involves finding the love of their lives in each other and together they are meant to live happily ever after. Sometimes the agreement only involves two people starting a relationship and loving each other dearly, but the final outcome is not fixed.

Some souls only join in order to have children and to learn from each other, before they go their own separate ways, despite the fact that the children connect them to each other. Yet other souls meet and start a relationship so that one can take care of the other during an incurable disease. This may look like an unbalanced relationship, but most of the time you don't know what happened between them in previous lives and how they have divided their roles this time around.

Parents and children can also make soul agreements. For example, the child arranges with his mother that he will be the victim of abuse. While some agreements appear to be incomprehensible from a human point of view (obviously a human would never consciously choose such a situation), on the soul level other things are at play. On the soul level, it is about agreements between two individuals in order to work out issues and gain and generate experiences that allow them to achieve their life goals and sub-goals. Together, they create the right circumstances for this.

Souls also make agreements to fulfill their 'bringing' tasks and to work together on important projects. For example, you might have an agreement with a colleague with whom you establish a spiritual center; a professional football player may have a soul agreement with his coach, who gives him the space to grow, to shine and to entertain the fans; or perhaps you are hand in glove with your neighbor when it comes to helping out at school activities your children partake in.

An important aspect of all soul agreements is that on the soul level, agreements are made in order to direct the stage play of your life as suitably as possible – but you can always deviate from this and make other choices if you have second thoughts; you always have Free Will.

Janet is twenty-eight when she first visits me. She has a big problem with her cousin. As a child she was abused by him, she tells me, so she doesn't want to be anywhere near him anymore. Understandably, she is still angry with him. Janet also recently married and would like to get pregnant, but so far she has been unsuccessful. This is probably caused by her thyroid gland problems (for which she takes medication), but she isn't sure. She is a nice, sweet woman who is highly sensitive and mostly thinks and reacts in terms of black and white; there is no grey area.

Janet's situation is quite complicated. It so happens that I have also been treating her mother Elizabeth for a while, who is struggling with the same issue of abuse. But her mother is under the impression that the abuse, as it is engraved in her daughter's memory, may be better labelled as sexual play that went too far, or even simply finding comfort in each other. Both Janet's and her cousin's parents were in the middle of a divorce at a time and the children were sad and confused.

I understand what she is saying, but I explain to Elizabeth that it would not be very wise to say such a thing to her daughter, because it would give Janet the message that her mother does not believe her or that she should see or feel things differently. We're talking about trauma here, so this would mean she would not get the support she needs from her mother.

Besides, Elizabeth doesn't know what actually happened and she doesn't know how her daughter experienced all of it, which is the crucial point here. Even if, as a child, Janet did not stop her cousin from doing what he wanted to do, this doesn't mean anything. Very often, children who are forced to perform sexual acts don't show any signs of protest. Sometimes they don't know yet that it is inappropriate and do the things they are asked to do because they like the other person. Later on, sometimes years later, when they realize what actually happened, they may feel very guilty about it.

Alternatively, if the abuser in question is physically stronger, these children may be so afraid that they decide to comply to save their own lives. Or they dissociate by withdrawing from the body in order not to have to experience it. Sometimes children are indeed involved in sexual play and they go further and further, and then later realize that you're not 'supposed' to do these things with a family member. Then social morale also becomes a factor and the behavior is condemned. In these circumstances, while at first there was no real problem, the problem is created afterward.

That is why you can never judge these things and the best thing you can do is support the child involved as (s)he comes to terms with the trauma. Whatever happened or seems to have happened, it's a big problem that has to be dealt with. The exact events are not relevant anymore; the way they are dealt with is.

It is clear to me that Elizabeth is very concerned about her daughter, despite the fact that their versions of what happened are somewhat different. Meanwhile, Janet does not feel her mother supports her enough because she does not choose her side unconditionally. She remains neutral. That hurts, which is understandable. On the other hand, Elizabeth doesn't want to lie and simply looks at the issue from a different angle. I also understand that she does not want to pretend. Mother and child seem unable to resolve the issue between them, at least not by talking about it.

I get to work with Janet and look at the causes of her childlessness. I see a baby and I hear 'two years' so I tell her I think she needs to let go of the idea for the coming two years. That would remove the pressure, at least for a while. Apparently, it's not the right time; her child's soul is not yet ready, or something else has to happen first that we have no knowledge of. Whatever may be the case, we will use that time to work on Janet's thyroid gland problem and the issue of her abuse so the child will be able to grow up surrounded by as pleasant an energy as possible. And because everything you have dealt with yourself cannot be projected onto your child, Janet thinks this is an excellent idea.

I see that in her abdomen there is still a lot of unresolved anger related to the abuse, and that the future child (which will be a son) is having trouble with that. In the present situation, he would have to grow inside a mother who hates little boys, which is not a very pleasant thing to look forward to. I am told he has difficulty with the negative role she has assigned her cousin and how this has made her feel about men in general.

I have no opinion about what actually happened back then. I only conclude from the way Janet talks about this that she still sees herself too much as a victim, and that this is not in accordance with the present situation. After all, she's a grown woman now who has her life on track and, for the most part, has dealt with her past. Nevertheless, one way or another she keeps clinging to something from the past, an old image, which lowers her energy level. Talking about it is not very fruitful, so I decide to let my hands do the work. This will ensure that the right thing happens.

In layer 8 I come across a past life. Janet is a Chinese woman who lived about 400 years ago. As a child, she fell down a mountain and ended up with a spinal cord lesion, so now she cannot walk. She lies in the cabin all day long and doesn't see other people. She is lonely and feels abandoned. As is the case in her current life, her thyroid gland is overstrained. The thyroid gland is situated in the throat. It is the organ that has to deal with all earthly suffering and transform it into consciousness, so it has a very important task. Her thyroid gland works too hard because of the psychological pain she is enduring. There seems to be no purpose to her life. She just lies in the cabin. She can move her arms, but what good is that to her? She is lonely and feels abandoned and neglected.

Naturally, I remove the old pain and all that sadness. Then I encounter two limiting beliefs. The first one is 'life is suffering' and the other is 'people walk away if I show my true feelings'. These interferences impact her present life, so I rewrite them to 'life is there to enjoy' and 'it is safe to show my true feelings – I know exactly who I can show my true feelings to and who can deal with them properly – and if someone does something that I have trouble with, I am fully capable of dealing with that'. In this way, they are reprogrammed and the residual energy is removed. Next, I treat her hormonal system. I focus specifically on her pituitary gland, so she can feel her life purpose again; and on her thyroid gland, so she will no longer suffer from sad situations. I do this in aura layer 10, the one you use to create your future (more about this later).

Because Janet's issue with her cousin is in layer 8, I know it is about a soul agreement between them. They have agreed upon entering this issue together. Of course, this doesn't change anything about the unpleasant earthly facts, but it does make the situation more understandable.

Later, I also come across a disturbed field in Elizabeth's eighth layer. So Janet and her mother also have a soul agreement, which I infer from the layer I have to work in. Her mother is carrying another field because she feels responsible for what happened. It looks like a large bowtie-shaped pair of sunglasses and in layer 8 this is related to her eyes.

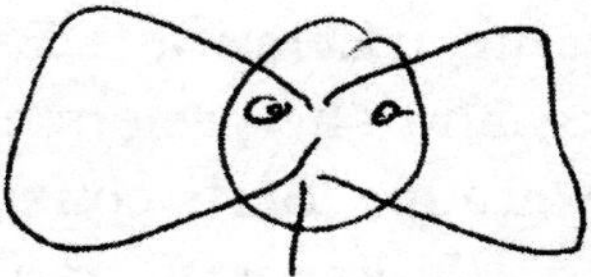

Figure 5: The blockage in Elizabeth's eight layer

Previously, Elizabeth felt guilty because she had not noticed what was going on between her daughter and her cousin, but now she mostly feels responsible for what happened. This makes her eyes hurt because of what she is seeing, because of the frustration and because she and her daughter are stuck in this issue. I remove the problem; it is over and done with. She has struggled enough and learnt to have a more balanced view of things, so I am allowed to remove it and soon Elizabeth is calming down.

Six weeks after the final session, Janet tells me she is pregnant. Her son Dennis is born exactly two years after the initial interview.

Bert is a giant of an engineer in his mid-forties. He is unemployed, has had numerous jobs and doesn't really know what he is capable of and what he wants. He is stuck and has noticed that other people don't really enjoy being around him most of the time. They think he has a strange sense of humor and looks at things from a very peculiar point of view. Fortunately, I like his humor and we set to work.

In aura layer 8, I come across two relevant lives. In the first, he is a woman. It takes place in the ice age. Everything is white, frozen over, cold. This life is on Antarctica and the woman freezes to death.

Next, there is a past life in Lemuria*. 'Bert' is a woman who is quite rigid in her views, and she prefers clarity to insecurity or not being part of the group. 'Bert' constantly adheres to the prevailing norm and strictly keeps to notions of what men and women are 'supposed' to do. This is her way of holding her own in the community, although I get the impression it's not the best way to go about things, otherwise Bert would not be left with his current blockage.

Bert is still suffering from this in his current life, because in that past life following the rules cost him his life. So in his current life, he doesn't like rules and he has a tendency to think outside the box, which so far has resulted in his being unemployed. However, I expect him to get a job in the near future, which requires thinking up new and different things. So I see a bright future for him, but in the present situation his wife is the breadwinner. The soul agreement I come across in layer 8 is with her. This agreement allows him to explore different modes of existence.

We clear everything up so his mind comes down and I hear the words, 'No work also means not the wrong work...,' I repeat the words to him and he bursts out laughing. He totally agrees.

Let us turn one final time to Nate, the young graphic designer who struggles with food allergies and is obstinate. Nate is also paranormal, but he isn't interested in it. It does bother him, though, because he doesn't take his sensitivity for energetic stimuli seriously. This causes headaches or sleeping problems, because at night he has uninvited visitors. It's high time he does something about this paranormal issue.

In layer 8 I come across five past lives. With Nate, it's always about large numbers, which initially causes a big problem but later brings about enormous progression. I perceive a dramatic increase in tension in Nate's nervous system, especially in his arms. This proves to be caused by his paranormal giftedness, which cannot be suppressed that easily anymore. This puts new pressure on his nervous system, because he has to learn to deal with the energies he experiences. It's just like a baby gradually moving from breast milk to liquid food and then solid food. Your intestines have to learn to digest this food and, for the most part, it is the same with perceiving new energies; your body has to get used to them and learn to process them.

There are relevant lives in layer 8. The first one takes place 293 years ago. Nate is a woman and lives in a remote park. She is a 'seer', a clairvoyant, and helps other people with her gift. She has no family anymore, is childless and has no husband either. Other people think she's scary, but most of the time she is very lonely.

Then there is another life, 260 years ago. Again he is a woman, and 'Nate' has a service job, this time as a cook. Again, the theme is serving. In the next life that emerges, he is a woman who lives in Wales. She works as a governess and has her finances well-organized, but the children under her care are not her own. She does not have any children of her own. Serving others and loneliness are again the themes here.

There is also a life on the coast of southern France. I see a poor woman who unloads racks of fruit on a ship. It's hot and dirty and sticky and there's mold on the fruit. The mold produces a gas the woman can't stand and unfortunately she dies.

Next, there is a past life that hooks onto his left shoulder. It takes place in the Middle Ages and, once more, Nate is a woman. Again she is a 'seer' and this time she is killed with a sword, because she delivers a message the receiver didn't want to hear. It's a case of literally killing the messenger.

In summary, the lives in which Nate did use his paranormal gift only resulted in serving others, very little personal happiness, great loneliness and even death. So I understand his hesitation about using this gift in his current life. However, what Nate does not realize is that what happened in those lives was part of soul agreements with other people. These agreements can be found in layer 8. He hasn't made this kind of agreement for his current life, so things will not turn out as negatively as in his past lives.

After clearing up the eighth layer, and carefully going through his light body and nerve bundles, I go to the seventh layer. Nate is allowed to start a new phase of his life plan. He chooses to apply his paranormal gift. He chooses to see using all his capabilities. All he has to do is to find the right format for this life, but that doesn't seem to be a problem for someone who has such a visual profession.

While working in Nate's eighth aura layer, I wonder why these lives are not 'simply' found in layer 6; they seem to be showing Nate's issue in a strictly personal way, which can normally be found in layer 6. I think and think and suddenly it dawns on me: *I* am the person he has the agreement with! I am allowed to help so he can continue with what he has to learn and with working out the part he has brought with him. This quickly gives me a lot of knowledge and experience about reading and clearing past lives. I think it is a wonderful system and I am thankful for how well it works in actual practice.

Aura Layer 9:
Group Goals and Soul Agreements

As is the case with aura layer 8, aura layer 9 is about agreements and goals. However, whereas in layer 8 these are agreements between two souls, in layer 9 more than two souls are involved. Layer 9 is where group agreements and goals can be found.

In layer 9 there are agreements to learn things together, to teach things to each other, to perform certain tasks together as a group, and to come to Earth to do certain things as a group soul and work together with other group souls. Often the bringing and getting parts are mixed in the sense that one (or more) group member learns something from other group members, while the group as a whole has come to create something. Sometimes you don't understand what makes the group so closely-knit, because from a human point of view there is enormous variety in terms of contribution. In such cases, the answer may be found on the soul level.

When group agreements are at play, the origin of the soul doesn't really matter. The agreements can be between people from the same soul group or between people from different soul groups. You can compare this to football players: they can play for the national team or they can play for a foreign team in the premier league. In the former case, they are selected based on their origin; in the second case, their origins are diverse and the team is mixed. In aura layers 16 and 17, more can be found about soul groups and their agreements.

Apart from these concrete agreements, in this layer I have also come across the morphogenetic fields* of certain themes people have turned out to be connected to. Because of these fields, every person with illness X is connected to another person with illness X. If you look at the world as a weather chart, field X could be seen as high-pressure area. That high-pressure area has a particular energetic charge that all patients who suffer from illness X contribute to and are influenced by, because they are all members of the same group. Therefore, I see these fields mainly as an example of a common theme people are connected with and can work on together.

What do these agreements look like in practice?

Ida is forty-five-year-old woman who is in the middle of a dismissal procedure. The company she works for is closing down, which means Ida will lose her job. Of course, this is not what she wants to happen. I guide her through the process and come across a painful issue in layer 9. There is residue of the abortion she has when she is still married. Her husband doesn't want the child and she herself doesn't know what she wants – she's too confused – so she lets him have his way. The theme here is 'not making your own choice'.

The issue of her husband leaving her for somebody else links up with this perfectly. Unfortunately, he leaves her just after she has received her part of her parents' inheritance. And because they are married in the community of property, he claims half of it. On top of cheating on her with another woman and having done this for quite some time, he also makes off with half of her inheritance. This can be found in layer 9, which means it was 'premeditated' on the soul level. Ida, her parents and her ex-husband had a deal. Ida would marry her ex-husband, he would cheat on her and her parents would not include an exclusion clause, which would have left him empty-handed. This was the ideal set-up for Ida to be confronted with the themes of 'trust' and 'making your own choices' and deal with them. Fortunately, things turn out relatively well for her.

Judith has just turned forty and is suffering from depression. I detect a connection with the depression field at her shoulders. This field has its origins in a past life and has become active again because she is the same age now as she was when she developed depression before. In that life, it broke her down; this time, we will remove it. I do nothing complicated, really; I simply break the connection and remove the fields, all in layer 9.

Marius is struggling with something that makes me chuckle because I know all the people involved. Marius is a good friend of mine. One of his best friends is married to a know-it-all whose favorite subject is spirituality. In itself, there's nothing wrong with that, but the woman in question, Jo, rarely stops talking. And although Marius does his best not to enter into discussions with Jo at weddings and parties, she always manages to challenge him publicly to share his views. Every once in a while he takes the bait, leaving him angry with himself afterward. After the umpteenth confrontation, I suggest doing a past life reading and doing a session if necessary. Marius is eager and there we go.

We are in Switzerland where he lives as a man near the Carthusian monks in 1543. Jo is a kind of rector and also a man. Marius is a smith and does odd jobs; he isn't part of the Carthusian community, but lives outside the community as a 'heathen'. There is a fight because 'Jo' wants to convert him. Eventually he says in no uncertain terms that he does not believe in God (which, by the way, is not true – he has his own faith, though he isn't very religious) and he is excommunicated. Although strictly speaking he cannot be excommunicated because he isn't a member of the Carthusian community, that is the word I hear; he is cast out. His family suffer greatly from the practical implications of this exclusion.

The relevant themes are: 'Who is right? What is faith? What are dogmas?' Apparently, there is still work to do for Jo and Marius, and it seems Jo's husband has to resolve certain issues as well, which makes this a group agreement enabling the trio to tackle these themes seriously. At Marius' request, I clear up the ninth layer and remove these connections.

Since that session, Marius has not been bothered so much by Jo's attempts to provoke him. He feels there is more distance between them, which allows him to look at the game Jo is playing from a neutral point of view...most of the time.

George has been looking after his children full-time for years since he and his wife divorced, but one way or another he has been unable to get his life going. In layer 9 I come across two relevant past lives. One of them takes place on an island just off the southern coast of Argentina and he is a woman. This life is about 110 years ago and the woman is mentally disabled. This makes her a bit clumsy. For example, she is incapable of doing the housework herself. She seems to originate from a tribe that looks like the Maoris. 'George' remains alone his entire life: there's no husband, no children, and she's not part of the community. She feels stupid and wonders: what use am I? From a societal point of view, she doesn't seem to contribute very much, but she does speak with the birds and communicate with the animals. Her soul just wants to *be*. Due to her disability, she doesn't have to make life choices. She doesn't have to do or earn anything; she is loved anyway. This recognition is also relevant in George's current life.

A life near the Galapagos Islands pops up. He is a twenty-three-year-old man who dies of a wound inflicted by a red lion fish, which pretends to be coral, but unexpectedly manages to injure him near his spleen, where the poison does its work. I see 'George' swimming around a large group of jellyfish and I see how he takes care of his brother (younger by eight years) for five years, after the rest of the family fall ill and die. When almost his entire life falls apart, 'George' stops living, he does not gain new experiences, he gets stuck and he only continues to breathe because he feels responsible for his little brother. He lives on autopilot, but he doesn't really live anymore.

There is a lot of sadness around his heart. He feels lonely and I can see a symbolic orange clown fish like Nemo, saying, 'Go with the flow, keep it playful, don't fight too hard, go with the flow....' George takes that message with him while I remove old issues in layer 9, the layer with the agreements that caused him to be mostly on his own.

Dorothea is a middle-aged woman who feels like an outsider to her own life. This makes her angry and sad. Her feelings are related to two past lives in layer 9.

The first one is in northern Italy, near Trieste. She is a mother of six children who need to be taken care of and she herself suffers from bronchitis. She struggles with being self-effacing and being part of the family. In fact, the load is too heavy for her and she wants more space for herself. In her current life, this wish is fulfilled because she has plenty of time and space for herself, but it's not quite what she had in mind.

Then there is a past life in southern Italy, where she is an eight-year-old living on a lakeside. When she becomes an orphan and is admitted to a Catholic children's home, she renounces her true faith in order to prevent herself from being excluded by the people who take care of her. She does not want that to happen, of course, so she acts sweet and nice to make sure she can stay there. However, inside, it embitters her.

The soul agreement I come across here is an agreement between Dorothea and her caretakers. She was given the chance to be who she really was, to be honest, but she was afraid to take the risk. She didn't want to be the odd girl out. In her current life, she is faced with the other side of the coin. Thanks to her husband and her family, with whom she has her current agreement and she feels a lot of distance, she experiences what it is like to be an outsider and what this does to her.

Although Sandra usually has a way with words, she finds it difficult to hold her own in discussions with her husband. She thinks he is smarter, because he has two university degrees and she has 'only' done higher vocational training. It's also true to say that he has a quicker mind than she has. On top of all that, if she gets emotional, the whole thing falls apart and every discussion escalates into a nasty fight.

When we look at an old issue that caused her to clam up and which blocks her throat chakra, resulting in her not being able to express herself very well, we discover two interesting past lives. In the first, she is a three-year-old girl living somewhere in the former Soviet Union. She is torn to pieces by a wolf that grabs her throat. She accidentally lost sight of her parents and is crying in fear when the wolf discovers her on the tundra. She dies with the understandable thought 'it is not safe to make a sound', which I replace with 'I open my mouth when it benefits me'.

I remove the residual energy and we go to a life in which she is five years old and abandoned by her parents. She is too small to take care of herself and, as a result, she dies with the thought 'it is not safe to be alone, I will not survive', which is attached to her right knee in layer 9. This has caused her to be afraid of arguing with other people, because she is afraid her husband will leave her and she literally will not survive. That is why in her current life she has learnt not to speak in certain situations, because she's afraid she might say the wrong things, enabling others to make her verbally 'dumb' and crush her with their intellect. She overlooks the fact that she is no longer that five-year-old girl and that she is fully capable of taking care of herself now.

In this case, she has soul agreements with her husband and children.

Thirty-eight-year-old Daphne is head over heels in love with Raul, the man she recently met but who is already as good as living with his girlfriend. Madly in love, Daphne found herself kissing Raul, despite already being in a relationship with Bart. The physical attraction between Daphne and Raul was so great that they kissed passionately in the pub. And when she was finished kissing him, that same night she kissed Bart. She can't understand her own behavior, because she has always been monogamous before. For that reason, she visits me to find out what's going on.

The kissing can partly be traced back to a past life in Greece. Daphne is a man, a fisherman, and Raul is a woman, the widow and sister of a good friend. 'Daphne' is a man of loose morals and a similar lifestyle, which conflicts with the traditional Greek social rules. In Greece, there are strict standards and values concerning how to act after somebody has died and there are guidelines relating to the mourning period, such as wearing black clothes, etc. It's all quite formal and 'Daphne' doesn't have the courage to express his feelings to the woman he loves because, according to the rules, he should wait a while.

He dies unexpectedly during a shipwreck. There is a storm near Lefkas and he drowns. He never told her he loved her and dies without having revealing his feelings. So it is understandable that the two of them, who at the time did not express their love to each other, are now very quick to do so on a physical level.

After that, there is a past life in former Yugoslavia, near the Albanian border. Chronologically, this life takes place before the life in Greece. Again, Daphne is a man and Raul is a woman.

They are married and have three daughters, the eldest of whom are twins. Their middle daughter has cerebral palsy and is therefore physically handicapped. According to 'Daphne', this makes her unmarriageable and she is a millstone around her parents' necks. He has a lot of difficulty accepting his disabled child. He is a harsh man who has serious communication problems with his wife 'Raul' when it comes to their daughter. The themes are 'your mission in life' and 'being loyal to yourself and doing what's right'.

Then another past life emerges, this time involving Bart. 'It feels so familiar,' she says of their relationship. 'We can talk about anything.' The reason for this can be traced back to their life together in Peru. I feel icy cold. Daphne is the eldest girl of seven children and Bart, Raul's friend, is there too. I see a bird species that looks like geese, but I don't recognize it, and I deduce that 'Daphne' tends birds.

There is a great deal of sadness and poverty and 'Daphne' dies of scurvy when she is just fourteen years old. 'Bart' is her younger sister and they have a tremendously close bond. In her current life, it is advisable to consider what things are appropriate to say and what things are not. After all, Bart is no longer her younger sister and the old familiarity might have gone one step too far. She will learn how to protect herself by knowing when to be an open book and when not.

All lives are connected to Daphne's ninth aura layer because they concern group agreements. Both Raul and Bart, who are good friends, know what Daphne is doing and feeling and somehow this is the way for all three of them to resolve the past life issues that are still bothering them.

Finally, there is Eileen. She is a nice, spontaneous eighteen-year-old girl, but she lacks self-confidence (she rarely thinks she is good enough) and has a great need for safety. She won't take risks very easily. She likes it when other people need her, because that means they won't let her down. She also admits she stays with the wrong boyfriends for too long.

Her journey back in time starts with a life on the Russian tundra. She is an eight-year-old boy who is taken by surprise by a storm. This issue literally blurs her vision for a while when we talk about it. The fear of not seeing right and getting lost again is attached to 'her' eyes. After all, it caused him to develop hypothermia and get killed. While I am reading, I remove the painful residue and right behind it I see the life of a fetus still inside her mother. She is five months old. She is supposed to come into the world alive this time, but her mother has already had three miscarriages and no longer believes in a positive outcome. She is very negative – *too* negative. Eileen's soul finally chooses a different path because this negativity is not in accordance with what she intended to experience. The result of this is a miscarriage in the latter stages of the pregnancy.

In her current life the pattern is different: she puts a lot of effort into doing her best when somebody – according to the agreement – is negative, for example her critical father and her boyfriends. This causes her to cling to negative people and she finds it hard to let go of them. As of today, she will have a choice: Do I really want this? Where do I want to be?

Then there is a life in the Alsace in France. She lives there between 1900 and 1923 and she is a man. I smell citrus, which one way or another seems to be connected to her family's death. They all die from an illness during the time of the First World War. Nothing has any *meaning* anymore.

Next, there is a life in which she is undernourished. I hear 1942-1946 and, being Dutch, I instantly think of the winter starvation in the Netherlands. I turn out to be wrong. She is a three-year-old girl living in Ecuador. She is undernourished because she simply refuses to eat. Her parents beg her to eat, but she will not do it; she gives up.

The Ecuadorian life is followed by a miscarriage. She will be a boy, but decides at a very early stage that she is not ready to come to Earth yet.

And then she is ready and she is Eileen, who has now decided to live with everything that comes with that and who now really experiences her life.

A woman, her partner and their unborn child. Losing part of your inheritance to your ex-husband. Endless discussions with your best friend's wife. Losing almost your entire family and being lonely. Not being able to feel at home with other souls in an orphanage. An unfulfilled past love, a woman and her sister. These are all painful relationships that are now worked out in a group, so that all relevant issues can be resolved, enabling the souls that are involved to grow.

The beautiful thing about aura layer 9 is the group agreements, and the fact that the basic energy of all group members becomes purer when at least one member decides to work on a relevant issue and resolve it. In this way, this member also makes it easier for the other members to develop and make the most of new opportunities.

Aura Layer 10: The Creation Field of Possibilities

In contrast with the aura layers that hold agreements with other people, the tenth aura layer is a creation layer. I call it the Vortex and it contains your heart's desires and future manifestations, soul memories and dreams.

This layer contains the representation of the things you dream of and would like to see become a reality. They are the things your soul desires most. This layer also causes you to strive for certain things and, with the help of this layer, you can determine whether something is in accordance with who you are. Through your feelings, you can determine whether something resonates with your heart's desire or it conflicts with it and you had better say no to it. Apart from the creations of the soul, aura layer 10 contains the wishes you would like to realize for yourself as a human being: a beautiful house, a loving relationship, an interesting job, three healthy children.

This layer also contains soul memories from past lives (including intermediate phases and places) that can detract from the achievement of your life goal by affecting or determining your views and ideas. Finally, Layer 10 is the gateway between different dimensions. In other words, the past, present and future are linked in this layer.

Aura layer 10 works like a vortex: a vortex looks like a tornado and it moves everything that swirls around in it to its center, its eye. When you create things, you see them in your vortex in the form of images. You make a sort of blueprint of them. In due course, the manifestation of these things gets closer and closer and more concrete, until eventually you can touch them and they are materialized.

Let us compare this to building a house. First, you dream of a house. Next, you do your math in order to ascertain if you can afford to have it designed. You start looking for a building site, you set to work with an architect, you design the house and you pick out a contractor. Meanwhile, you make all kinds of decisions about kitchen tiles and bathroom fixtures, window frames, light, colors and sizes, and all those decisions ensure that your house eventually becomes what you intended.

It's the same with this creation layer in your aura. You put everything in it that is important to you in your life and if all these things fit together, they become your eventual life design. This causes you to attract certain things and, if everything goes right, these things are attuned to each other.

However, this is not always a smooth process because people may have (expressed) contradictory desires. If you want a south-facing garden, this means that during summer the garden will catch a lot of sunlight. And if you change your mind on further consideration, you had better change your design. Changing your design takes place in the tenth layer, because you create your future from your vortex. That is why it is very important that this funnel cloud does not contain old debris, i.e. large obstacles from the past. When these are removed, you can attract for your future what is best for you and the things you want can be created and come to you. If there is debris blocking this, the cloud can lose its sense of direction, which means it is lost to you.

Whether or not your dreams and heart's wishes become a reality depends on various factors. Many books have been written about this subject (for instance *Ask and It Is Given* by Esther Hicks, *The Secret* by Rhonda Byrne, *The Deeper Secret* by Annemarie Postma) so I won't go into it any further here. What this knowledge about the existence and workings of aura layer 10 adds to these theories is that every creation stays in aura layer 10 until either it is released or has become manifest. Very old desires can still block you in the form of 'debris' without you being aware of it.

And sometimes an earthly creation simply cannot be realized. Sometimes the things you want as a human being don't become a reality. The reason for this could be that the wish is not in accordance with your soul's wish or creation or those of others. Or it is not congruent with who you are at that particular moment, which prevents it from coming to you. So this can also be a soul issue, and soul issues are always a priority.

The difference between past lives in this layer and those in other layers is that this layer is fully devoted to the creation of your ideal life. The other layers also affect your emotions or the way you think, but they only affect your response to events; they don't create anything new. In layer 10, you can see the representation of what you 'have put in the air' for your future. Both your consciously expressed wishes and the consequences of 'action = reaction' (karma) can be found in this layer.

It is all in layer 10, the layer that belongs to the layers that connect you to your fellow human beings, because everything you create has to fit with what others create. Therefore, your creations will always be attuned to those of others and rarely will something be created that is harmful to others if those people have not given permission for it on the soul level.

When there is a blockage in your tenth layer, it becomes more difficult for you to attract and live according to your ideal life. In that case, you will not be able to follow the life you planned before you were born. The following cases will show you the different types of blockages that can be present in aura layer 10.

Take, for example, Steve, a six-year-old boy with Down's syndrome. He is all over the place when I visit him at home for a session. The problem lies in layer 10; something hurts his ears and sends his brain into overdrive. This overburdens his brain and causes him to get stuck. Sitting in the garden, I let the energy related to this problem drain away while Steve enjoys a slice of bread covered with chocolate spread. After that, everything is fine and he can move on in his own way.

Next, another child, nine-year-old Lawrence. He suffers from the aggression displayed by other children and doesn't know how to deal with it. Lawrence is a real New Age child who reads the colors of my aura and tells me how many past lives I've had. He is impressed, because I've had more than he has.

I come across one of his own past lives...I think. I see him as a scared dinosaur. He is a light brown herbivore who can't handle aggression. This old issue is still very much present, so I remove it. This goes smoothly, but to this day I don't know if it was a literal image or a figurative one.

Ilse's story is quite different. She does not take herself seriously enough and is confronted with that at work. Even now, when she is studying for her dream job, she shows resistance, undermining her own future.

The core of the problem turns out to be a past life in which she is a sick man who is fifty-three years old and lives in Morocco. He is stabbed to death by his own daughter because he has given her away in marriage. He wants to find a suitable husband for her, to make sure she is taken care of – after all, he will die soon because he has an incurable disease – but his daughter worries she will end up with a nasty husband. She doesn't know her father is ill and she is just angry with him. Her anger makes her try to prevent the marriage by killing her father with a knife.

Out of love for her he looks for a husband and out of fear she kills her father. This is to no avail because, as a punishment, she still has to marry the man her father chose for her and it turns out not to be all that bad. So she has killed the father without reason.

The daughter's feeling of guilt from this past life still affects Ilse in her current life in the form of an energetic attachment in layer 10. It causes her to doubt the purity of our own choices, just like when she was that Moroccan man. This prevents her from taking certain steps, making decisions and expressing herself.

I remove the energetic attachment and Ilse changes radically in the following months. She really stands up for who she is and what she does. The change in her personality is so dramatic that people no longer recognize her when they see her. It is a beautiful thing to witness.

Joe, who visits me for a business consultation, is shifting uncomfortably on his chair. I ask him why, because it's a bit out of character for him, and because acute problems always come first during a session and his behavior tells me there is an acute problem. He turns out to have slept with a good friend. It was nice, he says, but also a one-off thing. The thing is: it scared him a little because afterwards she acted totally different and now she wants a serious relationship. Joe obviously does not. He loves her because she is a dear friend – a friend, by the way, who has regular one-night stands, which made him think she saw the situation as such – but he does not intend to start a romantic relationship with her.

I try to find out why this bothers him so much and I see that the friend in question is temporarily having feelings for him because of their shared intimacy. However, the feelings are not mutual, because for him their relationship is good the way it is. To take things further is not in line with his life path and threatens to put him off course. I remove the energetic hook with which it is attached in layer 10, so we can move on with attracting his ideal life partner. Eight months later, he has found her.

Bart has an intractable character, to put it mildly. He is squarely built, doesn't like any fuss or cockiness and doesn't want other people to tell him what to do. He is a policeman and the themes we are working on are 'enforcing the law' and 'obstinacy'.

A life in Indonesia emerges. In 1865, 'Bart', who is a female slave, kills someone. It does not matter that it was self-defense; the law is put into effect very strictly and he pays for his actions with his life. He draws the following conclusion: 'People who enforce laws are short-sighted because they do not take the circumstances into account'. We rewrite that conclusion, because in his current life and in his job as a policeman he judges himself, which creates a tremendous amount of internal tension. We clear up the layer and Bart can move on with his career.

Cora has completed several Native American workshops and is very involved in creating things. Or rather, she wants so much so fast that she is disappointed about her own creational power. She is not content with how quickly things are coming to her.

In layer 10 I see a symbolic wishing well. I see her escrow, the horn of plenty filled with everything she wants to create. All kinds of theories, Native American techniques, all her wishes and thoughts come together to form a kind of cement mush of everything she wants. I see a lot of contradictory desires that can never simultaneously become a reality, but they are still there and block the stream of good things coming to her. I explain to her that it isn't very useful to wish for one thing one day but to try to achieve the opposite the next day. The universe gets to work for you according to what you ask from it. And if two things are each other's opposites, there is a conflict in your tenth aura layer.

So I clear it up and organize it. Now it's her job to choose what she really wants and to let go of the rest.

Emma is a nice, willful eighteen-year-old woman. She is stressed out and I have to mind my Ps and Qs when I talk to her. She is allergic to 'vague terms' such as 'spiritual', 'paranormal' and 'past lives', and blurts out everything that comes to her mind. This works fine for me, because it allows me to know exactly who I'm dealing with. So I keep my choice of words as down-to-earth as possible. I don't feel the urge to convince her of anything and I believe in the basic principle that 'you came to me for a reason, so there must be something I can do for you'. Meanwhile, I have noticed that she is paranormal and, from experience, I know that when somebody is so strongly opposed to these tendencies, a past life is usually involved. This proves to be the case with Emma.

First, I feel a big lump of emotions and accumulated stress. I let part of it drain away and then I come across a past life in layer 10. I ask Emma if she believes in past lives. The answer, of course, is NO, so I tell her I will do this part of the session without saying anything. But no, Emma is interested and asks me to say out loud what I come across while I am working. So that is how we do it.

I see three red berries and then I see her in Mongolia. She lives very primitively, with two wolves at her side. I see her die in 1844 when she is eighteen years old. In that life, she is part of a community of four people; three women and one man. The man is a 'healer', a Shaman. But Emma, who in that life also has a way with words, does not treat him with respect. She gives him lip. That stings him and an energetic tug-of-war ensues. I see the two of them walking through the village, meeting each other, exchanging looks and the energetic thunderbolts are flying. The Shaman obviously feels threatened by Emma's power.

Next, I see him forcing Emma to eat the three red berries. The berries are actually phytomedication, an antidote, but when you eat them without having an ailment, they are very toxic. So she is poisoned. She seems to be ill, but in reality she is murdered. After her death, her soul lingers as an entity. She isn't ready to leave right away. The final conclusions she dies with are 'paranormal people cannot be trusted' and 'I was too trusting'. The latter is quite different in her current life, which causes her to create a different life to what is possible for her. In total, I remove three issues of this kind before I can continue working with her.

These are very important limiting issues for her, because until today they have prevented her from using her intuitive gifts and have kept people at a distance who could teach her how to apply her latent gifts.

Figure 6: Blockages in the rational side of Emma's body and aura

Next, in layer 6 – the layer of personal traumas from your current or past lives – I come across two issues that present themselves as big grey fields with a different structure. Field 1 is situated on the right side of Emma's head and consists of all kinds of emotions she has absorbed from others without being aware of it (because, for the time being, she is unable to deal with her clairsentience). In field 2, there is a lot of anger between her neck and waist on the right side of her body. Most of it is unreasonable anger – disagreeing for the sake of disagreeing! It is anchored in her heart chakra. This issue is entirely her own and partly has to do with her parents' divorce and everything she finds difficult to process. I 'vacuum' her aura, as I am used to, and soon afterwards Emma is a lot calmer.

My next paranormal client is Seb, a radiant twenty-four-year-old man who is beautiful both inside and out. I always feel happy when I see him and he has this effect on most people. We worked together years ago and now he is back, because he is affected by energies in his environment. Like so many of my clients, he is hypersensitive and easily takes on the pain and moods of other people. He is like a sponge in that respect. Also like other clients of mine, he doesn't feel like actively doing something about it. However, he will have to, otherwise this nice gentleman will get stuck and ill.

When we begin I see he is short of breath, his vocal cords feel a bit strange, he is in for some changes and it's about time for him to make some choices. I can tell from looking at his body how he braces himself and what has attached itself to the tops of his shoulders. His back hurts and he is full of doubt. He thinks negative thoughts and there is so much going on, there are so many things that make him insecure. His third eye* is closed and it is pulling at the back. Actually, it's open, but it spins at an angle with one side closer to the body than the other. I suspect I will come across a past life with bad experiences as a seer or something of that nature, and I start reading.

For Seb, today starts with a life that ends in 1772. He is a woman living in Norway and the area near his cerebellum (back of the head) and brainstem, where all the large nerves of the body originate, is overstressed. 'Seb' is paranormal and the back of her third eye has been too busy. This has caused severe pain in her nervous system and a short fusion in her body systems.

Before this, there is a life in 1682. He is a woman, a Hungarian witch whose life consists of talking to and living with animals. It is a very lonely life. The pain cuts right through me. These two lives would be reason enough to leave the paranormal alone in his current life, but there is more.

Something very peculiar follows: a life as a man who dies in 1604. He is French and is stabbed to death by a friend when he is eighteen years old. His friend stabs him in the stomach. This came completely out of the blue and it still makes him insecure in his current life; danger can arise when you least expect it. I tell him he was killed by a friend and that the boy knew exactly where to stab him. Then I sense that he knows this friend in his current life. I ask him to list a few names of people in his circle of friends. With one of them, I feel something of a yes. I tell him this starts to feel familiar, but that we aren't quite there yet. It turns out to be this person's brother, Ben. And suddenly Seb bursts out laughing on the treatment table. His friend Ben's nickname is Ben the Butcher, because he works in a slaughterhouse.

How different is Mariela's story. She is a timid woman who has difficulty saying what she thinks. Whenever things feel *too much* for her, she has a tendency to avoid the situation, to leave the room or, if these options are not available, to dissociate: she hangs over her body, as it were, and is 'somewhere else' for a while. She has gone through a lot in life, such as her partner's suicide, and in the session we will look at the reason why she struggles with saying what she thinks.

In aura layer 10, we come across three issues that prevent her from manifesting the good things she creates for herself. The first issue is related to a past life in South Africa. She is a man who is killed in 1939. This issue turns out to be linked to a difficult life in Spain. About 330 years ago, she lives there as a man who is deaf and dumb and is raped. Because she can't speak, she can't express the painful emotions resulting from the incident. She decides she is incapable of judging what people are like and that she cannot trust others. She does not even trust herself, and she is literally unable to express herself. After all, she can't speak. This is too much for her and that is why the issue is still relevant in her current life. Now she is capable of giving words to her emotions and the blockage is cleared.

The third issue involves strange beings. These beings look jagged, as if they are dark-edged pieces of a puzzle, and I can see them 'stepping' outside of themselves: they are all dissociating. One moment they are inside their skin and the next, they are outside of it. Sometimes they crawl into a different cloak (which doesn't seem to be a good thing and is the risk involved in dissociating, namely that an entity embeds itself in your energy field). I see that this is the field related to her dissociation and that it is meant to teach her something. I disconnect Mariela from it so she does not have an automatic escape route anymore and has a better chance of consciously going through her experiences. This ends our work in layer 10. Now she can do what she was born to do.

Hannah stumbles in on crutches with her ankle in a cast. She's not even my client today; she is his mother.

Together with her boisterous children, who are four and six, she came all the way by bus, because her eldest has an appointment with me. Unfortunately, she got off at the wrong bus stop and had to cover quite a distance on foot. A nice start. I ask her what happened and she tells me the ankle was a planned operation, but that on her way to my practice she sprained her wrist – and that having to support your full weight with it while carrying a large bag full of children's toys on your back is not very comfortable.

Acute issues always come first, so I decide to treat her first. And while her sons are fighting over the only handheld computer game console in the back, I apply the best first aid remedy I know of for the aura, in case of accidents – the etheric pocket rescue – to Hannah's wrist. Next, I remove the stress from her aura in layer 5; the rest follows in layer 10. This accident will not have any unpleasant consequences for Hannah. I'm done with Mum. On to her child.

One treatment that has a great impact on me is Antoinette's. She is mother to four children, three of whom are around thirty, but the fourth, a boy named Merlin, died six weeks after he was born. He had a heart condition and died because one of the nurses made a mistake by administering twice the right amount of medication to him. Merlin fought for his life, but he died. This was twenty-nine years ago.

I treated Antoinette five years ago and now she asks me to help her because she is in the middle of a dismissal procedure. Apart from that, there are problems between her children, which is very difficult for her, but she can do nothing about it. Finally, she recently had a migraine attack.

The first thing I sense is her fear of not having enough money and losing her job. This fear is attached to her stomach and makes her feel nauseated. Then I look at a spot near her lip. I ask her what it is and Antoinette says, 'I've been meaning to ask you about that. It seems to be getting worse.' It makes me shiver and I hear 'not okay'. But I am not a doctor and I am not able or allowed to make a diagnosis. So I say to her, 'As soon as we're done here, you call your GP to make an appointment and have him look at it. Not tomorrow or the day after, but today.' She understands me and does what I tell her to do. Later, it turns out she has skin cancer and she is operated upon soon afterwards.

But that little spot already makes me think during the session. In layer 10 there is a connection to her employer. Something unpleasant has happened to her old boss, which she is quite spiteful about. On the one hand, I understand her reaction, but on the other hand, I don't. What good is it to you when somebody else goes through hardship, even if in your view that person has treated you unfairly? Why gloat over it?

Just to be sure, I clear up that field and I can sense very nasty aggression, something that has been accumulating for years. I happen to know her former boss and I know something about the work climate of the company in question. There is a lot of gossip there, which has almost been too much for some of the people who work there, but I am still surprised about the effects something like that can have on people. It's almost like passive smoking.

I continue in layer 10 and remove veils of energy that have been there for several lives, so Antoinette can make better use of her intuition. It allows her to perceive things more clearly and she doesn't have to work so hard at thinking about things anymore. Her brain can be used differently now and her creative side can blossom. I also include her pituitary gland in my treatment of layer 10, so that the information stored there can get flowing and help shape her life.

While I'm working and Antoinette is lying on her back on my treatment table, I sense we have a visitor. I suspect it to be Merlin, her deceased son. But because I don't have a lot of experience with channeling and talking to dead people at this point, I am afraid my imagination has got the better of me and it might be someone else.

I ask Antoinette if perhaps she is feeling something (after all, she is also highly sensitive). 'Yes,' she replies. 'I can feel Merlin is here.'

Ah, yes, right. I say, 'That's right, and he's standing here on my left.'

And from that moment, everything goes smoothly. I tell her I perceive him as a tall grown man with dark brown hair that is longer than usual. I think this is quite remarkable, because sometimes babies remain babies in the spirit world and sometimes they develop into adults. It's clear that Merlin has done the latter and he is now a grown man of twenty-nine.

He has a very calm and pleasant energy, a radiant light, and it is wonderful to work with him. Initially it feels a bit awkward, because his mother feels a lot of emotion and instantly fires several questions at him, which prevents me from clearly understanding his answers. But I soon find a way to get both of them to answer in turn. Antoinette asks a question, I translate his answer and then his mother can respond to it. He also answers questions that I ask in my mind, because there are things I would like to check while they are having a conversation and I don't want to put an unnecessary burden on his mother.

Merlin tells us he's doing fine and he gives his mother all kinds of advice about how to deal with the spot on her lip (see a doctor), her job (don't worry and don't fight your dismissal, but finish the negotiations and all will be well financially – he even gives her the date of her dismissal, which later turns out to be right) and her children. Merlin promises to mediate between the children in the form of some extra spirit guide work on his side.

Then his mother asks the reason for his passing. After all, he only lived six weeks. Such a short life, it seems to be so useless! She starts crying and is obviously still very sad. Then Merlin starts to talk. He tells her that he chose her as his mother because he knew she would love him very much and miss him dearly, but also because she would be capable of understanding why it happened. He explains to her that his life plan contained his heart condition and that it allowed him to experience what it's like to fight for one's life. He wanted to develop a fighting spirit. He needed that, so that was his life goal. And after six weeks, he achieved it. So for his soul it was perfect, but for his mother it was not.

Then his mother asks, 'Have you forgiven the nurse?' And Merlin says, 'No, I haven't.'

For a moment, I don't know what to say. I ask him again and again he says no. So I take a deep breath, muster up all my courage and say out loud, 'Antoinette, he says no,' and instantly Merlin adds, 'Because there is nothing to forgive.'

He pauses and then continues, 'She did exactly what we had agreed on.' I repeat out loud to his mother what he says. I didn't see this coming. And it's one thing to know this kind of thing in theory, but it's quite a different thing to hear it from the lips of someone who has passed away due to what was (from an earthly point of view) a medical error.

Of course we have plenty of questions, which we fire at him. It becomes clear to us that Merlin consciously chose his short life, and that the way he died was planned. I ask him if this is always the case and he says it very often is, but not always. He indicates that there is nothing to forgive when somebody stands by his or her agreement under difficult circumstances, and that the whole thing was very hard for the nurse for a very long time. It marked her for life. But that was also part of the big plan and her soul path.

Merlin says he now works as a spirit guide at neonatology wards in different hospitals where premature babies and children have to fight for their lives. He guides souls that can choose if they want to stay and – if they do – need a lot of fighting spirit. For some of them, it is predetermined that they will not make it and it's just about the experience of the whole thing. Others can choose whether they want to stay alive at the moment they are fighting for it. Yet others will simply survive because they still have a lot to do in this world.

What touches me is that Merlin tells us he literally had to go through the experience of fighting for survival. This allows him to represent and pass on that energy to small children in intensive care.

An hour-and-a-half later, we have nothing more to say to each other and I have done everything I can in terms of treating

Antoinette, so we finish. I notice I have been crying almost continuously throughout this session because the experience was so moving. The energy is so loving and tender, and all I can feel is gratitude for having been allowed to be part of this today. Antoinette is deeply moved yet calm when we round off the session. Merlin and I make an agreement that he will help me with my work if necessary and he visits me on a regular basis. I am very happy with that.

Aura layer 10 creates your daily life as a result of what you wish for yourself and what you decide you want and do not want. This layer is about filling your life with the details after the existing life plan in layer 7, the blueprint designed by your soul, is already in place. The existence of a life plan may give you the impression that there is nothing you can do about it. However, this is not the case. From my conversation with Merlin, it has become clear that some life plans are fixed and others are more flexible. They develop organically, as it were, and can be adjusted along the way. For example, someone's date of death is not always predetermined, and sometimes a soul can decide along the way if and how it would like to move on.

I was also deeply moved by what Merlin said about needing the experience in order to be able to pass on a certain type of energy. I recognized it. I asked him if that is the reason I have experienced what I have. That is indeed the case. Merlin indicated that I can heal in others the things that I go through and deal with myself. It is my way of self-development and growth. We all grow and self-develop in our own ways, often as a result of adversity. And these adversarial forces allow us to make sense of our suffering. Sadness can erode us and it can hurt very much, but it also polishes and cuts the diamond in us all and makes a true jewel out of it.

It makes your soul glow.

Aura Layer 11: Specific Knowledge of Pre-Worlds and Other Times

In about 90% of all people, this mental layer contains no blockages. This is a good thing, because such blockages are quite serious: they affect a person's mind in no uncertain way. The blockages consist of troublesome residues and knowledge of pre-worlds, (pre-)lives, intermediate worlds and a special variety of past lives.

So about 10% of the population carry with them knowledge and information from those times. It is always about very serious responsibility issues. The way these are dealt with in a person's current life purifies that piece of knowledge and the whole process goes very deep. If souls carry this kind of information, they held positions of great responsibility on Earth a long time ago and worked with powerful forces. It always concerns the battle between Light and Darkness during times in which the world as it existed was destroyed and entire civilizations vanished, such as Lemuria, Atlantis, Avalon, Egypt, and during the various ice ages. The themes are often related to handling energy, light and information and dealing with power, position of power and balance of power.

For us as human beings, the essence of it is Light and power and how they relate to each other. This may concern heads of state, members of royal families, world leaders, dictators and sect leaders. It can also apply to members of a clerical order or spiritualists who worked with Light and Darkness and used black magic or other occult magic powers.

In our modern time, I see that the souls who are dealing with these themes are often people whose intelligence is above average. This is not surprising, because in our time of change and great contrast, making choices that support working through these issues requires a certain level of thinking. It also requires seeing the bigger picture even if the details cause you to worry.

The blockages in layer 11 are always anchored in the pancreas. The pancreas produces insulin and other bodily fluids that support the digestive process, not only of the food you consume but also of your experiences. Insulin makes sure you can allow in and absorb the loving part of your experiences. This is how you are nurtured. Love is the fuel that keeps everything going.

So, in layer 11 it's about spreading pure love and acting from a place of love (or learning how to do so) for the larger whole, on a global level.

Debbie is a six-year-old New Age child who comes across as a bit unworldly. She is a beautiful blonde girl with peculiar green eyes who can look at you as if she doesn't see you at all. Sometimes she does things that make me feel a bit uneasy, because she seems to be a bit sneaky, an earthly expression for impure behavior. I can see that she is a beautiful soul, but I can also see that she isn't there yet and she has a lot of work to do. Debbie doesn't make friends easily and she suffers from stomach aches.

I discover three entities in layer 11. They don't want to leave under any condition, because they are enjoying themselves tremendously and are quite successful in directing her behavior, so why would they leave? After all, it is much fun to make Debbie do nasty things. Considering the fact that Debbie is bothered by these entities, and is aware of her tremendous powers and will probably do something with them in this life, I think it wise to make the uninvited visitors go away.

In such cases, I ask Archangel Michael to take them with him, because they're no good and don't want to go voluntarily. Michael, the archangel with the sword of truth who feels very strongly about justice, picks them up and carries them away under his arm. Protesting loudly, the three of them leave.

I prepare a mixture of flower remedies* for Debbie to take for a few of weeks to support her in her process. It consists of the Australian Bush remedy Angelsword, which restores the true spiritual connection with her Higher Self and helps her keep her way of communicating pure; the Dutch Flower remedy Trumpet Vine (Campsis Radicans), which helps solve communication problems by enabling her to say in a soft tone what is troubling her; and finally, I add Poppy (Papaver Rhoeas). This will help Deb to allow herself to be vulnerable (this is linked to the stomach). This remedy mixture will enable her to live like a real human being, and to feel and learn to deal with her emotions. She will no longer be affected by the entities and she can learn to transform her own sensitivity into inner power.

Pedro is an ICT consultant in his early forties when he comes into contact with me. Since the divorce of his parents, he has suffered from post-traumatic stress syndrome, resulting in severe anxiety. He has been working on himself for years and has tried just about everything to rid himself of his anxiety: sedatives, RIAGG (Dutch regional institute for mental welfare), Gestalt therapy, psychotherapy, EMDR and 'self-medication with alcohol', he says jokingly – all without lasting results. That is to say, he can deal with his anxiety and he can talk about it, but it's still there and it emerges at the most inconvenient of moments. His wife is fed up with it, which is understandable. Because of his fears, he frequently lets her down as a partner, which leaves her with the responsibility for their family.

Pedro got my name from a friend of mine. Anything alternative or paranormal is not exactly his cup of tea and he thinks it's all a bit 'airy-fairy', but because he respects my friend highly, he gives me the benefit of the doubt. When I speak to him on the phone, I can already sense there's an abuse issue, though he doesn't say anything about it. I send him my anamnesis form, to get an overview of his medical history. The form also has a question about being abused, but he says he has not been abused. For a moment, I doubt my perception. Then I realize it's a repressed trauma.

We spend the first session releasing large amounts of tension in and outside his body. It becomes clear to me that Pedro is hypersensitive and registers and feels everything I am doing. It would not surprise me if he turned out to have paranormal qualities, but at this moment it's too soon for that. He still has too much excess baggage.

In the second session, we look at a number of relevant traumatic issues. He witnessed a terrible divorce between his parents and the nasty fights preceding it. And then there is the abuse issue. He gets nauseated when I look at it and I carefully ask him if he has ever been sexually harassed by a man. He says, 'Not that I know of,' but he also says he feels there is something there because he is feeling so miserable. I keep a sharp eye on him and remove the whole issue.

I discuss it with him afterwards. I do this at a later date because otherwise, he would have to deal with things on too many different levels: energetically, psychologically and emotionally. And there is a good reason why he suppressed it at the time, so it would be wise to take into account the pace his own body wants to go at.

I see images that show he was sexually assaulted by his next-door neighbor when he was nine years old. I don't say anything out loud, but I do ask him if he can remember this man. The moment I mention him, Pedro tells me the man locked him up in his cellar. This is the only thing he can remember at this point. I tell him the image I see doesn't mean everything actually happened as I see it, and I ask him to wait and watch which images emerge without drawing any conclusions about them.

I make sure his mind stays clear and in the here and now, while at the same time he attunes to events that happened thirty years ago. He starts shivering and admits the man touched him. 'But,' he asks me, almost in a begging voice, 'I don't think he did anything bad. I wasn't raped, was I?'

I can see that he was not raped in the literal sense of the word, but I can also see that something did happen. I give him the reassurance that I have the impression that he was not raped and, for the time being, I don't get into it any further. If the memory does not emerge of its own accord, I won't tell him either. I don't want to influence his memories. I follow the directions of his soul. I make sure everything that comes up is cleared, which is a lot.

Figure 7: Attachments of the different kinds of blockages on Pedro's body

I give him a week or two to process all of it and then we set to work again. Once again I reassure him that what I saw is not necessarily the way it actually happened, but Pedro says everything I saw was right. His memory is coming back. To me this is a good sign, because I have personally experienced that your body is your greatest friend in times of trauma. And when something is too difficult to understand or process, your body puts it away in a dark, faraway corner until you are strong enough and ready to remember it and deal with it. We talk about how this pedophile tried to give Pedro an erection without undressing him. He tried this three times without success. Nevertheless, it had a profound effect on Pedro's life. I work on the fields that come loose and Pedro becomes calmer and stronger by the minute.

During the next session, a past life in Africa emerges in layer 11. Pedro is a seven-year-old girl who lived around 150 years ago. She is taken over by a feminine entity, so she is possessed, and at night she walks into the desert all by herself. She dies scared and alone, eaten by three wolves.

In one of the next sessions, I come across an implant in Pedro's eleventh aura layer. An implant is an artificially inserted energetic object that disturbs the body's energy and functions. If, for example, you once died with a knife in your back, on an energetic level the knife can still be there and disrupt your energy systems. Pedro's implant is in his stomach chakra. I see numerous layers, *feuilles* I am told. Everything looks nice and soft, but eventually I find the implant. It has sharp points that break off easily and can stay behind, and it contains a plutonic demonic energy. Very carefully, I peel away the layers and try to push it upwards. When I have managed to do so, Archangel Uriel takes over the implant from me and lets it drain away.

Sixty-eight-year-old Maria is suffering from a shock when she visits me. After renovating her entire house, which took several months of time and effort, she comes home and sees that her newly renovated house is flooded. On the top floor, a tap sprang a leak and the water flooded into the house for hours, spreading over three floors. Now it flows down the wall, drips from the ceiling and trickles down the outside of the windows. When Maria enters my practice and allows herself to process what has happened, her body goes into shock.

During the first session, I only let stuff drain away and I can feel how the strange coldness leaves her body. I help her body and bodily functions recover to normal. The shivering stops and she can respond to what I'm saying. The next day, she sends me an e-mail. The subject line says, *A miracle has happened!* She says she feels fine again and is back on planet Earth. The inner coldness has gone and she has slept well. Nevertheless, we continue a week later, because her shock did not come out of nowhere. The week before, we did some first aid and took some emergency measures, but now we are going to track down – and hopefully remedy – the cause.

When she comes in, she tells me she had a dream that night in which someone tried to steal her purse. And during the dream, she realized it was *her* dream and that meant she could determine how the dream would end. Then the trend break came: she decided to create a positive outcome! And so she dreamt that she was able to prevent the thief from running off with her purse. As she tells me this, she shoots me a smile full of pride; she gets it now. She herself will decide how things will go and she is done with creating all kinds of negative scenarios, either in her dreams or in her life. I think this is quite a breakthrough and I am happy for her.

Next, I see if there is anything else I can do for her and I ask how she got along after the first night. She says she feels calmer. The uneasiness only emerged when the wind came and it started raining. Apart from that, everything went fine. We talk about the field that is currently active: being all on your own and feeling abandoned. This field is rooted in her childhood: she comes from a poor family and both her father and mother had to work to provide for the family.

As a child, she is all by herself when she comes home from school, because her mother cleans rich ladies' houses. That feeling of loneliness becomes active in all subsequent experiences: when she and her dominant husband move to another area where she pines away when she is still very young; when her child falls seriously ill and her (by then) ex-husband does not support her enough; when she herself develops a muscular disease and her friends abandon her; and when her second husband leaves her to take care of restoring the house following the flood. Everybody always seems to let her down. For the most part, she is all on her own.

First, I work on her liver in layer 9, because this will help her be less annoyed by other people. Group agreements are also agreements, of course, and things happen for a reason. Next, I go to layer 11 and find I have to let everything drain away through her feet. It does not have to be understood any longer, so I don't have to let it drain away through her brain, as this would only be an extra burden for her at this stage. It's about mourning. In fact, she is in deep mourning over everything and everyone she has missed but also needed. I am allowed to remove that large veil of mourning.

A week later, she comes in and almost dances around the room. She says, 'I've been in such a positive mood all week!' Remarkably positive, she says she hasn't felt like this in years.

During the session, she constantly has short coughs (the emotions are linked to her throat chakra) and she says she has been feeling a bit tired lately. Apart from that, she has gained weight and she's not sure how this has come about. I can feel that she has too much weight on her shoulders, but just keeps going and going.

In layer 9 – the layer with the group agreements, which in her case contains a group agreement with her husband and other people who have let her down – I notice that her chest feels a bit heavy. It's a depressing feeling. The same goes for her head. The rest of the body is fine.

I remove the field that is related to the pressure she is experiencing from continuing to work in her husband's business, which takes a lot out of her. Next, I focus on the residual energy related to her being all on her own.

After this final session, we have an evaluation. She is doing fine. She is still quite cheerful and enjoys life more. She also does more for herself, for fun, not just the things she *has* to do. Her sense of humor has returned, too. Whereas it used to have a bit of a cynical undertone and she could be a bit snarly, now she just makes funny jokes – all thanks to the flooding.

Jim has been the owner of a consultancy agency for years. He implements a spiritual way of thinking and living in the workplace. In other words, he helps people work from their heart. However, there is one problem. Due to the economic crisis, at the moment he has no assignments. From a human and spiritual point of view, he has done everything in his power to turn things around. He does a lot of acquisition work, he keeps in touch with clients and submits tenders, while at the same time he makes his wishes and needs known to the universe and uses affirmations to help them become manifest. Having done that, he lets go of them, has trust in God and surrenders to the process and the flow of his life in such a beautiful way that I suspect there to be a halo over his head and think he is ready to be canonized. Meanwhile, however, he has drawn on his savings in order to pay his employees and he is at his wits' end.

I expect part of the problem to lie in layer 10, his creation layer. When I start working, I am told, 'When I adjust my thoughts, I adjust my circumstances. Love is the way. Work more with your heart than with your head.' This surprises me a bit, because Jim comes across as such a loving person that he might have invented the word, but I don't conjure up these words myself; I am the speaking voice of his spirit guides.

They continue to speak through me: 'As far as your business is concerned, you surround yourself with the right people, but you could open your heart even further. You could make more profound connections. When you do this, you can work on a deeper level. You are ready for more depth. The unconscious belief that heart and business don't go together is still there. You inherited that from your father. In a business setting, it is easier for you to interact openly with men than with women. Without being aware of it, you have women do the deepening part of the work. By not entirely opening up, others have to work harder.'

Next, we (because I notice that Jim can watch with me) see a life as a nun in layer 10, which took place around 1630. It is about giving with no strings attached, without wanting or expecting something in return. As a nun, he vows never to cling to earthly possessions. But that vow belongs to that life, not to his current one. Nevertheless, it is still affecting him. We replace it with a vow that makes him laugh, but which is also 100% right for him: 'I like living a pure life and being enormously rich, even if this is not my reason to do or not do things.'

Next we see a black slave, a man who is stabbed in his stomach with a knife or a dagger. It is about the fight against white people – but two wrongs do not make a right, so how can fighting ever accomplish anything good? That is the belief behind it. But sometimes you have no choice but to fight and letting go is not the way. We put this conundrum right and work on his chakras. I cleanse and align them, because they are deformed as a result of the above-mentioned fields, and I notice the hidden limiting belief 'you have to do something in order to deserve it'. I explain to Jim that the simple fact that he exists is enough. He is a child of God, and simply 'being' is enough. The old belief now detaches itself and can be removed.

Suddenly we are in Egypt, where we see two lives. In the first, he is the master builder of a temple in the year 4000 BC. He is killed for what he says. But before this happens, he leaves behind signs in the temple that represent his 'truth'. What makes it remarkable is that John can describe the interior of the temple and he even thinks he knows which one it is. He decides to visit it, to see if he is right and what this does to him.

Then there is life 2 in layer 11. Again in Egypt, he is the elder sister of the person who is his wife in his current life. That younger sister has fallen in love with a man her father does not approve of. 'Jim' does not try to convince their father, but remains on the side lines. Due to this lack of action, his sister remains unhappy in her love life for the rest of her life and 'Jim' feels regret and guilt for the rest of his life. He carries this guilt over to his present life, and he has a tendency to compensate for this in his interactions with current wife. We work on it.

Then we work on a field that is typical for layer 11 and entirely about purity. It is very clearly about the ancient knowledge of working with Light and power and the consequences this might have. I cleanse the field and ask Jim to keep me posted. I indicate that I have the impression that he will just be able to manage, and that the big assignment he is in the running for (and which has been postponed several times) will come his way, but that it will take just a little longer than he thinks – about eight weeks. He says he hopes I'm right, but he also hopes it will go faster because of the financial implications.

Nearly two months later, he tells me he has indeed brought in the assignment. This means he will have enough turnover for the coming year.

Jim's story cheers me up because it gives me hope. Apart from the fact that he is now doing fine, his case also confirms a natural law: as you sow, so shall you reap. And when things are done with a pure intention, and when somebody lives and acts in trust, this is a very inviting prospect.

Apart from that, the examples in layer 11 make something else clear. Most of the time, it's not very difficult to feel loving and act in a loving way toward other people when everything is going according to plan. It is quite a different story when, for example, you are challenged to maintain that lovingness when you feel different as a child, when you feel isolated and lonely as an adult, or when you feel abandoned by the universe and all its beneficial laws as a businessman.

When there is nothing left outside of you that you can hold onto, when there is no straw left for you to grasp, then the trick is to find out how you can return to your loving state of being. That is the lesson that can be learnt from layer 11. And when you have found your way in this, you can spread pure love and act from love for the larger whole, on a global level, regardless of your circumstances.

Aura Layer 12: Past Lives Jointly Healed Through Family Karma

Aura layer 12 is a highly interesting layer to every person who has (or has had) relatives – to everybody, that is. It contains all blockages and agreements concerning family karma and family energy.

In this layer, soul agreements and their corresponding processes are entered into between people who are related to each other. The basis is family ties, whether biological, adoptive, by step relation and/or by marriage. It is about soul contracts, the compliance of which not only affects the individuals themselves (those persons whose souls entered into the contracts), but also contributes to dissolving joint group karma, thereby enhancing the level of the joint family energy. And that is what all family members profit from.

This is how it works: your personal energy is the sum of your own soul-connected energy, part of the family energy, plus a fair amount of energy of the entire group of relatives. In addition, you have parts of energy in your system that are connected to your relations, friendships and groups of people you relate to and to which you belong. They constitute different clouds of energy, together making up your total energy field.

Family energy has a rather defining nature. Especially during the first half of your life, up to about your fortieth year, it is the actual base of your existence. Imagine your ancestors and other relatives as a group of people behind you, supporting you. What would you rather have? A bunch of quarrelsome people or a loving company with an eye for nature? Usually the latter feels best, unless quarrelling is what you like best in this life. In that case, you will feel most supported by the first type of family.

If you choose to be born, you will select a family whose energy fits your purposes, energy that suits whatever you have to experience here on Earth. It is the basic energy you obtain by birth and that is why it is so important.

So aura layer 12 contains the soul agreements between relatives. But how does it differ from layers 8 and 9? For those sometimes include agreements between relatives, as well.

Layers 8 and 9 deal with agreements that only affect the group members involved. In layer 12, the outcome of the agreement affects all relatives, even those who have seemingly not been part of the family for years, because all relations were broken off and they never see each other anymore. Of course, when you work through something properly in 8 or 9, thereby enhancing your own energy and raising your enlightenment level, your next of kin are usually very pleased because you are feeling better. However, this does not change your relatives.

And that is the difference with layer 12. If a member of the family works through an issue in this layer, the energy field of his relatives changes too. This happens automatically and often without anyone noticing. It will become somewhat easier for the family as a whole to address and subsequently overcome certain issues individually. If expressed in terms of light and dark, it raises the entire family's light level in aura layer 12. Similarly, a family member engaging in dark practices lowers the family's light level a little.

Basically, if you want to change the world, start with yourself. So address your own issues and your relatives will possibly benefit as well. In this way, you almost imperceptibly contribute to a better, more loving world by taking on your own task and fully committing to it. It's also the best way to help a relative. Because they resonate with you, their energy field becomes more comfortable. Being aware of this makes it easier to decide on choices that fit your soul path.

Sarah is the mother of Ben, a ten-year-old boy with Down's syndrome. His intellect is comparable to that of a two-year-old child. Now he is getting older, his mother is finding it more and more difficult to communicate with him. He cannot talk properly and he is increasingly intractable, partly because his two younger brothers have surpassed him in every respect and he will never be able to catch up with them.

His mother plays a part in this as well. She is often tired and irritable and can't always summon and radiate the calmness Ben needs to understand her. I see the two of them together, feel what is happening inside Ben, and subsequently I can put them both on their way.

Sarah is an easy talker. She is a verbally strong woman who thinks and talks quickly. In fact, she is a real chatterer. And she is much too fast for Ben, whose head literally starts to tingle when his mother asks him to take his plate to the kitchen. Because moments before, she asked him whether he wanted to have another sandwich, while she was talking to me about everything that was going on and, at the same time, pouring him something to drink and telling him to drink it. An overload of information and too many stimuli for his head, I notice.

And so he reacts cross-grained when she asks him to take his plate to the kitchen, for he is already over-stimulated and just wants to get away. He can't take in any more information.

I am allowed to take a look and I see that when Sarah was pregnant with him, everything was still alright. They understood each other and they were connected. Now Ben is struggling with his limited capabilities and his mother is feeling how her life is being influenced and restricted by her son's limitations. Apparently they have struggled and experienced enough, because I see those parts being illuminated and I hear that I may remove them, enabling Ben and Sarah to move on to the next phase of their lives.

From aura layer 12, I therefore remove the part that has to do with letting go, how Ben should behave and react. I cleanse his head by removing the surplus tension and by balancing his hemispheres. As with everybody else, this is located in layer 3, the individual mental layer, his thinking.

Then I suggest a little experiment to his mother: thinking in pictures. As it happens, Ben is a picture thinker and his brain is very capable of processing and understanding pictures, even in large quantities. His mother, however, thinks in a logical, linear way, expressing herself in words. That requires a lot of energy from Ben, because he has to turn these words into pictures and his handicap makes it even more difficult. This results in Babel-like confusion. I explain to Sarah how I get Ben to consent to my treating him. First, I visualize myself sitting on a chair next to Ben while he quietly undergoes my treatment. I finish with a picture of a happy Ben with a clear head. I send him these pictures telepathically and he gets the message. Despite his former intractability toward his mother, I encounter no difficulties in my treating him.

After I have left, his mother starts practicing picture thinking. She notices the effect, but she also finds it takes a lot of effort and she can't always summon the required patience, as it is so much easier for her to think in words.

This is a good aura layer 12 example because it shows two souls in a family line healing their powerlessness. Ben feels he fails due to his condition and his mother encounters some limitations of her own. Yet I clearly see how, as souls, they chose each other. Ben is going to learn how to deal with limitations and his mother, among other things, will learn to use her intuition, which she has refused to do, up to this moment. She doesn't want to feel too much because she finds it rather awkward; however, she must if she is to establish genuine contact with her son. If not, she will wrong both him and herself considerably. Thinking in pictures and thus getting her message across, and receiving in pictures what he wants to explain to her, will certainly require practice for some time...and patience from both sides!

Arnold is a fifty-year-old therapist who doesn't get on with his father. The man is always criticizing him and Arnold never seems to be able to live up to his father's standards. Arnold spent a long time looking for the ideal job. Now he has found that job – he is a paranormal therapist with a strong feeling for home-made, supportive, botanical remedies – and he has fallen ill. He has Lyme's disease. In this case I am the appointed practitioner who, being a specialist in the higher layers of the aura, will help him cleanse the necessary issues in aura layer 12 to support his speedy recovery.

In aura layer 12, I find family karma from a past life as a mentally disabled person. It is directly linked with his sixth aura layer. Here, I can see a trauma from his present life that relates to his sensitivity for energies, as well as the mentally disabled brother of a childhood friend. This past life deals with him being not so bright, having a mental disorder. Both items are still bothering him and I notice that they may be removed, for I see them become active and illuminated.

I vacuum the layer and a different life appears. In ancient China, Arnold is a man living among plants. He is not allowed to study. This makes him angry with his parents and angry with the all-dominating system. He finds it rigid, but his anger does not help. Although he acquires little theoretical knowledge, he learns a tremendous lot. He acquires a lot of knowledge in a wholly different manner. As he is out in the open all day long, all his life, he knows everything there is to know about trees and plants and their healing powers. But because it does not gain him an official degree, to him it carries little weight. In his present life he is smart enough, but he does not feel he gets the chance to prove it. However, he doesn't recognize his own self-acquired knowledge, thus doing to himself what he resents in others.

Yet he gets all the nature he has asked for. He just can't remember it was at his own request, because he submitted the request so long ago, during a life that is now being shown.

In the life preceding his Chinese experience, Arnold lives in the north of Sweden. The country is covered in snow most of the year. He is happy, yet wishes for the lush green life he will be given in China. There, his lack of nature is duly compensated; he gets nothing but nature. Unfortunately, he has other wishes in his Chinese life, lacking something completely different: theoretical knowledge. However, his life amidst green nature results from a life in white snow.

While treating Arnold, I notice that all knowledge he acquired during his past lives is now being released. In addition, Lyme's disease gives him breathing space and an opportunity to withdraw inwardly. This process of focusing on his inner self helps him feel comfortable with really living from his inner source. He can rediscover and apply his botanical medicine.

To me, it is remarkable because I know Arnold to be a nature-lover who, with a little help from his father, chronically underestimates his own knowledge. I notice this part can be closed now, after extensively working through the various aspects concerning self-respect throughout a series of lives. Arnold sees leaves and twigs fluttering around him while I cleanse the layers of his aura.

Neil is fifteen when he shuffles into my practice. He comes from a home for children with personality disorders, where he is temporarily staying because he is said to be unmanageable at home. He is far too cheeky toward his parents and the Youth Care Office thinks the home will do him good. When I ask him to take off his cool cap so I can treat his head, he turns out to be just a nice lad who is sensitive, rather than suffering from some disorder. I can see that his family home is situated on some tricky energy lines, water veins and earth rays and that he is very sensitive to the energy in the house.

For the whole of that session, we work in layer 12. Neil appears to be dissolving family karma at a very young age, which I admire. First I feel the turmoil in my head, so I remove the excess stress in order to continue to lay the foundation for the rest of the treatment. Then I repeat this at his stomach and his third eye. There is turmoil in his abdomen, as well. He is so unmanageable at home because he absorbs too much from his family members. As it is a large family and so much is going on with each of them, this can overwhelm him. In an attempt to release this tension, he rants and raves at his father.

He acts as the black sheep of the family by taking on as much energetic junk as possible from his various relatives, making sure only one person is burdened with it – Neil himself – instead of the entire family. In a word: self-sacrifice. He is obviously paranormal (just like his father, for that matter), and he tells me enthusiastically that he wants to become a metallurgy teacher. A man with a mission. In addition, I can see him coaching young people in dealing with the same paranormal gifts he has.

Next, I am introduced to four entities living in his twelfth layer. The first one is profiting from his grief and intensifying it. When I disconnect it, I can easily guide it toward the Light. The second entity is a six-year-old boy, a proper tale-teller. He is able to stick to Neil because his youngest sister frequently squeals on him, often unjustly. Consequently, Neil gets a scolding and, as a result, he feels misunderstood and sad. No wonder, as he takes on all kinds of burdens from her and in return she squeals on him. Of course that hurts. Despite feeling at home with this tell-tale energy, the six-year-old boy neatly follows me when I take him away. After I have cleansed the corresponding field as well, he has no reason to stay any longer.

Entities 3 and 4 are twins who died in a car crash at the age of fifty-four. They are angry about their abrupt end, because they did not think it was their time yet. They simply do not agree and they instigate Neil to do certain things. The brothers are not as meek as the six-year-old boy and it takes some more time and energy to get through to them. At last they leave and Neil is free from entities now.

Then his maternal grandmother appears. She doesn't agree to his being placed in a special home, either. And although he is in the wrong care facility, she is happy now because she sees that things are beginning to move and he is getting the right support, my treatment being part of that.

William comes to the fore. To me, he looks like Grandmother's twin. Neil tells me he thinks it is her handicapped twin brother. I can see he resembles Neil a lot. He looks on wide-eyed at what we are doing: for the very first time, he sees how his sensitivity works. He is learning by looking at his sister's grandson. He too is very surprised, just as Neil's grandmother was.

After that, I empty a large field of junk belonging to others (mostly relatives) and sticking to Neil. The field resembles a festival ground at the end of the day. In fact Neil is a beautiful, small Light that can grow into a huge beautiful Light if he learns to keep out other people's junk and to choose what is good for him. Energetically speaking, he will do all right then. I do have to tell him, though, that he is susceptible to alcohol and drugs, originating from his great-grandparents on his mother's side. He reflects for a moment and agrees. His grandparents were alcoholics. I don't know whether he will act upon my remark or whether this is something he must one day experience because it is part of his life plan. It doesn't matter; it's up to him. I finish off and make an appointment with his father to clean their home's energy. This will make Neil's life a lot easier.

Annie is also susceptible to addictions. Apart from having an alcohol problem she also has relationship problems: she is jealous of the families of her brothers and sisters. Being a favorite aunt is not enough for her, as she is all alone; she has neither a life partner nor kids.

In her twelfth layer, four lives are of importance. In the first, she is a female Eskimo living on her own. I can see her as a hermit, very lonely.

Then a life as a male in the US emerges. He joins the people who are going to colonize the Wild West, but is afraid of what he will come across. He tries to suppress this fear of the unknown by drinking alcohol, thus creating a drinking problem. This life is immediately succeeded by a life as a prostitute. She is a poor woman who drinks heavily. Lack of money forces her into prostitution. In that particular life, she sleeps with scores of men. Therefore, she wants her present life to be completely different. In this life, a nun is her confidante and energetic role model and that, of course, does not attract men very easily.

In her next life she is a lower-caste girl in India, in 793. Not particularly pretty and dressed in orange, she is responsible for washing the elephants. I am told she belongs to the third-lowest caste, but I am not familiar enough with the subject to understand it fully. I read Sudra (a lower caste) and I get the impression that there are variations within this caste as well. 'Annie' is rather different from the others and she feels very lonely. She thinks she will not get on in life due to her appearance, when in fact it is because she belongs to her particular caste. She draws the wrong conclusions as a fact and feels turned down for the wrong reasons.

The preeminent themes in this layer are 'loneliness' and 'controlling fear by means of alcohol'. We cleanse all items and a few weeks later she tells me she has had a bottle of her favorite liquor at home for a week. She only took one small glass, whereas formerly she would have emptied that bottle in just one night. Progress has begun.

This is not the case yet with Yolanda. She comes to see me because of eczema and a small spot on her right knee. For years now, she has been taking care of her disabled older husband. That is not always easy, but she puts a brave face on. In layer 7, the life plan layer, I encounter a past life greatly affecting her present life's development, as it is connected to her life plan. She is a German man who has a burn on his right knee caused by boiling oil. His behavior is forced and he keeps going, despite the awful pain. The theme is 'pull yourself together and do not complain of pain'.

Another important life emerges. In layer 12 I can see her as a German-speaking girl. She is living in Switzerland in a health resort, suffering from eczema and fixed in a plaster corset to cure her back. She is eleven years old, far from home and missing her parents badly; she feels very lonely. Her present husband is the physician in attendance. His name is Ulrich and he is Swiss. I can see him as a physically strong, wise-owlish man who loves skiing. 'Yolanda' absorbs his wisdom when she needs it and she looks up to him. After all, he is a real man! She copies his manner of thinking and doing, automatically shifting to her male energy, acting strong and tough even though she feels very differently indeed.

By taking care of him in her present life, their contract has been fulfilled. She has compensated him for what he did for her and her supposed debt has been settled. Of course it is not a real debt if it is according to agreement, no matter how much another person does to support you. It's great and sometimes even admirable how someone supports someone else, but sometimes it's just prearranged; and so, from a soul perspective, it is the most appropriate thing to do. However, that does not diminish any achievements here on Earth.

I cleanse layer 12 and I hope their marriage proves strong enough, for I suspect Yolanda will no longer place her husband on a pedestal.

A lot of people have problems with one or more relatives. This may reveal itself at birthday parties with an icy atmosphere, lost contact, tedious funeral arrangements and lack of understanding of each other's thoughts and visions when an inheritance has to be divided among the beneficiaries. In such circumstances, there is much work to be done at the soul level. Indeed, the struggle and the ongoing search to resolve these matters jointly yields awareness. Letting go of your childhood patterns and the standard parts you are expected to play is difficult.

However, trying to be your true Self when entering into new relationships based on who you are as a soul, rather than your traditional position in the family, hugely deepens your relationships. By being loyal to yourself and by expressing your own values within your family, you add substantially to the level of light in your own twelfth aura layer. And as you are connected to your family in this layer, their twelfth aura layer will become a little lighter as well. This extra ray of light has a contagious quality and may also affect other layers. Just as a blockage in aura layer 12 can negatively affect the lower layers, that extra ray of light in 12 enables your relatives to dissolve their themes in the lower layers more easily.

So Sarah and Ben contribute to a stronger family energy by addressing their powerlessness. Arnold learns he has to define his own self-image in the face of the criticism of others, thus doing his bit for the family. His father's behavior is frequently found in families: giving and receiving criticism and, in doing so, healing karma.

Neil, the alleged black sheep, sacrificed himself for the entire group. His family energy is much lighter and easier now, enabling others to make more progress than before. To them, the only drawback could be that for the most part, they will have to do it themselves, as Neil will not take over from them anymore.

And Yolanda and her husband worked on family themes their entire lives and are now dissolving them permanently. And that is good, especially for Yolanda's family, as many of her relatives suffer from cancer. Her contribution to raising the family energy makes it a bit easier on those who are ill.

Aura Layer 13:
Living among Others as a Human Being; Physical Consequences of Your Brain Affected by Your Fellow Human Beings

Aura layer 13 is the first of three layers that connect you to all other living beings and all people who have passed on. I call it the Field of Humanity.

In aura layers 13, 14 and 15, your life is affected by a field formed by all people together, which connects everybody to everybody else. It is created by people who are alive now and people who have existed in the past. You can compare this field to an atmosphere. When you are having a good time with a group of people, you create a certain atmosphere. You cannot touch it or see it with your naked eye, but you can feel it. An atmosphere is like a cloud of mist. You can't grab it, but it does have an effect. It is the same with this energy field, the cloud of energy of the Field of Humanity.

The central theme that can be experienced in these layers is 'what does it mean to be a human being among other human beings?' As a soul, you know exactly what life is intended for and you can see the bigger picture. But as a human being, you can get stuck. As a result, you sometimes think the play we have all agreed to perform on Earth is reality. You forget you are a soul wearing a 'cloak' and you think this reality is all there is.

Of course, the difference between being a human being and being a soul comprises more than just the cloak: as a human being you can experience emotions, which you cannot as a soul, because as a soul you don't have a body, which is the instrument you use to feel the impact of your experiences. Your body allows you to experience things as a human being that you cannot experience as a soul. Moreover, souls can't feel physical pain, because they don't have a physical body. Your body contributes to your developmental path by allowing you to experience and deal with certain events and pains. Therefore, the soul often chooses a human cloak in order to become more complete and grow. That choice is mostly based on a goal the soul has for itself, as well as a goal for the soul group living on Earth: humanity. If part of the soul's goal is related to humanity, you will find it in aura layers 13, 14 and 15.

In layer 13, it concerns the physical part: for example, the bodily consequences of life as a human being, rather than a horse or dolphin. Animals are not connected to the Field of Humanity in this way and therefore are not affected by it.

For a human being, it largely works like this: at the beginning of your life as a human being, you attune to the physical Field of Humanity, because you still have to learn what it's like to have a physical body and you still have to find out how you operate an earthly body. In doing so, you notice how the Field of Humanity affects the workings of your brain, how it ensures that your body is functioning properly. So you learn this by energetically copying the art of your predecessors and fellow human beings.

So you vibrate, move and dance along with the vibration of the mother field. In turn, that large cloud of vibration you are connected to does something in your energy system and brain. It affects the chemical substances and hormones produced there. For every individual human being, this has a different effect. This makes sense, because when we are hungry, for instance, one person feels better after eating a bar of chocolate, while this can make someone who is suffering from diabetes feel miserable. Depending on your body and constitution, it is easier or more difficult for you to process chocolate. The same bar of chocolate can affect different people in different ways and it is the same with the energy of the Field of Humanity.

If your life plan or life goals do not contain anything about consciously contributing something positive to this field, it is a calm field for you that has a supportive function. If, on the other hand, you are born to participate in it and contribute something to it, the Field will trigger the relevant issues in your aura layers, causing blockages to emerge that invite you to do something with them. Going through your life themes increases your consciousness, which you then add to the Field of Humanity. In this way, the system works perfectly.

So the thirteenth aura layer is a high-level physical layer in which the Field of Humanity affects the chemical processes in your head. The chemical processes control the bodily functions and the functioning of the body. The Physical Field of Humanity also controls the hormonal processes, and it affects the electrical processes and stimuli in your brain. In doing so, it partly controls the functioning of the brain. It has a profound influence on you. For example, it regulates the production of substances that make you feel happy or depressed. It can also inhibit the firing of electrical impulses in the synapses by neurotransmitters, which causes your nervous system to be constantly stimulated, resulting in possible physical symptoms.

When your body is ill and you find it difficult to accept and cope with (in other words, if you have trouble fulfilling part of your life assignment), there is a blockage in aura layer 13. Also, in the case of Transient Ischemic Attacks and cerebral infarctions, part of the cause can be found in a blockage in layer 13 or a life goal connected to this layer.

And although this is a 'physical' layer that expresses itself mainly in the form of physical infirmities and illnesses, it also affects certain habitual thought patterns. If the tension in certain brain areas is too high and is not released properly anymore, the electrical impulses can cause people to get stuck in their way of thinking. In this way, family and group thought patterns are negatively affected; whereas if both brain hemispheres are well integrated and all the cells can do what they were designed to do, there will be a lot less excess tension, which allows people to combine their thinking and feeling and to be more balanced in their opinions. And in people who have residues of knowledge of pre-worlds in aura layer 11, a negatively charged layer 13 adds to the problem.

Examples of experiences that have a great impact on this aura layer and have been added to the physical Field of Humanity by people through the ages are: experiments on human guinea pigs and the testing of electro-shock therapy on people who are 'mentally ill'.

Amber is four years old and quite a handful for her family. She is boisterous, unmanageable, she does not listen very well and she has had difficulty sleeping for the past few months. With her parents' consent, her grandmother has called me in for help because she is worried, not only about Amber but also her grandson Jacob. Jacob is Amber's two-year-old cousin who also has trouble sleeping. However, there is one big difference: Jacob has trouble falling asleep and Amber has difficulty sleeping through the night.

Through the phone, while talking to their grandmother, I already sense that Jacob can see entities, which makes him very uneasy when he is lying in bed, and I also sense a number of difficult fields in his house. With Amber, I see a connection with her grandfather, which is very complicated because grandfather Bob committed suicide three years ago. I am told I will see Jacob first and Amber the following day. Grandmother will be present on both occasions and this is how it is planned.

In Jacob's home I remove a number of fields and entities that make life difficult for him. While I am doing that, I notice Jacob's mother is quite angry with her deceased father-in-law. When she asks a question about him, I get dizzy. I sense his presence, but then my perception is blocked. It is clear that is not supposed to happen, so I explain that I am being blocked. I don't worry about it, because we only agreed on me working on the house in relation to Jacob's sleeping problems, so that is what I do. However, at the same time I notice that his mother has the implicit expectation that father-in-law Bob will come, allowing her to have a serious word with him. She does not get the chance, though, and at the end of my visit she says it has not been any help; Grandfather did not drop by.

The following day, I meet cousin Amber and I have a premonition. I think grandfather Bob is around and he will drop by to have a word with us later. Amber is a small girl who is not fully grounded. She comes and sits down next to me. She is literally stiff with tension, especially in her neck. I can feel this in my own body and when I say it out loud, her mother confirms it. She pays regular visits to an osteopath, but so far this has not really helped her. This doesn't surprise me, because I see two causes: a connection with her grandfather Bob, who causes something very peculiar, and a problem in her thirteenth aura layer.

Amber's brain functions differently from that of most people and she builds up tension quite quickly. Too many well-intended directions from her mother and grandmother don't make this any better. Be careful not to fall down. Hold your cup straight, Amber, don't do that, don't touch the.... This puts enormous pressure on her, which makes it yet harder for her to listen. There is also an attachment in layer 13 that causes her to be very sensitive to what other people think of her, and she has a tendency to eat sweets in order to release her uneasiness. I explain things to her mother and start clearing everything up. Meanwhile, Amber sits fairly quietly next to me, which in itself is a small miracle for a girl this boisterous.

Then we go upstairs to Amber's bedroom. It is icy cold because it's freezing outside. Something peculiar is going on there. I see a field across the street, which just reaches Amber's bedroom. The field is related to her grandfather's suicide. He used to live across the street and the residual field is still there, causing her restlessness. Considering Amber's bed is not inside the field, normally the field would not cause a lot of problems, but Grandfather has a habit of frequently visiting his grandchild to check how she is. He is worried about her and is unaware of the fact that his energy, combined with the field, causes her problems.

I detach the field from her bedroom and roll it up like a carpet, pushing it out of the house. I don't have to remove it completely; this is enough to help everyone concerned. From now on, grandfather Bob can visit his grandchild without causing harmful reactions in her.

Then he starts talking to me. I ask him if it's all right if we go downstairs first, because I expect a long story and it is very cold upstairs. When we are downstairs in the warm living room, he starts talking through me to Grandmother and her daughter-in-law. It is quite a special experience. Grandfather turns out to have been an alcoholic who saw himself as a big loser – a twit, as he describes it himself. He didn't expect his death to cause so much grief. I explain to him that the grief is unnecessarily great because he took his own life. A natural death would have been sad as well, but it would have caused a different kind of grief.

Bob understands and tells me more about the how and why. He just did not want to live anymore. He drank a lot, which did not bring out the best in him. He acted more cheerful and funny than he actually felt. Stepping out of life seemed the easiest way out; it felt like the best solution for him. Grandfather also tells Grandmother that it is in no way her fault. There is nothing anyone could have done. He was determined to step out and just waited for the 'right' moment.

Daughter-in-law Lisa is in tears when she hears all this, because she also thinks she should have been able to prevent it. Bob is very clear and straightforward when he says, 'It is no one's responsibility, except my own.' He also says to Grandmother that it is not up to him to give her advice (after all, they have been divorced for years), but that he can see she worries too much about the children and grandchildren. She is constantly afraid that something bad might happen and, as a result, she interferes with the upbringing of the grandchildren a bit too much. He says, 'Let the children raise their children. Just be their grandmother and enjoy it!' He says you never know when you will die and you have to enjoy life while you can. With tears in her eyes, Grandmother says he is right and she is happy she can let go of her sense of guilt.

To Lisa, Bob says with a lot of love that he thinks she is such a sweet woman, and he thanks her for her understanding. She has never judged him for his choice, no matter how greatly it impacted her life. He also says this is the reason he had the courage to come today. His other daughter-in-law is still angry with him and he does not have the courage to confront her yet. He has dealt with a small piece of what he has done and he now sees what he has caused in the lives of the bereaved, which is quite a shock for him. Unfortunately, he already felt inferior and this realization only adds to that feeling. For this reason, he will first continue coming to grips with everything that has happened until he's ready for the next step. But I can feel that Lisa's love for him does him a lot of good.

He continues by stating that he and Amber are very much alike in terms of sensitivity and giftedness. This upsets Grandmother. However, he is quick to explain that they are both highly sensitive, but that he was not able to deal with it because he didn't know what it was. He only knew he was easily overwhelmed and he found it difficult to deal with his emotions. That's why he drank them away. With Amber, on the other hand, it's already clear what she is like, so she can get the right support in learning to deal with her sensitivity. When grandfather Bob clarifies this, I understand why he likes visiting his grandchild. He understands her very well and can learn from her from a distance about something which he did not seem to be able to do himself.

I thank him for his explanation and wish him good luck. I understand from his words that Bob is still learning the things he was unable to learn here anymore. He is on his way to discarding his inferiority complex.

Dennis is a seven-year-old boy with ADHD, who sees red, green and white eyes in the air, while I do not. He has a vivid imagination and is capable of making up everything he says, so I am prepared for anything, but I soon discover he is not making things up at all. What he sees are the eyes of entities. He can't see the rest and the eye color indicates whether or not he can trust them.

The red ones are aggressive bad guys, the white ones are neutral and the green ones are the good guys. And because he talks about them as if we are in the middle of a *Star Wars* movie, it all seems a bit implausible, but he is absolutely right. I only remove the nasty entities, and I teach him how he can make the distinction between the different types and call for help whenever he's in doubt. Next, I show him how he can protect himself against uninvited guests.

Then I enjoy the whole experience for a minute, because I very much enjoy discovering new things. I also realize that every person perceives parts of the Field of Humanity in his or her own way.

Leah's once-only session is a birthday present from her friend. Her friend liked her sessions with me and hopes I can help Leah with her sleeping problems. She suffers from a serious type of sleepwalking, which makes her go to the kitchen to fry eggs and walk up and down stairs at night, which of course can be very dangerous.

I explain to her that I expect it will take two sessions in order to tackle the whole problem and I see something related to different time zones. It reminds me of the time I went on holiday to Australia and when I came home, my body was still functioning according to Australian time for weeks. It was as if I was not entirely here yet and part of me was still in Australia. It kept me awake while everybody else was sleeping and vice versa. I sense something similar in Leah, but the time interval is greater. I suspect a past life is involved.

I also notice the problem is attached to the back of Leah's head. It extends to her maxillary sinuses, and she is obviously paranormal. The thing is: she doesn't want to do anything with it. She cannot close herself off from what she picks up and, as a result, she is very restless and was thus diagnosed with ADHD by her GP. Furthermore, on her anamnesis form she indicates having had anorexia. Her communication chakra is closed off and although she talks a lot, she doesn't have the courage to say certain things out loud.

In layer 13, I come across a life in which she was a five-year-old boy living in Australia. He is an aboriginal and there is a problem with his food, because he has eaten too much of a certain plant and, when eaten in those amounts, it is poisonous. The poison kills him. As a result, Leah does not trust her own judgment and she is also a difficult eater. She is afraid of making another judgment error.

Then another life announces itself. It is again in Australia, but this time she is a thirty-three-year-old woman. She suffers from a cerebral infarction and is disabled for the rest of her life. As a result, she does not trust the good in life and has completely lost her trust in herself. I see that part of Leah's soul has stayed behind in this life and decide to do what the Indians call a soul retrieval: I retrieve the part of her soul that was left behind and bring it to the 'here and now' and make her soul 'whole' again. The part that was still in the Australian time zone affected her sleepwalking and if everything is right, all clocks are now synchronized. I can see another issue, but going into that would be too much for one session, so it will be dealt with next time.

I do address the third issue, however. It is about self-confidence and it's linked to her third eye. She is afraid of seeing or believing that she sees things right. So she is not insecure, but she doubts her perception, which is a residue from her life as the aboriginal boy. I am allowed to clear it up because from now on, things can be different. Her current life issue of not wanting to hurt other people is also something we have to work on, but we will keep that for next time. Otherwise, her body will not be able to process all the energetic changes and she could fall ill as a result of having received too much new information.

Francis suffers from autoimmune encephalitis, a severe illness that causes inflammations in the brain without any external influence or known cause. Initially, the doctors don't really know what to do with it. Once a big strong man, Francis is now an insecure hothouse plant who can't do much himself and starts crying at the drop of a hat.

Since his wife is under my treatment, she tells me about his illness. I suggest I take a look. At that stage, I don't know if I can be of any help, but because I can feel energy flowing through my hands when we talk about Francis, I suspect I can. Unfortunately, Francis isn't really into this 'airy-fairy' stuff, so I first have to be approved by the ballot committee. So I visit him and we are introduced to each other.

Fortunately, he gives me permission to treat him, so I start tuning myself to his energy. I experience some kind of sea in my head, which is a very peculiar feeling. I have never felt it before. I can't put it into words, although I am feeling and experiencing a lot. It comes and goes, it pulls and pushes, but I have no idea what it is. This is new for me, because I usually have a way with words and can call emotions by their names. After a while, I say out loud that I am feeling all kinds of things, but that strangely enough, I can't express those feelings in words. This makes Francis happy. He feels recognized. He has had this problem all his life. I feel moved, because sharing this desperation with him also allows me to feel connected to him.

I carefully set to work and remove the worst stress from his body and aura. When I support his head with my hands and close my eyes, I see the image of his brain and lots of pixels in deviating colors, which clearly don't belong there. I focus on the blue and black ones and neutralize the contents of his brain. For the most part, this goes well. There are still a few red pixels left, which I will work on next time. Francis falls asleep in my hands during the treatment. When someone this ill allows me in, it gives me a wonderful feeling. I see it as a sign of great trust. He has the same energy as an unborn child, very delicate and vulnerable. He totally surrenders while his head is resting in my hands. It makes me feel soft and thankful.

There will be five more treatments. During the next one, he tells me his emotions have been bothering him a lot less since the first treatment and that he feels less burdened. Using psychometrics*, I detect that his left eye on the emotional side of the body is not working properly. It's pulling a bit and its vision is impaired. Moreover, his brain hemispheres do not work together properly. I can feel friction. His heart chakra hurts, which extends to quite a large area; his sadness is considerable.

For the treatment, I start in aura layer 7, the life plan layer. Just like last time, he is making soul choices for a transition to the next phase in his life. Aura layer 12 is next: it is about an emotional issue in his brain, toward the front, above Francis' left eye. This is where the core of the problem lies, the cause of his illness. This is where the blockage is that caused the encephalitis. Francis says his doctor also said this was the exact spot where it all started. It feels good to get this confirmation.

So the attachment point of the illness is situated above his left eye, in the prefrontal cortex, and it started in his twelfth aura layer. Standing beside his right hip, I focus on the spot above his left eye. When I start, his cerebellum at the back of his head also hurts. It's a tough problem and I suspect it is related to the part of the brain that deals with, selects and processes emotions. I look it up in my medical books and this turns out to be the case.

Next, in aura layer 8, I come across an issue related to layer 12: it is his soul agreement with his wife, who will support him during his illness. The next part of the problem, which we are working on starting from layer 12, is in layer 4. This is the transition from subtle aura layers to the basic layers of Francis' aura and the bridge to his individual field. After layer 4, Francis' personal emotions emerge in layer 2: the despair, the pain and the sadness caused by his illness and the loss of many of his bodily functions.

After this part has been cleared up, I stand on his right side, because his emotional left side is hypersensitive, and I treat his cerebral membranes. My own cerebral membranes feel dry, as if they have become smaller than their contents; they have shriveled up, as it were. I have the impression that Francis' cerebrospinal fluid has a different composition due to the encephalitis; the concentration of waste matter is too large, which attracts more fluid in order to normalize it. As a result, there is not enough fluid in the surrounding tissues, including the cerebral membrane.

The first time, I worked on the brain contents and neutralized them; now I work on the fluid balance. I do this by cleansing the part of the cerebral membranes above Francis' left eye, where the cause of the problem is. Next, I cleanse the part above his right eye, and after that, the right side and back side. I finish off with his left side while standing on his left side, as well. Next, I sweep everything together and let it drain out of his aura. It looks as if I am sweeping a pavement around his head, collecting everything at one spot and removing it with a dustpan and brush, a different technique. Then I have to collect and get rid of the waste matter. This hurts in my hands and it is a heavy, intense energy. Furthermore, the lump of energy in Francis' neck can't be removed just like that. There is a past life attached to it.

This life immediately precedes his current life. It ends about 80 years ago, in 1924, and Francis is a woman. She faces many emotional challenges and decides that in her next life, she doesn't want to feel anything anymore. This decision affects the feeling center of 'his' brain and has made him experience his emotions as the sea I felt, all his life: intangible, difficult to experience and impossible to put into words. I rewrite this as follows: 'In that life, it was difficult for me to experience those emotions. Now, in this life I am able to experience, deal with and let go of the emotions I encounter when they have had their warning function.' It is a beautiful, strong and loving restatement that cannot work against him in a possible next life.

Francis says he hears a buzzing sound, similar to the sound you hear when you are near a power house. This is not very surprising when you know it is coming from layer 13 and related to electrical impulses. After the treatment, the sound slowly fades away.

Figure 8: Blockages in Francis' aura

We agree that I will not tell him what exactly I have done, so I don't influence his experience and instead get an honest impression of his response to the treatment. However, I do write everything down and I will tell him what I have done when I see him again, after he has told me about his experiences.

During the third treatment, Francis is suffering from cramps in the extensor muscles of his hands and legs. He sweats a lot and is much angrier than before, so all kinds of things are being released. The buzzing sound is back, but it is slightly different. I suggest he consult his doctor and find out if vitamin B12/B2 might be of help in relation to the cramps and I set to work in the twelfth layer. It is about the courage to face this emotional issue, because there is an extra emotional charge from a past life.

In layer 17, I remove the field that causes changes in his crown chakra. The field prevents him from being able to tune in to his Higher Self, preventing him from knowing which road to choose and causing him to avoid important decisions. After that has been put right, I reconnect his crown chakra to his pineal and pituitary glands. Francis hears the buzzing sound again, through his crown chakra.

In layer 15, he accumulates the emotions he picks up from his parents because he doesn't know how to deal with them. This affects his adrenal glands and is related to leading a 'subservient life'.

In layer 13, I come across a courage issue – being courageous in standing up for your views and beliefs, regardless of whether people agree with you and the consequences this has. I can literally see blind, black spots until this issue is cleared up. So he really did not and could not see.

Then we go to another courage issue in layer 13: the courage to stand up for your emotions and the potential consequences this has (other people might reject you). The issue is situated on his left side. After all, it is an emotional issue, and I fine-tune it to the other courage issue.

In his heart, I feel the sadness he has gone through in his life and I understand he often keeps his mouth shut to avoid hurting other people. I cleanse his lymph nodes through his thirteenth layer. I also remove the blockage in his oral cavity by releasing the stress from his speech nerve. This allows him to speak his mind and physically be able to speak and say things out loud.

A month later, the prednisone he's taking is causing problems. His overall condition is a bit worse. The muscle cramps have greatly improved because he has been taking B2/B12 and we have found that the absorption of B12 is disturbed by other medication he is taking. In layer 7, Francis again makes the choice to move on. Then, in layer 10, the layer in which he creates his future, he comes across a blockage. It is his wife Michaela. He has to approach his relationship with her differently. He has to stand up for himself more and do more things on his own. It is a painful and sad issue, because at the moment he does not feel his wife understands or recognizes him for who he is.

Next, I detach the field of his encephalitis in layer 11 via the back of his head. The buzzing is back in Francis' head. Through his head, I work on the neurons responsible for the stimulus conduction in his brain. I do this in layer 10. It turns out there is a connection with his left adrenal gland and I remove everything through the back of his head, just like I did with the encephalitis field.

Another month later, I work in layer 5, the blueprint of his physical body. I focus on his heart and bronchi in relation to the cramps, and on his sadness about his relationship, which isn't going very well. Then we go to layer 7. I ask him, 'Do you really want it?' Yes, his essence says. But he is still afraid. The fear returns in layer 8. It is the fear that Michaela will leave him. I remove the fear, because it's of no use and if she ever does decide to leave him, he can worry about it then. I also remove an entity who is reinforcing the fear. The angels Orion* and Angelica* help me with their energy of purity and protection, especially with rounding off the old and starting the new phase.

During an added consultation by phone, I feel slightly nauseated, which is coming from my abdomen. There is no organ involved; it's pure exhaustion. There is a temporary increase of information and stimuli, which Francis can't handle, and I think he is doing too much. He is improving very quickly and is able to do more things, but his physical rehabilitation program in the hospital uses up all his energy, so there isn't much left for his healing process.

He insists he is reasonably fit, but he feels too tired to me. It is about seeing now and having the courage to see other details. I again treat the control center of his nervous system through the pituitary gland, and in layer 10 I remove the emotional issue regarding Michaela, who still does not take him seriously. She treats him more like a patient than as an equal partner and keeps her distance; she shields herself. This blocks a happy future together.

Over the following month, Francis achieves various milestones: he goes to a sports game, he travels by train on his own and goes to a music event all by himself. All these new stimuli have made the buzzing sound worse, but for the most part he has no complaints. He is just very tired. He still shakes, which I can't do anything about, unfortunately; it's caused by his medication. However, I can do something about his hormonal imbalance relating to his third eye. Its vision is impaired and he has trouble focusing with it.

Once more, in layer 7 I ask him what he wants. I hear: a big change and a different choice with regard to his driver's license. He wants to go to the next phase and he wants his driver's license back, because he needs it to get back to work.

In layer 9, I again balance his pituitary gland. Finally, I am allowed to detach Francis from his family issue with old thoughts and patterns. Apparently, he has gone through enough, enabling him to decide for himself how his brain works and how he will use it after having worked so hard. He had the courage to heal his family karma and experience his beliefs and emotions, regardless of what the people around him thought of that.

Next, Archangel Raphael* uses my abilities as a trance medium and works through me. He fills both of us with pure Light. After that, Francis is also nourished by Archangel Michael* through his neck, enabling him to speak his truth from now on. We round off and I have done everything that is possible at this stage. I am happy to see Francis is doing well and is self-reliant again.

In summary, Francis' thirteenth layer contained a universal issue shared with other beings, people who are also working out this theme. This affects brain function to such an extent that in Francis' case, it resulted in an autoimmune illness. Francis has chosen to heal this issue on behalf of his family karma in layer 12. The softness in this man, the despair, the pain and his sadness tell me it was a very tough issue. I admire him greatly for his courage.

Other people work out individual issues in layer 13 that are not related to layer 12 and family karma. They develop themselves by having an extra handicap. In this case, the handicap is being sensitive to the field that represents what other people think and can disturb your own brain function. This causes you to think more negatively about yourself than necessary. At first sight, this seems to be a very complicated system. But it is also ingenious.

Aura Layer 14: Living among Others as a Human Being; the Consequences for Your Creation Power When Your Thoughts Are Affected by Your Fellow Human Beings

Just like layer 13, aura layer 14 affects the functioning of the individual person. This happens under the influence of the field constructed by the whole of humanity, which connects them: the Field of Humanity. Just like layer 13, it is created by all human beings who are alive and have ever lived. In layer 14 the field affects you on the mental level – it affects your way of thinking, how you think and what you think. Consequently, it also affects the way you experience the world and your worldview.

This Mental Field of Humanity indirectly influences your creation power, because what you think and believe is possible determines what you dare to wish and create. So it is about your worldview and designing your life based on that worldview. It is about the question of how your creation of your life and everything in it is impacted or determined by your worldview, what you consider normal, possible and good. What can and can you not ask for yourself, when are you greedy or arrogant? How do others perceive you when you create everything you really want to create? Do you still belong? Would you perhaps lose friends?

In this aura layer, we come across the reasons you are not aware of, which prevent you from creating and allowing your ideal reality. This layer also contains the underlying fears, or better said: the views, assumptions and thoughts that prevent you from developing your ideal image and therefore cause fear. So your thinking creates your fears.

This layer has quite an impact on your worldview, the way you look at people and the way you look at life itself. It determines your perspective on everything, including God and religion. When you start working on this layer, you will follow your soul's choice and not always the example of the field or the large crowd. As a result, healing soul issues on this level contributes to the purification of the disturbance in the way humanity thinks as a whole, and it helps humanity as a whole develop to a higher level. In this way, the Mental Field of Humanity, which also feeds layer 14, evolves.

Raul is a sensitive thirty-eight-year-old man who isn't sure what he wants to do, as far as his career is concerned. He works as a consultant, but his heart is no longer in it. If you love your job, you can establish a lot more and most of the time you are better at what you do.

Raul's mother is a psychiatric patient and living with her after his parents divorced has left its tracks. Every time his mother visits his family, his mind becomes unclear and hazy. He has learned to separate his own energy from hers, which protects him from taking over her emotions, but there is still a haze in his head when she is around, which only clears up a few days after she has left. It looks as though he is also carrying a trace of that energy with him. Nevertheless, he is usually a very enjoyable and sharp-witted man, so something peculiar is going on.

In layer 14, we come across two past lives. In the first of these, he is a woman who suffers from a psychiatric illness and dies over 100 years ago, in 1890. The top of her head was damaged at birth and this has caused her crown chakra to be closed off. As a result, she does not have a mental GPS to tell her what is pure for her, which prevents her from connecting to her Higher Self or God, her spirit guides or angels. She is fully closed off and becomes very lonely and aggressive. Her third eye is heavily overstimulated, because she can't use her crown chakra to interpret the information she receives through her third eye. It's all too much for her. It's as if she receives dozens of letters written in Russian every day, when she can only read English. A lot of information, but none of it is useful to her. Apart from that, her nervous system is overstrained but she isn't allowed to 'leave' Earth. After all, she has run away from a similar experience before and now she must endure it. She has given up before, in her previous life.

In that life, she is a three-day-old baby who also has a closed crown chakra. All the pregnancy hormones have made her mother overly emotional. Her mother pours out such an overload of emotions on her that she is frightened out of her wits. Not only is she suddenly inside a physical body, but she is confronted with all those feelings coming from her mother. Terrible! It's too much and she can't handle it. She does not want to live like this and she leaves her body. She dies. So it's no wonder that Raul is very sensitive to the psychiatric aspect of his mother's life. He is no stranger to it, because it is still there in his energy field and got activated when he was confronted with it again.

After treating Raul, I cleanse his house, especially the study, because his mother is staying there when she is with them. When I am doing this, I find that the previous inhabitant of the house also had mental problems and there is still a residual field of it in the house. Raul's mother's energy felt perfectly at home in this environment and regularly replenished the field that was in the study. So whenever Raul thought he could quietly work in his study, he was given the whole works. In itself, this doesn't have to be a problem, because there are residual energies everywhere and you don't necessarily have to notice them. But Raul was carrying his problem with him, which caused him to react to those energies.

After layer 14 is cleansed, Raul can open up to his inner awareness of what he would like to do, without resonating with someone else's old energetic charge. After his study and fourteenth aura layer have been dealt with, Raul's haziness in his mother's presence is a thing of the past.

Derek has quite a different story. He is a very charming young man in his early twenties who, despite his insecurity, exerts a lot of attraction to homosexual men, although he is a heterosexual and is not interested in these men. An older man of means has been approaching him for quite some time. One day, this man drugs and sexually assaults him. This experience is stored in his fourteenth aura layer, and the fact that he was unable to prevent this experience has resulted in a conviction that he can't do anything right. He used to have this thought once in a while before the experience, but now it is fixed and has a paralyzing effect on him.

Derek thinks he is stupid, that he is incapable of doing anything and that it is no use trying to achieve what he would like to achieve most – all because the Mental Field of Humanity contains a lot of thoughts of people who think like this. If this field were only filled with positive thoughts, Derek's problem would be a lot smaller, because in that case he would be fed with a positive attitude toward himself. So a lot needs to be addressed here. I cleanse his aura and I also remove the images, so Derek will no longer be haunted by nasty thoughts and will be able to start shaping his life.

A few years later, he visits me again. He is doing very well, but he still gets emotional when he thinks about ghosts. He is scared to death of them and wants to do something about that.

We set to work and I notice his grandfather joining us. He passed away more than twenty years ago and he has dropped by to tell me what happened back then. When Derek was still a very little boy, he could see entities and he was scared of them. But when his grandfather died and visited him with good intentions, he really got panicked and Derek has been afraid ever since.

Grandfather is visiting us now to put things right and to help his grandson. I ask Derek, who is lying comfortably on my treatment table under a flannel, to expose the palm of his left hand. Next, I ask Grandfather if he can make contact with his grandson there. He does this and Derek feels a stream of warmth entering his arm through his hand. I am not doing anything; I am only watching how the two of them are enjoying their renewed acquaintance.

Next, I work in his tenth layer. This is the layer he uses to create his life and in which he can come to terms with having contact with people who are deceased. I expect there will be a career switch, which has been coming for a while but has not yet been realized. I remove all the fears that are blocking his having the courage to make contact with the spirit world and I talk to Derek about how he can do it safely.

For a while, he keeps the dead at a distance. All of them, except his grandfather. Only when he can recognize and understand his grandfather well enough are others welcome to come. It is very important to him that he feel safe and that his self-confidence not diminish. Meanwhile, he will practice in a playful way and will call me when he has doubts about the things he perceives, and we will have a look together. Better safe than sorry. Relieved and reassured, he leaves my practice.

Claire is a mother of three sons who all have sleeping problems. She calls me because a friend of hers has recommended me to her. During our telephone conversation, it doesn't take long for me to sense water veins running through her house – and entities. I make an appointment to cleanse the house and, just to be on the safe side, I put my folding table in the back of my car. I suspect I will be doing more than just cleansing in that house. I travel across half the country and arrive at Claire's home.

She tells me that since we made the appointment, things have been better in the house. It seems to be quieter. I chuckle and tell her that entities can hear what we say and know what I am going to do. I think they kept quiet for a while, hoping Claire would cancel the appointment. I go to work in the house and remove several fields and entities. I treat her son in layer 17, which is described later in this book. Next, I treat his mother.

Since the birth of her eldest child eight years ago, Claire has regularly suffered from severe lack of sleep and has been home from work for six weeks due to nervous exhaustion. Three night-revelers and a job in mental health care take their toll. She bursts into tears very easily and struggles with that because she thinks she is such a cry baby. This also happens when I enter the house and she apologizes for it. I tell her not to say sorry when she has done nothing wrong and I explain that she is only reacting to my energy. She can see the positive storm coming, so to speak; the tide will turn and she can sense that without being aware of it. It is mostly relief I see on her face. Because she knows a lot about psychology and psychiatry and how trauma is caused, from an earthly point of view, I am interested to find out how she will respond to my energetic interpretation of things.

This goes quite well. She is a smart woman with a great sense of humor, which sometimes turns into self-mockery, but she understands the parallels between how things work on a psychological level and how they work on an energetic level. She picks it all up very quickly. I have noticed she has a similar gift to mine, so I go into more depth with her. When I explain to her that her sister feels like she sucks up her energy, and that it's not only the negative stories she tells which Claire thought made her so tired, but that her sister literally walks away with her life energy...she bursts into tears. And when I warn her that this also happens when she talks to her sister on the phone, I can see this startles her. She thinks about it for a moment and confirms it wholeheartedly.

I teach her what she can do about it: to begin with, her aura extends several yards from her physical body, which makes her very vulnerable because her energy is spread over a large space. So I teach her how she can make her aura smaller. This is not very difficult to do: you just tell your aura to retreat to about one yard from your physical body, for example, and after some practice (and only if you really mean it) your aura will do what you want it to do. She can hardly believe it's that simple, but it is – If you know what to do, of course.

Next, I tell her that if you say to yourself, 'I receive the information but not the underlying energetic charge,' you will absorb other people's words but not the unpleasant energy accompanying them. And if you say, 'I decide what I do with my energy,' it's more difficult for other people to suck up your energy and it stays with you. And in case she will be confronted with very difficult energy-suckers, I perform an aura exercise** with her so she has a made-to-measure solution, in case of an emergency.

While we are talking about it, I can feel the spot that starts to hurt when something unpleasant comes in. The human body functions wonderfully, because the pain signal in her left scapula tells her too much is coming in. Her body tightens up and steels itself, which causes the pain. This spot is different in everybody and in her case it is her left scapula. In my case, it's my neck, while other people might suffer from stomach aches. When you know your personal canary in the coal mine, you can always keep it in mind.

I also notice Claire is not very well grounded and in fact only touches the ground with her toes while we are talking. She pulls up the rest of her feet. I ask her to rest her feet flat on the floor. When she does that, making sure her legs are parallel to each other instead of crossed, any excess tension can drain away. It's actually a good thing that I'm noticing this, because it tells me this is her second signal point. When she grows tense, she automatically lifts her feet. So now Claire knows: pain in her scapula means 'there is too much coming in', and when her feet leave the ground, she is tenser than she thought.

Next, I remove a past life immediately preceding her current life, in which she is a fifty-one-year-old man who is overworked. All this life, 'Claire' has worked very hard for his children because he is divorced from his wife. This life causes Claire to have a tendency to keep going and going, and now this is going to change. Then I work on her stomach chakra, third eye and crown, so her mind becomes a lot calmer. This is enough for a first session.

The next session takes place in my practice. Since last time, Claire has experienced more personal space and she has done things she enjoys. Based on her anamnesis form, I sense which themes have to be addressed today. We come to one of her greatest fears: several of her relatives are in mental homes, some of them because of depression (her greatest fear), while others have an alcohol or other addiction and one has religious delusions. I instantly see two past lives related to the depression, so I think we can do something about that.

She was also sexually assaulted by a serial rapist when she was at university. My vision starts to get blurry, here. This makes sense, because when she was assaulted, her head was pulled back so she couldn't see anything. For one reason or another, this is relevant. Then my eye falls on her left arm and hand. There is a big scar there from an arterial bleeding she sustained in her childhood when she fell through a glass door. We will also look into that.

As always, I check with my spirit guides to determine whether these are all the important themes for today's treatment and they confirm this. That's good to know and I get to work. By calling the topics by name and talking about them, the blockages in Claire's aura are activated, which makes it easier for me to work on them. Sometimes I can see them literally light up. Today, this is not the case. However, I can feel precisely where they are, because they feel like throbbing prickly chestnut shells. I go by them one by one and do what I have to do. Today's theme is 'the two sides of aggression and anger – are you allowed to let it all out, or do you suppress it and become depressed?'

We start in layer 9, the group agreement layer. So this is a theme she agreed on before she was born. There is an addiction issue around her stomach, relating to a client of hers with an eating disorder. So she picked up this energy at work and the residual energy is still there. But it won't be for long. Next, we address the addiction issue of both Claire and her family. She herself is vulnerable to alcohol. I clear up the issue, but I do not disconnect it from the mother field. This means Claire will remain connected to it.

This is the first time I am not allowed to disconnect somebody from a difficult field. I am used to doing it, so I have to think for a moment before I understand why it's different this time. I am only told that the disconnection would not be very beneficial in this case. I realize this is true, because in Claire's line of work, she needs access to that field. If she loses this access, she will no longer recognize addiction when she comes across it in her practice. I check with my spirit guides if this is the reason. They confirm it and I explain to Claire what I am doing. She totally agrees.

Then I come to her throat chakra and the assault by the serial rapist. While I am working on it, I realize there was a reason she was able to tear herself loose. There is no contract or blueprint for her life in which this was deliberately included as a learning experience. So it was not an agreement and it was not meant to happen. She did not sign up for an experience like it, so he did not succeed in raping her. I realize this might be difficult to read if you are a rape victim, but again, it is about what was decided on the soul level and not about what you like or do not like as a human being. In these kinds of situations, there is a vast gap between these two, which I know from experience. It is not one of Claire's issues, so she should be safe now. I remove the old stress and her throat is opened. From now on, she can express her anger more easily.

Next, in layer 13 I come across a lot of anger and aggression. As I said before, there is a big scar as a result of an arterial bleeding. I do not touch her, but Claire can feel her scar and her fingers start tingling as a result of what I'm doing. This surprises me, because I'm working in layer 13 and most people don't notice that physically. She does, which makes it plausible that she is also paranormal. We will see.

She needs her left arm and hand to pass on things in a figurative sense, and to create things. She needs them to make her emotional side more concrete and to create her life using her emotions, so she can start her own practice, because that is what she would really like to do. When her left side is working better, she can finally create things, both from a rational and an emotional perspective.

In the emotional side of her aura layer, I see a life in which she is a Frenchman. In that life, 'Claire' is psychotic and experiences every emotion imaginable. He often talks for hours on end. Sometimes he isn't talking gibberish, yet still people do not believe him. This infuriates him. He has also been treated as a thief because he is confused, and he is even put in a prison cell. His left wrist is chained. This also angers him. This experience is related to the scar on Claire's left wrist.

The counterpart of this life is on the other side of her aura: a life as an esquire, a landowner. In 1642, he is stabbed to death with a dagger. He is stabbed in his liver to the right side of his chest. The right side is the rational side. The spirit guide tells me in English that he was stabbed by a 'delusional person' so I know it happened in an English-speaking area. The esquire did not see it coming and has difficulty coming to terms with the untrustworthiness and uncontrollability of it. He can't do much with it rationally. He can't even get angry about it, because that would not be reasonable.

I calmly let everything drain away until Claire's aura feels balanced again and I think I'm finished. I am about to round things off when her right arm suddenly starts to move. It really draws my attention without doing anything special. It has been lying next to her body all the time without me noticing it, but now it has my full attention. Her right arm tells me it was overburdened because it had to take over a lot of stress from the left arm. It wants to get rid of this stress. I have never heard an arm talking before and I know the signal comes from her Higher Self, but it still feels like her arm is speaking to me. It's a very funny thing to experience.

Anyway, I release the stress from the lower arm, as requested, up to the elbow and ask 'humbly' if this is all I have to do. It is, and Hilarion* comes to help me 'stitch up' the aura in order to allow the issues that have been cleared up and operated on to heal further.

Julia is a beautiful, youthful looking woman of around sixty who has a warm personality. She comes to me half in shock due to the sudden passing of her sister. The worst of it is now over, but there is still some rigidity in her that causes her to walk around a bit numbed. She wants to have contact with her sister and, although I am not specialized in having conversations for the sake of conversations and would like to do more than just talk, I can see beforehand that her sister will come and help during the treatment; so I agree to make an appointment. Apart from her grief, there are two more things that strike me about Julia: She is clairsentient and she gets really frustrated with other people. Sounds, movements, noises when they are eating, all kinds of imperfections irritate her. She says this so expressively that she makes me laugh. But she also exaggerates it, which makes me suspect there must be something underlying it.

We begin in aura layer 6, where the irritation is. It originates in past lives, which I am not shown. I remove the causes and Julia develops a softer look to the world around her.

In layer 8, there are a number of painful experiences, starting when she was about six years old. She has never had maternal love, which still brings her great sadness. This issue – the result of an agreement between two souls, namely hers and her sister's – is attached to her stomach chakra and we clear it up. This makes Julia a lot calmer.

In layer 11, her sister joins us. I channel her and she talks about the lack of maternal love and the consequences this had. The consequences are linked to knowledge of other times and positions of power. We are not told the exact workings of this, but that doesn't matter as far as the clearing up is concerned, so we continue steadily.

In layer 14, the room suddenly gets very crowded: Archangel Gabriel* and Archangel Metatron* come with 'glad tidings', as they call it. I repeat this out loud and jokingly say to Julia, 'You don't think you're pregnant, do you?'

No, they are referring to the Tree of Life and spiritual growth. Their message is: 'You are a Light, a Light for other people. You are a torch in the darkness. Give unconditionally – but when you give, lay down certain conditions. Choose consciously what and when you give.' It is clear to me that they are talking about an extraordinary kind of Light in a very earthly appearance. And that is the beauty of it:

Julia, who has been sharply and venomously ranting about all the things that annoy her, not only has a spirited personality but also a beautiful soul quality, which the angels say she can give more of to other people.

The Greatest Light, of course, is not sitting on a high mountain like a hermit, levitating above the ground and meditating until it is canonized. It lives in people and spreads the Light to others through its deeds. I think this is a challenge for every human being: how to combine your soul quality with your humanity.

Julia is almost ready to start doing this. First, there is one more thing that has to be removed: a past life in 1707 in which she is a Russian woman charged with heresy. She is paranormal and listens to the wrong sources (entities). As a result, Julia's crown chakra is still blocked in layer 14. And because she was very sensitive to what other people thought about this issue at that time, the great Mental Field of Humanity has also influenced her all this time, which has caused her a lot of concern. As from today, however, this will be very different.

A small encore: during the session Julia keeps asking me the name of her spirit guide. I ask him and I hear 'Magblup, Maggblap, Magduhduh, Machuduhduh' – in other words, I cannot hear it right. In an attempt to be of service to his protégé and tell her his name, with my help, her spirit guide pushes the first part of his name out with so much energy that his energy dies off with the following syllables and I can't hear him properly anymore. So I can only hear the first part of his name. Unfortunately, it is not a name that can be communicated through images. This is a shame, because that would require less energy and it would also be easier for me, because literal hearing is more difficult for me than picking up an image and translating it.

Several times during the treatment, I ask him to spell his name letter by letter. It's no use; I can't understand him. Then I get an idea and I write down 'Machu' and ask, 'Is this right so far?' I hear, 'Yes.' This encourages me and I start spelling myself. I cannot understand his spelling because it seems as if he is drunk, but he can understand my spelling perfectly. And I can understand his 'yes' and 'no' very clearly. So I spell until I come to E, F, G YES and I know the next letter is a g. Eventually, I get the name Machuguell; it sounds a bit like Maagugwellû. It was not the easiest thing in the world to do, but it worked.

When I reflect on why spirit guides always have such strange names, at least in my view (the three spirit guides I mainly work with are Beatrice, Mutawi and Itmam, and in other people's books I read names that are even more exotic), I would like to ask mine about this. Then something hits me. The name is a sound, with energy.

Beatrice, who supports me with my personal issues and experiences as a human being, is called Beatrice because she recognizes herself most in who she was in her life on Earth as a woman named Beatrice. Mutawi, who helps me with my development as a healer, is an old Native American and has also taken along the name he had in his last life. This was a life in which we knew each other. And Itmam, my advisor and tower of strength when I am working in high and abstract fields and realities, comes from the Pleiades and has a sound that reflects his energy. Spirit guides do not communicate like we do; they communicate with energy, vibrations and frequencies. So it might all sound a bit strange.

When I have figured this out, I ask if I am far off. In his solemn way, Itmam says, 'I am entirely satisfied,' and the mystery of strange names is solved. Moreover, Julia can call her spirit guide by his name now, although this is not necessary. Your spirit guides are there for you anyway. It's just pleasant when you can call someone by his or her name.

When Itmam says, 'I am entirely satisfied,' in such a solemn way, it cheers me up, because while I am hearing him, I can also see his image. He looks like Sam, the big blue eagle from *The Muppet Show*. I watched the show as a child and I remember Sam as the big, stately eagle who always looks serious with his large eyes and who speaks in a solemn voice. This is exactly what my spirit guide Itmam sounds like.

So I affectionately call him my big blue Muppet eagle, which may sound a bit disrespectful, but it's not. He feels like a very precious friend who is continually with me and always answers my questions. His answers are mostly relevant and to the point, but he might just as well say, 'You know that, so why do you ask?' So I have learned only to ask questions when I really don't know the answer, or to call in his help when I have already done part of a reading. Then I ask him if I have done enough and he gives me confirmation, or he tells me some detail that I have to pass on to the client.

Figure 9: My personal guide: Itmam, the blue Muppet eagle

Itmam is a mix of very serious and abstract energies and loving warmth. He also has a great sense of humor. He is very quick-witted, which I love. He regularly teases me and, to be honest, I tease him back. I respect my spirit guides very much and I am thankful for their input. I have been working quite a while with my auxiliary forces. We are good friends, really, and good friends know where they stand in their relationships and make fun of each other once in a while.

Literally hearing what your spirit guides are telling you is not something everybody is able to do. I have only been able to do this since I fell ill and started working with angels. It was when my personal barriers were gone. This happened when I was around forty years old.

And although not everybody can hear the voices of their spirit guides, they are with you all day long and they are working for you. They send loving impulses to you, such as sudden inspirations, a particular feeling, a knowing, conversations during dreamtime; you are connected to your spirit guides day and night and you can benefit from your team of advisors. They add to your own intuition with a protective energy and are always concerned with your spiritual welfare, while at the same time respecting your right to exercise your Free Will.

In aura layer 14, our Free Will is affected by the Mental Field of Humanity without us being aware of it. For instance, when people thought human beings could not fly, it took a lot to be the first one to make wings and attempt the job. Every thought representing the belief that things are not possible has an inhibiting effect on the minds of inventors of new technologies, on the minds of people who try to find solutions for the world food problem, and so on. People who go beyond this, who don't pay attention to the so-called earthly reality and have the courage to dream and create new possibilities, are part of either of two groups: they have no blockages in layer 14 and therefore are not affected by what everybody else thinks or has thought; or they do have a connection with layer 14 and are affected by it, but deep inside they feel so clearly what they have come to do on Earth that nothing can derail them.

No matter how difficult this path may be, they will stand for the things they believe in and in this way create a better world, not only by what they actually do, but also by improving the energy of the Mental Field of Humanity through dealing with their issues in aura layer 14. And this benefits everybody else, because we are all connected to it. When enough people have enough courage to grow in layer 14, there will be a critical mass and a domino effect. In practice, this means that enough positive thoughts have been created to counter the existing negative thoughts. This would lead to such an enormous number of positive thoughts that the negative tendency of the field in question would be softened. This, in turn, would weaken the influencing power of the field and more and more people could then free themselves from their inner voices telling them something is impossible.

In this way, they would be able to think positive thoughts and believe that what they create can also become a reality. As a result, large groups of people will start thinking in terms of possibilities instead of problems, which will instantly change the world. It allows people to apply their creative power fully. Then healing in layer 14 for the whole of humanity will eventually be realized.

Aura Layer 15: Living among Others as a Human Being; the Spiritual Field of Humanity and Healing on the Group Level

Aura layer 15 is the third layer of the Field of Humanity. It is a spiritual layer, which means it is about your life path, living the essence of your life and adding a higher or new consciousness. In this case, the higher or new consciousness is added to the Spiritual Field of Humanity. This creates new consciousness, which is what layer 15 is all about: creating new consciousness as a group in order to make great positive changes possible. However, this is only possible when the challenge is taken on.

The challenge often manifests as disasters that impact large groups of people, such as earthquakes or big floods or heavy rainfall or a tsunami. It can also be a plane crash with victims on board the plane and surviving relatives at home; they would all be members of the group working on this layer. It may also be a wall, genocide, or groups suffering from the same incurable disease or epidemic disease. Another example is incest, with the main group consisting of both the perpetrators and the victims. Both groups also work certain things out in subgroups. The everlasting fight for Jerusalem, football fans and their opponents, native populations who feel threatened and have difficulty accepting other cultures and customs and develop xenophobia – there are as many themes as there are groups and as the soul, you always sign up for one or more themes based on the nationality and the groups you choose.

So aura layer 15 is the layer in which people go through the same learning experience as a group. They share their often painful processes and, in doing so, they observe group agreements in one big step, or release group karma or their Light level. It's a kind of pressure cooker method, and the road to travel is anything but easy.

Sometimes the group consists of relatives, but most of the time this is not the case and various kinds of people with different backgrounds are involved. These people do not only work on their karma or make considerable jumps on the soul level; the amount of consciousness the group gains as a whole adds more light to the Spiritual Field of Humanity than the smaller amounts the individuals would have added separately. The sum of the experiences of all group members is more than that of the separate individuals. This explains how aura layer 15 differs from aura layer 9.

In aura layer 15, blockages can be created when group agreements in layer 9 are not observed and if this negatively affects the course of life of an individual too much. The issue that then has to be dealt with by the person in question takes extra effort and therefore contributes to this person's Light level, but also upgrades the Spiritual Field of Humanity, which is a pleasant fortuitous coincidence.

David is a good-natured seven-year-old blond boy who is not entirely of this world. Perhaps a better way to describe it would be: he is not entirely on this world *yet*. He belongs to what I call the group of misunderstood New Age children*. He has had many kinds of therapy over the past few years because, according to experts, he does not behave like other children. So he is labelled with all kinds of so-called disorders, such as ADD and dyslexia, and he sees a child psychologist, Cesar therapy, a speech therapist, and special swimming classes for motor-disabled children, all because David has difficulty concentrating and making contact with other people.

When I see him, I know what is going on fairly quickly, because in my case he does not break eye contact and he talks nineteen to the dozen. I suspect this is because he likes my energy, which does not put an extra burden on him. I don't want anything from him. He is having a good time in my practice and it calms him down. I have finished in twenty minutes. Usually sessions with children don't take very long. They have fewer persistent problems because they haven't been resisting them for years on end, and in their current life they haven't built up a lot of old wounds because they simply haven't been in their bodies for a long time yet.

In David's case, the blockage is in aura layer 15, which is activated when too much information comes in, resulting in his brain short-circuiting. This is something many New Age children suffer from and it is exactly the way they develop themselves in this layer. They contribute to the raising of this large Spiritual Field of Humanity.

Meanwhile, I cleanse David's aura layer and I clear up the disturbance in his brain. He chuckles because it tickles a bit. 'It's like you're stirring in my head,' he says. Next, I realign his throat, brow and crown chakras and allow him to pick one of my brightly-colored Quintessences* the protective drops I put in the aura as a bandage for the person I operated on. I have him spread it over his wrists and bring into his aura. He chooses Maha Chohan*, which is going to help him say what he feels from his heart and also maintain a clear communication with his own soul, despite the hustle and bustle of the outside world.

Jake is a forty-three-year-old man who has difficulty opening up to his girlfriend. He lived on his own for years before meeting his current partner at the age of thirty-five. As a child, Jake was sexually assaulted and, as a result, he has a blockage in his fifteenth aura layer. In this case, it is about the group of victims of sexual abuse.

I come across three lives that need cleansing. The first takes place around 305 years ago. He is a woman who loses her husband in West Germany* on the Swiss border. Her husband dies, but she cannot let him go. Energetically, 'Jake' sends out the message, 'I am taken, I already have a partner,' so he does not attract future partners. He has kept this up throughout several lives and now it can be cleared up. His present sister-in-law turns out to be his then husband. They meet again now in order to realize they can break the pattern and move on.

Before this life, another one seems to be relevant in aura layer 15. He lives on the North American-Canadian border in 330 A.D. He is a trapper. His facial features look like those of an Eskimo. He has fallen down and hurt himself. He can no longer walk and his wife takes care of them. But he loves her more than she loves him, so all she does is physically take care of him. It becomes clear to him that he has different expectations to those of others around him, and that he does not share their world views. He develops this issue so strongly that in his current life, he is still somebody with a very original view on things who makes his own choices.

Then there is a life in 800 A.D., where he is living at an Italian court. He is still a child, the son of a cook. I hear 'hot air', which makes me chuckle because I think it is a wonderful expression. After all, the air in a kitchen is very warm. 'Jake' is suffering from asthma and has to stay in the kitchen because, hierarchically, that's his place. After all, he is just the son of one of the employees. But hierarchy is also hot air, a lot of hoo-ha. Being near the fires is not beneficial to 'Jake's' health. Eventually, he dies at the age of nine as a result of an asthma attack.

So he sits there because he belongs there, not because it is right or appropriate. The issue developing here is: 'which rules do you follow and which standards and values do you adhere to?' It's about rules and being forced to do things. This affects his hypothalamus, which is the switching center between his nervous system and hormones. As a result, it has an effect on his entire hormonal system and his creation process, because, as I said before, in men this starts in the epididymis. In this way, he can't put his optimal life plan into practice. I realign him and now Jake can open up to his girlfriend and follow his own rules.

Let us return to aura layer 13 for a moment. Francis, the man with the autoimmune brain inflammation, stores the emotions he takes over from his parents in his fifteenth aura layer, because he cannot cope with them. This affects his adrenal glands, because serving someone else uses up adrenal energy. Normally, you have exactly the right amount for what you have come to do on Earth, but when you are carrying issues that belong to one of your relatives, for example, you will exhaust yourself. This is similar to a mountain hike: when you are carrying three rucksacks from fellow hikers, you are likely to run out of energy.

Here, it is about a group issue relating to emotions. In this case, it's also a family issue that must be carried by all family members. Therefore, I remove it from Francis and give it back to the family members in question. If I just let it drain out, this would prevent him from working on the issue and growing, so I give it back. Fortunately, this is accepted.

Mike is a member of a group struggling with their egos. This is a very large group (if only due to the size of their egos) consisting of people who all think they are very important. Today's specific question for Mike is, 'How can I live without an ego?' because he would like to be able to do that. Personally, I don't think it is possible to live without an ego because at times it can be very useful. The thing is: you need to know how to handle it. You need your personality in life to be able to make a distinction between yourself and others. If you did not experience that dividing line, you would continually lose yourself in other people. Once you know who you are, you can again (learn to) open up and connect with others. Mike's problem is that he actually knows when he goes too far and starts playing power games. On the other hand, he also sees himself as a warm, loving man who really wants to connect with a woman. It's difficult for him to unite these two self-images.

Mike sees the same images I see. We see Atlantis*. He is at the head of the church. He is a man, he's very judging and strict, and he does not take into account the human aspect in his decision-making. He denies his love for a certain woman and chooses the church. This is not bad in itself, of course, because it is just a choice. The problem is that he has denied his love for her. So it is about the denial and not about the choice being *wrong*. Being honest, at least with yourself, keeps you sharp and allows you to keep your ego in check.

Then I see the beautiful image of a see-through t-shirt painted with translucent globes. It looks like the spotted jersey from the Tour de France, worn by the winner of the Mountains classification. The shirt symbolizes Mike's ego, which is necessary because it holds things together. You need a personality and an ego to be able to exist as a human being, but you have to understand it is only the operating system and not the decision-maker. The message is: 'As long as you keep feeling, your ego cannot get the better of you.'

Mariah is a Dutch woman in her late fifties. She had breast cancer a year ago. She underwent radiation therapy and an operation and now she has difficulty recovering her energy. She takes care of her family and gives away her own energy. This is not very sensible, because it means she doesn't have enough energy left for herself. Moreover, her family does not learn to stand on their own feet or how to monitor their own energy levels.

Mariah also knows she has to organize her life differently. However, she does not know how to do that: 'Something is blocking me and I can't put my finger on it,' she tells me when I first see her.

That 'something' turns out to be a past life, among other things – a life in Africa, to be exact. She is a member of a tribe that has 'fair shares' as one of their norms. In addition, the fact that she is a woman means she has to comply with the adage 'you will do *anything* for your family'. In her current life, she is still living according to this adage, although it is no longer relevant for her. Her unconscious program is to empty herself by giving everything to others, despite her cancer and her needing energy for her own recovery. The issue is related to her throat chakra in aura layer 9, the layer with group agreements. The throat chakra, in this case, stands for expressing and giving back emotions.

The following session, I remove a cloud of her husband's powerlessness from aura layer 6, the layer with individual traumatic experiences. She picked this up from him when the rule of 'fair shares' was still active.

Then we go to layer 12. Her deceased father Herb, who is her guide in her daily life, comes to assist me with an abstract higher energy. I experience him as mild-mannered person and I tell Mariah that her father is here. He died years ago and Mariah is clearly moved. She tells me about her childhood trauma when she was locked up in a scary place, and while she is talking about it, I am allowed to remove the field. She can let go of it now and I can see a field with all kinds of old connections being transplanted. It's similar to a heart transplant. I see the weaving and creation of a replacement field, and then I see how it is filled with new information and light. I can feel her heartfelt grief and I am told it does not matter what kind of work she does, as long as she follows her heart. Father Herb tells me his relationship with Mariah has always been meaningful. His choice of words comes across as a bit unusual to me and I tell her that. She smiles and says he has been dead for quite some time.

During the follow-up treatment, I start in aura layer 10, her creation layer. In this layer, I come across the cause of Mariah's painful shoulder. It is about a life as a woman in which she is torn apart by a Bengal tiger at the age of twenty-one. The tiger tears her left shoulder to pieces and because at the time she was unable to do anything, it is now the attachment point of her powerlessness.

Then I see a rough French sea. I see 'Mariah as a middle-aged man looking out over the dark grey sea. There is a storm. He is standing on the shore watching someone drown. Because of the storm, he cannot do anything; it is too dangerous. He feels guilty and powerless for the rest of his life. As a result, he has the tendency to work too hard, to overcompensate. And Mariah is still using that old pattern. At her pituitary gland, I remove related past lives, so information of her current life can flow freely, enabling her to create the right situations for herself.

Then I have to do something very precise. I am going to cut Mariah loose from the general field of cancer and from the field of Dutch women with breast cancer. I don't use just my hands for this, because that would take too long. I use something not designed for this: the Biogenesis Wand. It's a glass stick created to add light where it is needed. I use it to bundle my own Light into a laser, enabling me to cut in those large powerful fields.

I am told I have to pay attention to the clean cutting sections and ease my way up from layer 5, up to and including layer 15. It is a pleasant thing to do and it's nice to cut Mariah loose, because she has made her contribution to the larger field. She has added her consciousness and I hope this will be sufficient. I also hope she does not have to deal with the issue again in some other way.

When I have finished, I re-check every section. When they are all radiating energy, I neatly 'stitch up' the entire area and fill it with new pure light. The angels Orion* and Angelica* help me with this.

During the final session I work in layer 3, the mental layer, although I expected this issue to be in layer 5, the blueprint of

Mariah's physical body. I have her lie on her belly and I work in her aura, from top to bottom. When the back side is as clean as I can get it, I ask her to turn around and I apply the 'method à la Annemiek'. It is my own way of removing persistent energy that is stuck somewhere. I sit at the head of the treatment table with my arms lengthwise below her neck and my hands cupped between her shoulder blades. In this way, I vacuum her back and remove everything I am allowed to remove. And while I am slowly moving my hands toward the crown, I clean up the entire area.

I notice I am actually working in layer 5 when I sense residues from the radiation therapy. I remove the dark oozing kind of energy. I flush her lymph glands, to prevent any lingering residual energy that could potentially cause new problems. Eventually, she is energetically clean. Both the fields in her body and those in her aura, where I am able and allowed to work, are cleansed.

A few months after the final session, I hear that Mariah is doing fine. After the first session, she was very emotional; after the second one, she improved very quickly; and since the third treatment, she has just felt calm and well. Now she knows how to manage her own energy – and that she is only responsible for herself.

Whereas in aura layer 14, releasing yourself from the Mental Field of Humanity contributes to a life with more creation power for all people, in layer 15, issues that are worked through and healed make it easier for other people to follow their personal individual spiritual paths. They will have less difficulty feeling what their personal life path is and they will more often make soul-based personal choices. As a result, the level of consciousness of humanity as a whole will grow more swiftly toward a new peak.

Aura Layer 16: Lifting the Earth as a Living Community to a Higher Level through Soul Agreements between Souls Who Have the Same Intention or Belong to the Same Soul Race

Soul races are groups of souls who were split from the Source as a group and therefore have the same original source energy. When God or the Core or the Source (or whatever you would like to call it) wanted to experience itself, it split up in subfields, as it were, and gave every group their own theme.

Let us compare God to the manager of a multinational company. He is the CEO and runs the entire company, which is subdivided into marketing, sales, assembly, customer services, PR and all kinds of other divisions. They are created in order to experience a different aspect of God and eventually grow back toward the Source. If you see the whole of life and the universe as an exercise, a way to grow (back) to wholeness, you will grow back to God and become one with God again.

Different divisions, called soul races, have different qualities, developmental paths and opportunities. And based on their specific qualities, they all contribute to the unification of the whole, in their own way. It is about working through duality, neutralizing differences, creating more and greater or clearer consciousness; there are as many soul groups as there are aspects.

In layer 16, two kinds of soul agreements are important. The first is the agreement between people who were born with the same goal and want to establish something together. They are not from the same soul race, but they do have the same intention: they want to make the planet a better place and they are on the same wavelength with regard to how they would like to do that.

They could do this by starting eye camps in the Himalayans and operating on thousands of people, preventing them from going blind – or by starting a new type of school catering for the self-learning capacity of children – or by organizing holiday camps for special groups such as city children, so they can leave their concrete environment for a while, come into contact with nature, learn something new in a playful way and, at the same time, have a great holiday – or by starting a naturopathy center with a mixed group of therapists, where sick people are helped with a made-to-measure therapy – or a group of architects who choose only to design and build in a durable way.

What all these goals in this layer have in common is that they are about nature or about people other than yourself. So it is about the Earth as a whole and all its inhabitants. Self-interest is not a goal, because you are in the service of others, which you can enjoy tremendously.

The second type of agreement that we come across in aura layer 16 is that between souls of the same soul race. For them, the Earth is a place they want to lift to a higher level. By going through experiences together, they can lift the energy of their own soul race. You could compare this to relatives who put aside their differences for a while when Grandmother falls seriously ill. Everybody jumps in to take care of her and that is the actual goal. But by doing this, everyone involved discovers new aspects in others; they adjust their ideas about other people and, by doing so, they grow. This is a pleasant bonus.

So the essence of layer 16 is: 'What have you come to contribute? What is the unique thing only you can be and do on this planet and with whom did you agree that?'

And just as everybody on Earth is connected to and affects each other, the Earth as a whole is also a Thing, a quantity connected to all its own kind. The Earth is connected to all other planets and stars, and what happens on Earth directly affects the other planets and stars and vice versa. That is why aura layer 16 is called *intergalactic.*

Danielle has a blockage in layer 16. She is a thirty-five-year-old communication expert, which is ironic because her reason for visiting me is that, in her private life, she either clams up or throws everything out. She struggles with maintaining intimate relationships and she has problems with her father. They do not understand each other and at her grandmother's (his mother's) funeral, it comes to a crisis.

In aura layer 11, the layer with knowledge of pre-worlds and dealing with great powers, Danielle has an old experience with an ex-boyfriend. This experience helps her make distinctions between wrong and right. Her ex-boyfriend is a pathological liar and the theme is 'talking nonsense'. She had fallen for it in previous lives and now she is doing it again. But that's okay, because we can do something about it.

Next, we come to aura layer 16 and see that Danielle and her father have a soul agreement relating to this layer. They belong to different soul races and therefore have totally different frames of reference. As a result, the communication between the two is very problematic. It's as if he speaks German and she speaks Dutch. To an outsider, they may sound the same, but they are two different languages. And sometimes Danielle and her father use the same words and they think they understand each other, but ultimately they have such different world views, the relationship is doomed to fail. This makes both of them sad and they have difficulty coping with it, because they both feel justifiably misunderstood and not listened to.

However, this Babel-esque confusion of tongues is there for a reason. It is a way to learn to make choices energetically instead of mentally and verbally. And that is exactly what the world is heading for. So Danielle and company do their part.

Annabel is a fifty-four-year-old woman who, after many years of being single, has met a nice man, but – and it's an important *but* – she isn't interested in having sex with him. So far, he has been very understanding, although he is clearly disappointed. The minute Annabel starts talking about it, my stomach contracts. It is closely related to her nervous system and her throat chakra is completely blocked. At the moment, she does not feel like having breakfast in the morning and I can feel a lot of repressed anger at her shoulder. This will be a complicated case.

We start in aura layer 3: her personal thoughts about the situation between her daughter and ex-husband Jacob. After the divorce, Jacob left the raising of their four children entirely to her, both financially and emotionally. For this reason, her daughter did not want to see her father again. However, her daughter is now an adult and she wants to contact him. Annabel is afraid that after all these years, she will lose her child. These are all strange ideas in layer 3, so they are clearly personal thoughts being fed by fear. Fortunately, we are allowed to do something about that and so we do. Now she is able to think more positive things again. On to the next part, which is quite tough.

In layer 7, the life plan, something emerges relating to another child. Annabel's son has gender dysphoria; he is a woman in a male body and is about to undergo an operation that will make him officially a woman. He has been taking hormones for months and he has changed quite a lot. The energetic attachment of this can be found just above Annabel's pubic bone, in her lower abdomen, at the same level as the sex chakra. Her transsexual son will become a daughter and his previously male energy will become female, so on an energetic level, her connection with her child will change. She can feel this, because a different bond is developing between the two of them. I help her with this transformation.

Next, we go to layer 16. She and her children are all from the same soul race and have come to work through a difficult relationship issue concerning sexuality and justice. The former, in particular, is a very earthly theme. Not surprisingly, this is linked to Annabel's uterus. Furthermore, being a rape victim, she still mistakes sexual power for sexual control, which makes her clam up. Her nervous system is hit hard because her body experiences sexual passion as aggression, so without being aware of it, she suffers from internal stress. Add to that her son's transgender operation, which also affects her second chakra, and all in all she has quite a lot to deal with. Nevertheless, the treatment goes quite smoothly and easily. This is a good sign; Annabel has worked hard and can tackle the next issue.

Eva would like to get pregnant, but although she and her husband have been trying to get another child for five years, so far they have not succeeded. In Eva's sixteenth layer, I meet her unborn daughter Sophie. She and her future mother are not from the same soul race, but they have a similar goal on Earth: helping people heal, especially people who have made negative choices in the past. Her mother, who is a medium herself, will help her with that and is already looking forward to it.

In layer 16, we come across a mutual past life for both Eva and Sophie. It is around 1830 BC and they live as mother and daughter in Mesopotamia. Eva is sacrificed to Sebeh, the crocodile god, and Sophie to a birdlike god. All this happens in order to bring about prosperity for those who sacrificed them. Given the fact that their previous life together didn't end well, it is very exciting for Eva and Sophie to become mother and child again.

Mesopotamia disappears and I see a dungeon, also in layer 16. It is a life in which 'Eva' is a boy who has been put in prison. High above his head the boy sees a little window, but he doesn't see a way out. He is in prison because he was hungry and stole food in order to survive. While I am clearing up the layer, we hear 'justice (Divine Justice) will prevail'. Eva doesn't have much trust in this anymore, partly due to this life. By removing the old distrust, it gets easier for her and I quietly hope the Divine Justice in this case will correspond with her dearest wish. I close her aura.

Egbert is a man in his early thirties who once suffered from anorexia. He is still very thin, which is caused by a candida infection* in his intestines. In layer 16, I can see that his nervous system is overstressed and his head is aching. The anorexia is related to a deceased loved one, his grandmother. It is his weak spot. On the surface, it is a longing for his grandmother: he only wants to be with her, he thinks. But underneath, he wants to escape from the things he is confronted with in life. He would rather be dead; that would be the easy way out. The grandmother in question is also in the sixteenth layer and I remove their unhealthy connection.

More family karma follows in layer 12. He is living near Egypt. Egbert has a high position in the government and something is wrong with the grain crop. He is responsible, so he is hanged despite *thinking* he did the right thing. Consequently, Egbert decides there must be something wrong with his thinking; he thinks he is stupid and he deserves any punishment he gets for this. He sees confirmation and support of this in all kinds of ways, such as his dyslexia.

The issue is comparable with his past life during the Atlantean age. He is a woman who collects knowledge. Now he is afraid of knowledge; he doesn't want to know anything because he is afraid of responsibility. In Atlantis, 'Egbert' knows a lot and when things go wrong with Atlantis, she cuts and runs away from her responsibilities, which is exactly what Egbert tries to do in his current life. In Atlantis, she leaves the man she loves – a scientist who she says is an astronaut – without saying goodbye and the emotional bonds with her Atlantean husband are still active. He is visible, but a large cloud surrounding him prevents him from moving on. I ask Egbert to say goodbye now and I am allowed to remove the cloud. Almost instantly, he grows calmer.

Finally, I see that now he can start using his fire knowledge, which comes from his Shaman background – in other words, he can use his power! His fear of responsibility has largely gone and he can view life in a more nuanced way from now on. It is not black or white anymore. Shades of grey are also possible. Settling issues is very important for him because it allows him to move on.

Someone who is also struggling with unfinished business, albeit from a very distant past, is Caroline. She lives in 1659 as an Arabic slave trader. In that past life she sells the person who will later reincarnate as her present boyfriend. Now, as Caroline, she is faced with the consequences of what she did in that past life. They are playing a complex power game with each other and he is into sadomasochism. When one day she refuses to go along with it, he forces her.

Although this happens according to the soul agreement between them, this rape has a lot of impact, of course. First, there is the grief and pain Caroline has to deal with. Furthermore, both Caroline and her boyfriend are triggered on the soul level and it prepares both of them to handle 'power' in a much purer away. Only when they are able to deal with their powerlessness can they use their inner strength and achieve what they have come to do on Earth. Their life goals are clearly related to power, although at this time it is difficult to say how this will turn out, because they are still in a preliminary phase. Unfortunately for them, they have to work through these issues, so I clear up layer 16 and explain to Caroline how it works. She understands and calms down.

A few weeks later, her boyfriend no longer feels attracted to her. The experience has been completed and the lesson is learned. They don't need each other anymore, so they each go their own way. She is on the right track.

Another woman who is struggling with power and powerlessness in combination with sexuality is Marjorie. She is a woman in her late forties and the daughter of a pedophile. As a child, she heard a lot of horrible things about her father. Unfortunately, he also abused her when she was a child and now she must live with the knowledge that he also does this to other people. She has mixed feelings toward him. On the one hand, she loves him, and on the other hand, she is repulsed by him because he is a pedophile and she strongly denounces his behavior. Verbally, Marjorie is quite aggressive and has a very critical side, which she expresses by magnifying other people's negative qualities. She comes to me because she is suffering from migraines. When I talk to Marjorie, it strikes me that underneath her radiant appearance a war is raging. Anger, panic, ambiguities, fears – she feels like a powder barrel about to explode.

In aura layer 9, the layer with the group agreements, we see her in Egypt near the River Nile. She is a sixteen-year-old washing girl who is doing the laundry. While she is rinsing, a storm breaks loose and she is hit by a falling uprooted tree. She dies on the spot. She is very angry with herself. Isn't she intelligent enough to be able to see the danger coming and assess it correctly? She *is* intelligent enough, that is not the problem, but this was an accident. It was not meant to happen and was not in her life plan.

Sometimes people die prematurely. Accidents do happen and not everything is fixed in life. Angels and other auxiliary troops aren't always able to intervene, so sometimes things go differently to what was expected. The death of the washing girl could not have been anticipated. One moment of inattention was enough. The field in layer 9 extends all the way to her thirteenth layer, in which the functioning of her brain is affected by her earthly existence. I conclude that the thunderstorm and static electricity have affected her brain. The resulting tension is now contributing to her migraine. I remove the original anger and we go to Groningen, in aura layer 16.

In Groningen, she is a sixteen-year-old farmer's daughter. Her mother doesn't say much and is depressed. They don't talk about anything; they only work on the land and life predominantly consists of surviving, because times are difficult. When Marjorie has her first period at age sixteen, she thinks she is seriously ill and will die. The painful cramps and the blood make up a horrific scenario and she is scared to death before she can muster up the courage to confide in her mother. Her mother takes no initiative to explain things.

When she is seventeen, her brother suddenly dies. Again, they don't talk about it. So the family motto is 'keep your mouth shut because then it is not there'. Marjorie gets married. Unfortunately, her husband beats her. Her new motto is 'keep your mouth shut, otherwise someone will hit you'. She is afraid and behaves very submissively. Her children take her as an example and also become very submissive. 'Just keep your mouth shut, don't say anything, just sit with it and keep your thoughts and feelings to yourself.' She is still carrying these issues with her and it causes an inner conflict with her anger about everything she sees going wrong.

The hardest part of the session relates to her father. The core of the problem can be found on the right side of her head. He is a cynical and negative man, and the examples she gives me cut through my heart. Apart from that, he is a psychopath and very manipulative. So he knows exactly what to say and do to appease her when she is still a child and then hurt her; and because she is still a child, she falls for it every single time. She is still partly beating herself up for the experience with the fallen tree. We remove this self-reproach and I see an image of how her father's remarks cut a hole in her skull, releasing pure poison. It affects her self-image and distorts her worldview. That is why she magnifies other people's infirmities.

The strange thing is that despite everything, she also says she loves him and I can feel that she's telling the truth. However, this love is not of the present; it dates from a past life immediately preceding her current life. It is a life in Switzerland and she is a lesbian. She and her father in her current life are both women. They appear to be old spinsters sharing a house to keep each other company, but secretly they are lovers. She still feels the love she felt for 'her father' at the time, but it doesn't correspond with the person that soul has become and what Marjorie feels, thinks and knows in this life. I clear up the Swiss life so Marjorie is free to determine her present behavior and feelings. A mutual acquaintance tells me her father feels she has become softer in her interaction with other people. I wonder if he looks at this as positively as we do.

The beautiful thing about Marjorie's example is that something happens here that takes place on more occasions in my practice: someone comes in with particular symptoms and these symptoms turn out to be 'only' the entry point. It is the earthly, concrete reason to make an appointment, which is beautifully arranged by the client's soul, because by the time I see a client in my practice, their soul already knows the serious stuff will also come to the surface because the (soul of the) client decides what I am allowed to work on. The client leads and I follow. That is the division of tasks. So Marjorie is released from a migraine, her aggression and her contradictory feelings toward her father.

The abuse and rape she underwent are a horrible way to work on these issues, but 'power' is the core theme here and things are purified. Marjorie and her father belong to the same soul race and decided to work on the issues to enable Marjorie to collect her powers and eventually be able to bring to the planet what she intended to bring. I can only hope the issue also provided her father with what he needed.

My sweet Labrador almost jumps up to the ceiling out of pure joy when Margaret comes in. Margaret is a twenty-five-year-old sociologist who is going to complete the paranormal therapist training I did years ago. We know each other because of our 'dog children' and because I have recently moved to a different town, I make a rare exception and allow my dog into my practice to cuddle her friend's owner. This means I will have to do some extra vacuuming, but it makes the two of them very happy and that makes it more than worthwhile.

When they are done cuddling, Margaret tells her story. She is in the process of changing jobs, feels very tired and suffers from headaches. She has come to me for a good 'spring-cleaning'. It will be a 'holiday treatment' because she is going on a trip before she starts her new job. I get to work and notice she is on a crossroads in her life. Although she has already registered for the training, she is not 100% congruent with the consequences this will have.

We start in layer 7. Margaret is indeed entering a new phase and making a new choice. She will integrate her paranormal gift into her entire being. Then the focus shifts to layer 11. Something is hooked to her intestines. I see a symbolic Merlin with pointed sleeves. So 'Margaret' is an alchemist, someone who can transform substances into gold and who can change things into something else. I see all kinds of laboratory gear, things that look like test tubes and simmering substances in cauldrons. Suddenly something explodes and is squirted into the room. It lands on 'Margaret's' back. It burns the skin away and she has a reaction to the poisonous quality of the stuff. She fights for her life for four weeks before dying.

She dies doubting her own capabilities. In her current life, she expresses this through her doubts about her own judgment and what she is capable of. It is a large field: the offshoots of the field extend from her neck, shoulders, along her back and down to the pelvic area. It is also pulling at her throat. She has to stand up for her own opinion and speak her mind. Because this issue is in aura layer 11, it becomes clear that she has worked with great powers and that things didn't go entirely according to plan.

Then, in layer 12, I see she is a Native American medicine woman living in Central America. The theme is transmutation, literally reshaping. In this case, it's about breaking down and processing a poisonous substance because the medicine women are bitten by snakes and have to process the poison. If they survive, they are said to be capable of transmuting any physical or energetic poison. In this way, the most wonderful powers are often developed.

I see an initiation ritual. She is administered poison and has to transmute it. She gets very sick and, although she does not die, she never really recovers. She is weakened to such an extent that in her current life, she prefers to let the cup pass from her. I completely understand, but because it's an old issue and has no positive consequences in her current life, I clear it up. The poison hurts in my body; it is a stinging pain. It's in layer 12 because there are more people in her family who are trying to work through this issue, so they can support each other.

Next, I see an old castle. I look a bit longer and see it is just a symbolic image. The field runs from her pelvic area to her knees, which are locked. Margaret is not very well grounded, which is mainly caused by this field. The field turns out to be related to her present workplace, where she must work two more days before her holiday. It is a kind of electro-smog affecting the lump in her neck. It also affects her thinking. I see how it works: Margaret has a field swirling around her, similar to a large cloud of fog. She is unaware of it, but it makes her feel cold and, shivering, she arms herself against it.

She locks her pelvis and does the same thing with her knees. It makes her cringe. She lifts her feet so only her toes touch the floor and she tries to ground herself as little as possible, because when you are grounded you start to notice how you feel. In her case, this would mean that she would feel the full intensity of the effects of that field. I remove it and I am happy she doesn't have to work there much longer.

Then I start tingling all over and I see silvery squiggly things in the air. They look like small fluttering parts of silver foil. They aren't attached to anything and they come and go whenever they feel like it. I go to layer 16, the field of the soul race she belongs to, of her ancestors so to speak. It is a deva-like energy that I have never consciously experienced before in a human being. It is wonderful to see, so delicate and fragile, and at the same time clear and powerful.

I see that her right foot, where she has athlete's foot, symbolizes the coarseness of the Earth. Elf-like, she is standing with both feet in the mud called Earth and her body and energy system are not equipped for that yet. This issue will affect her more in the future because it is related to layer 8, her personal soul agreements, which in this case I am not allowed to touch. I tell her this means she may encounter problems concerning interpersonal agreements. If that is the case, it will probably be caused by the fact that she is so sensitive and can deal with less than is sometimes convenient when you have agreed to work on certain things together with other souls.

This is similar to visiting an amusement park but being too scared to go on any of the rides because you're afraid of heights, for example, and then blaming someone else for having gone to the park together. Margaret now knows she has to start keeping in mind her sensitivity, and that some contact with others will be difficult, but that this doesn't mean this contact is wrong. She just has to find out which contacts are good for her and which are not. She asks me to schedule a quarterly clean-up session, which we do.

When she gets up, Margaret is a bit dizzy and nauseated. I give her some grounding exercises** and she later lets me know that whenever she performs them, she first feels nauseated and dizzy, but that she can see auras afterwards. Her path has begun.

The cases in aura layer 16 make clear what certain soul groups have come to contribute to the Earth. By tackling a blockage in the communication between people with different perceptions of the world, part of the gap is closed, which makes it easier for other souls to understand each other better. Consequently, the Earth has come one step closer to world peace.

The groups concerned with sexuality and justice, sexuality and power/powerlessness, and sexuality versus manliness or womanliness, have a different goal: by finding out what is wrong and what doesn't feel good, these people experience new things in different ways and find out how things should be. This is about finding ways to rediscover and experience sexuality in its purest form. In that pure form, sexuality is an expression of love and an honest exchange between the creative forces of two souls.

And it is not always about a longstanding romantic relationship. Even in a one-night stand, two souls can share that creative power and healing when they energetically form a matching soul combination and are sincerely connected to each other. As a result of those kinds of positive sexual experiences, mankind as a whole will find it easier to open up and connect to each other. This also brings mankind one step closer to world peace.

The deva part is a different story. A deva is a spirit that belongs to the plant world. You can see it as a guide, but it doesn't help a human soul; instead, it helps a tree or a plant. Souls like that of Margaret, which possess deva energy, support nature on Earth. They enable the Earth to recover from all the assaults made on nature. Therefore, the deva soul contributes to the growth process of the Earth toward its renewed balance.

The added advantage of this developmental process of the Earth is that it can remain the home and learning environment for souls whose consciousness grows quickly for a longer period of time. After all, their energy types keep matching each other.

Aura Layer 17: Cooperation and Healing between Different Soul Races

Just like layer 16, layer 17 is about elevating the Earth as a whole to a higher level. In aura layer 17, this happens through the cooperation and healing between different soul races.

On the one hand, these are soul races that work together very smoothly and, on the other hand, different kinds of soul races that have something to heal between each other on the soul race level. In the latter case, it is about uniting as soul races and fusing toward the Source, because in the past things have gone wrong and left scars. You could compare this to how Dutch and German people felt after World War II and how only now, more than half a century later, people in Europe have begun to cooperate more and let go of old prejudices. Soul races also carry a common history and by healing issues in these layers, they contribute to a more positive future.

The beautiful thing is that even if you have a different soul origin, you still have things in common: there are other subgroups who want to work through similar issues, souls with different backgrounds but the same intention. Therefore, cooperation is not very difficult at all, it almost happens naturally, but past issues can always emerge. This layer is also intergalactic. This means that making the right choices here also has an effect in other worlds.

To take an example from my practice, there is a group of people who belong to different soul races but work toward the same goal: lifting the Earth to a higher level. These four people are all paranormal therapists and Light Workers. The first person has come to spread Light and help people heal, and become more conscious and lighter during illness and the process of dying. The second person belongs to the same soul group and spreads Light and healing by teaching people how to make contact with their soul, how to develop their consciousness and how to heal pain issues from a space of Light, heart energy and pure love. Number three is from a different soul group and helps people heal and detach from the dark. This is her main task. Number four has come to Earth to invent, discover and use all kinds of Light Work instruments.

All four of them try to guide the Earth and its inhabitants to a higher frequency and consciousness and all four of them are doing valuable work. Altogether, it works very well because, in their behavior and method of working, they exemplify the unity they try to achieve in their work.

Andrew is a sensitive man who is very good at attracting and pushing away women. Most of the time, if the woman in question is interested in him, he pulls out. And when she disappointedly detaches herself from him, he changes his mind again. My spirit guide Itmam helps me see what's going on. I need this because I cannot see myself. This is because in Andrew's energy system, there are still traces of syphilis from a past life. At the time, this affected his eyesight, resulting in the impaired vision I have taken over from him now. I also feel an itching in my lower abdomen, which is not entirely unexpected in the case of a venereal disease. I notice it has affected his bladder. I 'rub' cranberry in his aura and construct a new 'drainage system' where the bladder is, in order to let the syphilis energy drain away.

It is related to 'attraction and repulsion'. Sexuality had been besmirched, which causes Andrew to be ambiguous about it. Angel Emanuel* gives him help in the form of a blue-white protective layer. Then there is a rose of white Light with a dark red edge. It feels like pure healing love from a very pure source. I see a white bridal bouquet while I remove four old connections or lines with the anti-light. These make him aggressive and represent his rage, anger and power/powerlessness. The underlying theme is 'stubbornness'. So every time he is angry, outraged or short-tempered, or meets someone who plays a power game with him, he becomes aggressive and stubborn. He stays in it and, because of the old syphilis energy, he cannot clearly see what's really going on.

We remove it so Andrew can work together with other soul races from now on. His foundational trust has been recovered. Several months later, he tells me his stubbornness no longer bothers him.

Jack lost his sister thirty years ago and would like to communicate with her. Initially, everything seems to go well because it doesn't take long before somebody comes to visit. However, it is his aunt, or rather, the soul who died in his grandmother's womb when it was five months old. She has come to tell us that his sister has reincarnated, so she cannot come. She is about three years old. That is possible, and even pretty logical after thirty years, but Jack is very disappointed and, to be quite honest, so am I. But I have a feeling this is not the end of their story.

This turns out to be right, because his aunt continues. She knows Jack is going to travel the world for a year and tells me he might see her in South America. I see a playing child in the waiting area at an airport and I hear, 'Don't try to find her. Just pay attention and feel. If it comes, it comes naturally.' I tell him I think his eye will fall on a dark-haired girl of about three years and he will find it difficult to look at something other than her. That is the moment he needs to feel and open up to what he sees and whatever happens next – because I have no idea what will happen. I do know that by having been brother and sister in this life, they have healed an issue between two soul races in layer 17.

Meanwhile, Jack has embarked on his journey around the world. I am very curious about his experiences.

Theo is a seventy-three-year-old man who has a direct connection with God. He can speak with Him on a daily basis, which makes him feel very comfortable. And when he is not communicating with Him, he feels unwell. Then he is lonely, because he has been searching for a new life companion for years. When I look for things that could be blocking the arrival of his new love, I come across some old traumas in layer 17. In his case, they affect his stomach. No wonder he likes sweets so much: once in a while, he eats away his tension with a tasty apple pie.

First, in layer 14, the layer in which your creation power can be mentally affected by your fellow human beings, I see an Atlantean issue. In that life, Theo is a high priest who foresees the downfall of Atlantis and keeps this from his family. If he told them, it would not change anything about their inevitable end, but his wife blames him for it nonetheless. (His then wife is now the sister of a friend he had when he was about twenty-four years old.) The theme is 'being holier than the Pope'. So he wants to do things more decently than necessary and is limited by what other people think is possible. After all, it is a blockage in aura layer 14. No wonder this lovely woman will not show up; the admission requirements are too strict.

Next, in layer 17, there is a life in Greece, just below Athens to be exact. 'Theo' lives there as a woman who loses her entire family as a result of an earthquake, and who is buried by the debris herself. Her legs are buried under the debris and she can no longer walk, but she does survive. Her heart chakra hurts. So Theo has experienced losing family for several lives, including his present life. The soul agreement was to experience loss so deeply that it had a purifying effect, which is quite something.

Then I see the image of Niki, a youngish Russian friend of his. He also knows her from past lives, because I see them as two Chinese people: she is a woman, he is a man, and although they are in love with each other, they do not have a relationship because both of them have partners. It is a secret love. In their current life, they can have a relationship because they aren't in other relationships, but it is their choice. It's just one of several possibilities.

I hope the healing has done enough and I tell Theo's spirit guides, 'As far as I'm concerned, that lovely woman for Theo can come.'

Matthew is someone who sometimes does things for the wrong reasons, to gain financial profit or get approval from others, for example. Or he does things so he can ask someone else a favor when he needs it, instead of just asking for it. In short, he doesn't always do things from his heart. When I try to find the cause of this, in layer 17 I see the bones of his skull and their frequency light up. Their structure is the hardest material in your body and thoughts that have been recorded in them are firmly fixed there. Consequently, the frequency or vibration of your bones (which is based on those fixed thoughts) is difficult to change.

This frequency is not as easily raised as that of other tissues, because it is a very solid substance that is difficult to move. After all, a block of ice – the solid form of water – does not turn into vapor in a second, either. It first has to be warmed up until it melts and becomes water. The warming up of the ice causes the frequency of the ice molecules to be raised, which transforms the ice into water. Then, the water is boiled until the steam goes up into the air. This also requires energy and is the result of raising the frequency of the water molecules to vapor. So the transformation from ice to vapor takes some time. This also goes for the bone frequency. For this reason, bone cancer can be very persistent and difficult to treat. When the underlying thoughts are not cleared up, they will continue to create the same negative vibration in a very durable form.

In Matthew's case, I mostly see the bones in his head with light and dark spots and I can see his cerebrospinal fluid. Next, I witness a trepanation. I suspect he was a guinea pig in a past life for some kind of doctor, which has caused him to draw very negative conclusions about humanity as a whole. This issue relates to humanity on a global level. It is linked in layer 13 and affects what he is thinking. The bone issue, the frequency of the bones and the cerebrospinal fluid I see clearly belong to layer 17, and something intergalactic is healed here. In the dark spots in his bones, I come across the distrusting assumption 'one good turn deserves another' and replace it with 'I enjoy doing what I like doing best and I will thrive financially'. Matthew likes my phrasing very much.

Then I see what look like iron particles floating around in his cerebrospinal fluid. There are seventy in total and they have a female energy (they are clearly of extra-terrestrial origin). They disturb the male frequency in his brain. That's why he feels more comfortable around women and avoids contact with men. He has difficulty attuning to men. I collect all the metallic slivers with a sort of energetic super magnet and hand them over to Ezekiel*, who purifies them further and lets them drain away.

Then we clear up an energetic residue in layer 12 and Ezekiel says, 'Now you can live and speak your truth.' Finally, Matthew can live from a place of love and communicate from his heart.

Matthew's son is named Norbert, a ten-year-old New Age child. He's a cheerful boy who loves animals and can play the piano wonderfully. But he has difficulty making contact with other children, because he reacts to things differently. You could say he is too wise for his peer group.

I see two past lives between Lemuria and Atlantis. (Determining timeframes is very difficult indeed, but even I think this is a very broad one.) I perceive an abandoned girl who is eight or nine years old. Others have broken all connections and bonds with her, so she is very lonely. I cannot see the reason, but I sense it is the same as it is in his current life: that he knows, understands, sees and predicts too much.

In the life that comes next, he is a very manipulative woman who, at all costs, tries to control everything in her relationships. She is very persistent in this. She is not an easy person to be around. Two lives in which contact with others did not go very well, but Norbert was also able to learn a lot about what works and what doesn't. In order to achieve his current life goal, he has to take one more step and succeed in showing his wisdom, at the same time connecting to others in a way they can handle. If he can do that, it will open up a new realm of possibilities, because I expect he could be a very good healer with his perceptive abilities.

Tim is the son of Claire from the chapter about aura layer 14. He is eighteen months old and, so far, he hasn't managed to sleep through a single night. He cries a lot, leaving his mother exhausted and desperate. Therefore, she asks me to help find out the cause of Tim's nightly escapades and help him with his problem. This turns out to be easier than I expected, as I soon notice Tim's bed is positioned on a water vein. Water veins are underground water streams that can cause a lot of trouble aboveground if you are sensitive to them. Tim is sensitive to them, just like the rest of his family. Water veins and Earth rays can be moved, but in this case I choose to move his bed because his entire family is sensitive to the water veins. When you move water veins and Earth rays, new trouble spots can be created. If you do it right, this will not happen in most cases, but I don't want to take any risks with three brothers who don't sleep and a stressed-out mother.

The bed can be moved without any trouble, so I check the rest of Tim's bedroom and move his bed. I use my Biogenesis Wand* to cut loose the field linked to the bed. I clear up the rooms so no entity will be interested in staying there anymore, because they have become too positive, and I try to tune into the entities that are there, because there are quite a number. Three of them disturb Tim's sleep and frighten him. They are able to do so because he is still young enough to see them, which at night, when you're alone in bed, is very scary. These transparent beings stare at him and don't give him a very pleasant feeling. It would make me cry, too. He can't make the distinction between an entity and a human being of flesh and blood, so it is unsurprising that he is scared.

The first entity is a fifty-four-year-old man. He died seven years earlier in an accident on a nearby motorway. He is very indignant about the fact that he died so suddenly and he has a very malevolent energy. He takes out his frustration on Tim by tormenting and teasing him. He is a real sprite. He was not a very pleasant person when he was alive and now that he is dead, he hasn't improved. When I ask him to leave, he initially refuses to go. So I ask for extra protection and Archangel Uriel comes to help me while I bring entity number 1 to the Light.

He is accompanied by Marius, who died at the age of fifty-one and used to work as a farmhand. Marius suffers from sore feet. His clogs hurt and I can hardly stand on my own feet myself. I usually work barefooted to let everything I pick up drain away, but my spirit guides advised me explicitly to wear my shoes this time. This has to do with Marius. Claire tells me Tim also has trouble with his shoes and this is caused by his uninvited guest. Marius is short-tempered and slightly built and also in the lowest position within the farm hierarchy. That hurts a lot and, when he dies, he has a lot of clogged up frustration and energy. Tim is also 'the lowest in rank' because he is the youngest of the family; an interesting parallel.

Then there is a three-year-old boy, who died about fourteen years ago in a nearby village. He suffers from stomach aches and causes his host to have stomach aches as well. I get the impression that he accidentally hooked onto the two obnoxious men. He lost his parents and was looking for them and the men took pity on him. They dragged him along. Because I am told that his parents are still alive, I ask if he can be picked up by deceased relatives he recognizes and trusts. I almost feel like an Ikea store announcer who announces that this three-year-old boy would like to be picked up at the play area, but it actually works in a similar way. It's difficult enough for a small child like him, so he is lovingly escorted by people he knows. It's beautiful to see how quickly he is picked up, and how Tim and his bedroom improve afterwards. Meanwhile, I remove the residual energy from his aura and smoke out the entire house with Peruvian Sacred Wood to clear the energy.

I tell Claire it will take about three days before the energy in the house has settled in the new version. I wish Tim all the best and I drive home. Two days later, I get an e-mail from his mother. The first night, Tim did not sleep well, but he did not cry either. The next night, all the sons slept from 7:30 PM until 7:30 AM. She cannot believe it, because this has never happened before. The only downside is that Tim objects to his afternoon nap. He isn't tired yet.

During the following months, I continue working with Claire and she tells me that sleeping through the night has become a normal thing for her children. I am very happy with this and I think the agreement between Tim and is mother is a tough one. He made sure she was exhausted, so she would try to find other ways of healing. She needs those in her work so she can achieve her life goal. In this clever but (from an earthly point of view) tiring way, Tim was very helpful to her.

Susan is the thirty-year-old owner of a boutique in a nearby village. She is an attractive, sparkly half-Italian woman with a husband who is almost as lovely as she and a sweet little daughter. Susan comes to me because she has a great dilemma. She has found out that her husband Tim visits prostitutes and downloads a lot of pornographic material. The moment she asks him about this, he breaks down and swears he will do anything to get rid of his addiction. But even if he succeeds in doing so, Susan will never know if she can trust him anymore. Her whole world has collapsed and she is at her wits' end.

Considering the fact that I have worked with her before when her mother passed away, she calls me and we make an appointment. Fortunately she knows about the natural law that things happen for a reason, and that people attract each other for a particular reason. She's crazy about her husband and does not want to lose him, but she also knows this is his process. Nevertheless, she realizes they have picked each other for a reason, so we look at her part, the reason why she – on a soul level – entered the relationship.

I find that her father shows similar behavior. He has several girlfriends alongside his marriage. Susan's mother knows and accepts it. She has no choice, she thinks, because she doesn't want to be left behind with her three daughters. So she accepts the fact that he cheats on her and drinks away her sadness. She becomes an alcoholic. Grandfather from her mother's side also cheats on his wife, so it is a familiar phenomenon and energy for her mother. Moreover, her grandfather and grandmother from her father's side are swingers.

So it becomes clear that entering extramarital relationships is a family issue, and that there are several addictions in the family. Susan is used to that energy; it feels familiar and, as a soul, she has decided to use this to heal something. She is confronted with it so often that it cannot be coincidence.

The first session starts with a difficult layer, aura layer 11, in which the knowledge and handling of powerful forces are bundled. It is the year 1745 and Susan is a thirty-eight-year-old woman. She lives in Eastern Europe on a farm and I see her riding a horse. In this life, she is concerned with physically keeping things going on the farm and she neglects herself and her own needs.

In the next life I see, she is living in Western Africa and has been bullied by her fellow villagers for five years. She would really like to belong, but she is excluded. When she is eighteen years old, she tries to steal another girl's husband. She doesn't succeed and is strangled by his jealous wife. It's a kind of primal cat fight, which costs her her life. She dies with the conclusion 'I'd better not say out loud what I want'. So Susan doesn't have enough courage to show others and go for what she would really like: a loving, honest relationship. We look at the field and replace her conclusion with 'pure choices always have a positive outcome and it is safe to say things out loud'. This balances layer 11.

During the following session, we are in Sicily, Italy, in aura layer 17, and it's about healing between different soul races. It's the year 1876 and Susan is a man whose parents and three sisters have died from illness. He cannot cope with the grief and tries to forget everything by drinking. By the age of seventeen, he is addicted to alcohol and his addiction theme starts, which he will work very hard on through several lives.

Next, we work in layer 13, the layer in which the functioning of your brain is affected by the Field of Humanity. Susan's life is set in Béziers in southern France and her present husband Tim is also her husband in that life. Their present two-year-old daughter is also their daughter in that life, which takes place around 1838. 'Tim' loves her very much, but she does not reciprocate. She just needs a man to keep up appearances. In the social environment in which a woman has to meet certain requirements and comply with certain rules (which, according to layer 13, is thinking clearly), it's easier to have a man at your side – preferably a bit of a wimp who lets you have your way at all times. For that reason, she chooses 'Tim', a man desperate for love, who is all too happy to be her husband. In this way, she can do anything she wants. The downside of the situation is that a lot more is possible. There could be a lot more love between them, if only she had the courage to open her heart. But she doesn't, so this is a missed opportunity. Fortunately, most of the time we get more chances and the two of them are back together in their current lives.

In aura layer 14, in which her creation power is limited by what others think, the following questions emerge: 'What is sincere love between a man and a woman, in its purest form? What is sincere love apart from how it is distorted or traded within relationships?' That is what she is trying to get clarity about in her life with Tim. After layer 14, we return to layer 17, in which I come across an archetypical field*: the field of the Lover. While she is connected to this field, it is otherwise impersonal. The Lover means passion and devotion, unlimited appreciation for somebody or something, and it can be self-destructive in the form of blind devotion*. I am allowed to disconnect her from this field and Susan can move on.

During the third session, we again go to layer 14 and come across a life in which she was born as a man in 1893. In 1907, he loses his father and feels responsible for the family. He lives a 'decent' life but does not follow his heart. He dies in 1916. When he dies, there is immediately another past life in the same year, in which Susan lives in Italy again. This life is in layer 3, which I have never seen before. Strictly speaking, it's not possible and it should be in layer 6, but it is in layer 3; there's no doubt about it. Suddenly, I see why. Part of Susan's soul was left behind in this life. As a result, it can be in the personal layer 3 and block her thinking there. Part of her thinks she is still that person.

I retrieve this part of her and bring it to the 'here and now' and I see a boy who is drowned by a friend who bullies him in 1919 when he is two years old. Again, 'Susan' lives in Italy, in

Calabria to be exact, and is an only child. He has a strict, rule-abiding mother, who passes on non-emancipated Italian beliefs about 'the role of men versus the role of women', 'sticking to your principles will cost you your life', and 'other people cannot cope with that'.

In her current life, these principles work against her, so we replace them with new ones: 'I accept that other people can have different opinions to mine. When they react to me in a strange way, this only says something about them.' Up until now, Susan used to make an extra effort to please others instead of letting it be their problem.

To enable her to change this behavior, we heal one more life. That life can be found in aura layer 7, her life plan. She is Japanese and lives between 1932 and 1939. As the youngest of three children, she does her best to make life as pleasant as possible for her elder brothers. She tries to compensate for the fact that their mother suffers from depression. She dies from an intestinal infection and takes with her the limiting belief 'as a woman, you should give until you drop'. We replace it with 'I always make pure choices' and we clean the corresponding layer. Susan can move on.

As you can see, there is a reason why Susan picked her earthly family. There are a lot of extramarital affairs and addictions in her past, so she wanted to be sure she would be faced with this theme so she could heal it. She is in the middle of doing this. 'How you should do things' according to your husband, neighbors, friends, family or humanity can affect what you can create now and how you shape your life. If you have enough reason to stay in your relationship with your husband, despite the fact that he is unfaithful to you and despite his shortcomings, it is your choice and that's fine – that is, if your choice is a pure one.

What someone else would do or think is irrelevant, because they look at things from a different perspective. They have their own background as souls, their own expectations of what they think is right, and their own preferences for what they find pleasing.

It's your life and you want to do something with it and experience certain things. Judgments of others can only affect you in a negative way and cause you to deny yourself the things you would rather do or experience. Clearing up Susan's fields has enabled her to follow her heart and make her own choices. In such cases, statistics about the chance of your husband relapsing are of no use. It is about your ability to deal with the situation. If you believe you can, you will create your own life – and that is a wonderful thing to be allowed to do.

Interlude: The Influence of Free Will – Don's Case

Don is a charismatic man in his early sixties who has been divorced from his wife Melanie for about two years. They were married for about thirty years. Don is bothered by the strings by which he is still attached to her. 'She doesn't seem to be able to let go of me,' he says. Later it will turn out that this pleasure is entirely mutual. We begin in layer 7, in which Don's soul makes the choice for a new turn on his life path, a deep change: letting go of his finished contracts with his ex-wife and letting old dogmas go. He will enter new commitments and live completely according to his soul purpose.

In aura layer 9, we come across the first past life between Melanie and Don, which is part of a group agreement between them and the children. I enjoy working on this because, as it turns out, Don is able to see what I see. In that life, Melanie is a mother and Don is her daughter. I can see 'Don' in a straitjacket, a black and blue laced-up straitjacket, which is symbolic for her life. They belong to the upper class; they are rich and the girl who is Don has a cold and loveless childhood. Dogmas are at the core of her life. You have to, you have to, you have to. You're supposed to do things like this and you can't do that, etc.

There are rules everywhere and not much room for individuality and being yourself. Her mother thinks she isn't sparkly enough, because she is a pale, shy girl. She isn't pretty; she looks quite ordinary. But ordinary or not, when she is about nineteen years old, it's time for her to be married off. So a party is organized at which 'Don' doesn't particularly shine. In this period, the themes of 'not being good enough' and 'doing your best in order to belong and fulfil expectations' crop up. 'Don' acts nicer and funnier than she really is. This makes her seem insincere, which pushes people away.

Despite her background and all her money, she never marries and she remains childless. She works as a governess all her life and, when she dies, she concludes: 'Never again!' So she knows what she *doesn't* want, but she doesn't know what she *does* want. She had no direction, so she went along with what other people wanted, just like Don is doing in his current life.

Then, in aura layer 12, the layer for healing issues in the form of family karma, we come across a life with the Cathars in France. It is the life preceding life 1. The tables are turned here: Don is the mother and Melanie is her five-year-old daughter. She is a beautiful, dark-skinned girl with long, wavy, dark brown hair. This time, it's about religious struggle. Her father has been arrested for his deviating religious convictions and his wife and daughter have gone into hiding.

In this life, 'Don' is the one who is dogmatic and rigid. She is mostly concerned with securing her own place in Heaven and deserving to be there. Her child is less important. It is there, that's a given, but 'Don' is focused on doing the right thing because she wants to go to the kingdom of Heaven. She doesn't pay much attention to her daughter. While in hiding, they are found out. Daughter 'Melanie' is the cause of this. After all, she is just a child and children have to move; they can't hide the whole time. 'Don' is hanged. She blames her child for dying like this.

Meanwhile, daughter 'Melanie' goes to a kind of orphanage. It's a shabby, desolate place and I can see a limestone-like stone in a mountainous area. She is poor. 'Melanie' blames her mother for all this and makes her responsible for every setback in her life. In this way, she starts the theme of reproaching Don. In their current life, this takes the form of 'you were never there'.

This issue, which seems only to be coming from Melanie because she is the one who makes the reproaches, turns out to be interwoven with Don's feeling of guilt toward Melanie, because he also had a part in it. He is the rigid mother who is only concerned with herself and her faith and, strictly speaking, he is the one who instigates the whole thing. Fortunately, it will happen according to their mutual plan – but from a human point of view, they might experience it quite differently, and it can make their marriage quite difficult. His spirit guide says to him, 'Other people do not make you guilty; you do this yourself.'

Then there is a life in aura layer 14, the worldview layer. This is the issue I was informed about two weeks before my appointment with Don, because it is also related to someone I know very well, my paranormal friend Rose. She and Don recently met each other after years of not having seen each other. Rose's and Don's spirit guides visited me on many occasions in preparation for this issue that concerns both of them.

We start with Don. His spirit guides say everything is fine the way it is, but it could be better, more pleasant and more relaxed for Don. It is about a religious issue. It is about dos and don'ts and living a coercive life. His spirit guides say, 'It is about love. What comes out of love is always good. It is the highest truth. Letting go of someone out of love is pure and noble.' (In Don's case: divorcing your wife can be pure and the right thing to do when it happens for the right reasons.) They continue: 'And allowing someone into your life out of love is the most beautiful and important thing you can do during your life.' While they are saying this, the angel of Eternal Love joins us and says, 'Love will exist through the ages. Can you feel it?' This is very appropriate for the two souls of Don and Rose, who have loved each other for several lives.

Rose and Don have met and known each other on numerous occasions and apparently it's important to work on that now, because it does not emerge without reason. There are three past lives that are relevant at this moment. They were best friends on two occasions: they were like brothers in Belgium and they had a life together in northern France. In France, they are knights. 'Rose' has a way with horses, while 'Don' is a short-spoken, difficult man. They go to battle side-by-side and die in the name of their faith. They are blood brothers on a crusade.

In the third life, they are husband and wife in the USA. In one voice, the spirit guides say it is important that they have never betrayed each other during those three lives. This is crucial for what is to come. In their life together preceding this one, they are fighting for their faith. This time it's not about the form, the faith, but about proclaiming what underlies it, its true essence: Ascension*. And again, they set off together.

The American version of Don is named Chris. He dies at age thirty-five. Chris has Norwegian roots; he is a light blond Viking with green eyes. Rose is called Amanda. She is thirty-seven when she dies and although she is of Dutch origin, she looks very British: long reddish brown fuzzy hair, fair skin with light freckles and hazel eyes. She is relatively tall for a woman. The year is 1846.

I see them when they are about five years old. I am shown a symbolic image. They drink from a golden chalice with blue sapphire and an agreement is made and sealed. They have been married off, but the marriage is based on an existing friendship and soul agreement. They are white pioneer children.

Once they are married, they set off as young adults in their prairie schooner. They start just above New York and move to the southwest, to the Hudson River, I am told. Amanda and Chris are preachers. They are going to propagate their faith (I think they are Presbyterians). They are continually on the road and spend a lot of time in nature. We can see them travelling through the fields. The love between them is almost tangible. So they are very happy, but they experience a lot of hardship. Working together and mutual trust are central themes.

And although their love for each other is very great, they do not talk about it. They mostly live in silence and don't talk very much. Amanda is very close-mouthed, while Chris is just calm. They don't share their grief over their unwanted childlessness. Chris and Amanda cannot have children. According to Chris, this is the will of God: 'He decides it was wisdom, He gives it to us, it is His will,' and that is all there is to it. However, Amanda starts doubting God and the justice of it all and, consequently, the purpose of their work and life. Amanda/Rose is still struggling with this in her current life.

Chris falls ill very suddenly. He gets meningitis and something affects his bronchi. Eventually, he suffocates. Amanda takes care of him and, during their final hours, they promise to love each other forever. Chris dies in her arms. He feels guilty about having to leave her behind in a hostile and dangerous area, where they are at the moment, but he is happy he can go to the Lord. During his lives with Melanie, he carries along a similar feeling of guilt, but added to this is the guilt he feels toward Rose.

During this reading, I have been clearing up for a while when I start to realize why this life has emerged: Rose and Don have a soul agreement to enter a relationship. Not just a relationship; they will get married and live together and work and grow. At least, that is their plan. And an unjust feeling of guilt from the past or attachments to a jealous ex-wife can affect current feelings. As a result, things can go wrong within a relationship.

I get on with my work and see a life in aura layer 9, a group agreement. It is in Ethiopia. Don is a woman. Then Don, who is lying on my treatment table, sees an attic with rafters. I see the wood of something that looks like Noah's Ark. It seems a bit strange and they appear to be different images. Suddenly, I see 'Don' and 'Rose' in that attic. They meet each other there and there is a short moment of eye contact. That is all. They remain separated when they pass each other each on their own sides of the room. The contact is necessary to maintain their connection through the ages and recognize each other and maintain their trust.

Then there is another life, again in Ethiopia and again as a woman. 'Don' is walking in the desert. She is looking for food, because there is a famine, and she is taken by surprise by a sandstorm. She suffocates while carrying her child. The child dies with her. She is angry with God. The fact that she herself is dead is one thing, but her child?

Don sees the corn loft tipping over and it becomes a boat, a ship. The Noah's Ark that I saw. The ship is not yet finished and it is docked. I ask Don which part is unfinished, because the ship is a symbol for his body. He says, 'My left shoulder, upper body and head.' I smile because it matches exactly what I am seeing. Next, I see the 3D framework and heal the connections. It's similar to soldering with a golden thread. I recover the light body and finish building it in layer 9 so it is whole again and can function better.

After more than two hours of hard work, we are done. At least, that's what I think. I say goodbye to Don and ask him to let me know what the effect of the treatment is. The next day, he sends me a thank you e-mail. He writes: 'Physically, I feel a lot of air in my throat. I already felt that when I left you yesterday and I can still feel it. The coughing has stopped and my throat feels pure and open. I also experience Melanie from a gigantic distance. Previously, when I thought about her, I got anxious and doubtful, but now I notice I think about her in a detached way. I don't actually feel affected by it anymore. Apparently, I have definitely said goodbye this time.' A nice result, of course, but this is not all.

One day later, Don sends an e-mail to Rose, who instantly starts to feel very ill. She is nauseated and dizzy and very sad. She doesn't understand why, because there is nothing nasty in the e-mail. Perhaps Don is a bit distant, but the contents are not such that they should make her sick. She asks my advice and I see that her chakras are in very bad shape. When I look more closely, I notice some connections have been violently torn out. It looks like a big storm has uprooted a number of trees. The earth is churned and the roots have been coarsely broken off. Her heart chakra and sex chakra are particularly affected. I start my repair work, but I soon realize it's no use. Don has single-handedly removed connections with Rose that were centuries old. I am not allowed to see what he said or did, but it feels like high treason to remove a soul partner from your life in such a violent way.

I don't quite understand and Rose understands it even less. They have only recently admitted their attraction to each other and nothing has happened yet from an earthly point of view. To me, it seems like someone running away from impending changes. Meanwhile, Rose is heavily battered and the unconditional trust she built with Don for several lives is instantly gone.

I am joined by an angel, who takes over from me. It is a very beautiful Light and he starts working. The angel – Ithuriel* is his name – says to Rose, 'Too much has already gone wrong in your life and therefore we intervene at this moment. Otherwise, you will not make it. This was not meant to be.' And while he repairs the golden thread between Don and Rose, he talks about how the Free Will of people can sometimes make them not do what their soul, the purest and wisest part of them, wants to do most. They are afraid, lazy, conservative or just obstinate. Every person has their own reasons.

He goes on to say that on more than one occasion people have not stuck to their agreement with Rose, and that is the reason she does not have children. Everything that is said makes sense to Rose and all she can do is cry. She objects that it would not be very stimulating to start a relationship with somebody who does not want to and who treats her like this. Ithuriel understands her and compassionately says she must not give up, because everything will be alright.

But everything will not be alright, and eventually the angels have to recognize this. Don's Free Will causes everything to go differently.

During the months after the e-mail, Rose gets regular visits from angels and Don's spirit guides. They implore her not to give up and to keep the faith. 'Just hold on a little longer,' they say, 'until 22 April.' That is what she does. After all, there's nothing more she can do, and when she meets Don a month later, she tells him about her experience with the torn chakras and the angel. All he says is that he doesn't know anything about it.

One day after Ithuriel's repair work, Don is also visited by an angel in the middle of the night. He wakes up and the two of them have a long conversation. But the angel gives him a riddle that he doesn't understand. He thinks it's peculiar anyway and the form of the message annoys him a bit. I think it was clever that the angel took this approach, because Don is so obstinate. If the angel had been more direct, Don would have undoubtedly disregarded him. And when I hear the riddle, I know enough.

It essentially comes down to the fact that nothing just happens to you in your life, but that you have chosen everything on the soul level. And because Don sometimes still puts himself in the position of the victim in relation to his ex-wife and becomes very obstinate the moment he thinks – justifiably or unjustifiably – that he is being forced to do something, the message is subtly disguised. He was never Melanie's victim and he also had a part in creating the situation with Rose. Now he has convinced himself that he doesn't want a relationship with Rose, but on the soul level it is a different story. In short, that is what this is about.

Two months later, Don and Rose meet up one final time. It's a pleasant get-together, but Don keeps his distance. Rose sees right through it and, after another sleepless night, she decides she will finally break off all contact with Don.

The next evening, the phone rings. Don's ex-wife Melanie has suddenly died. Unaware of Rose's decision to break off their relationship before it could even get started, Don calls her for support. After the conversation, Rose is so shocked that she calls me and asks for help. During the treatment, we talk with Melanie's deceased father, who is very agitated and angry about something. He explains a lot of things and keeps asking Rose to reconsider her decision and not to abandon Don. It is still important. Rose and Don not only need each other and have a soul agreement, but his grandchild and Rose have one as well. She will help him learn to handle his paranormal gift. Her father continues: 'And if Rose pulls out now, the marriage will not take place.' Marriage? A marriage between Don and Rose. So that was the original plan. But what can you do when the entire universe is cooperating in order to execute such a plan, but the people involved don't want to? Rose is faced with a big dilemma.

That week, Rose is visited every night. Her own spirit guides, Melanie (who has just passed away), Don's spirit guides and angels talk to her, and Don comes to her on the astral plane to find comfort. After a week without any sleep, she is so tired that she decides it's high time to set boundaries. If Don wants a relationship with her, he should pick up the phone. That is what she's thinking and she gets Don's answer the next morning. She gets an e-mail. He wants distance, he writes. Rose feels this is the fatal blow for their relationship-to-be and literally falls ill now. She develops a serious fever and when she writes a letter a week later to tell him what she feels for him, she doesn't hear from him for a long time. A month later, she gets a reply. He thinks she's a nice girl, but that's all; that is his message. It is 21 April, one day before the date indicated by the angels, and everything is clear now for Rose.

Three weeks later, she is harassed by Melanie, who has not gone to the Light. Or rather, she has gone to the Light, but she did not stay there. She is still so attached to Don and her idea that she knows what would be best for him, she has come back and keeps bombarding Rose with well-intended but unpleasant orders to start a relationship with him. Rose is so exhausted that, together with a few friends, we join forces and guide Melanie to the Light. Melanie is very afraid and really doesn't want to go. Eventually, two large angels take a protesting Melanie with them.

Meanwhile, Rose and I set to work again, because although one soul partner can pull out because he cannot handle the effects of a soul relationship, the other soul partner has to move on. The first session begins where Chris' life ends, during the journey with his wife Amanda as preachers in America. It is in layer 16, because Don and Rose have a soul agreement based on what they have come to do for the Earth. In addition, they belong to the same soul group.

Amanda's life goes on. She starts doubting God and wonders where the justice is in all of it. This means she also doubts their work and the purpose of life in general. Chris' passing is also part of her doubt and desperation. After his death, she is left behind, alone and vulnerable. She is in Arkansas. We can see goldmines that do not harbor any gold. We see crime, and Rose falls victim to a group of men. She is locked up in a kind of horse stable and forced into the act of prostitution. She prays, almost as a mantra: 'Why have you forsaken me now that I need you the most, God, why have you forsaken me?' She is joined by angels who give her Strength, Acceptance and Forgiveness. I see a very big heart. She is connected to God, but Amanda is afraid she is sinful now, although it was not her choice to have sex with those men. She is very afraid of the possible consequences regarding her road to Heaven.

And although she never carried Don's child when she really wanted to, she does get impregnated by one of the men. Her child is a stillborn boy born thirty-seven weeks into the pregnancy because his mother is beaten up. This is still affecting her in a current life. She thinks, *I am in all this misery and when I do get something positive, it is taken away from me. In the end, I will be left empty-handed.* Amanda says she felt Chris abandoned her prematurely. And now it happens again with a child. Eventually she dies in captivity and after her death, initially she cannot go to the Light. She is in shock and stays at the place where her body once was.

This issue is like a festering wound through the ages and I have been seeing images relating to it for weeks. I realize now I have seen those images as a preparation, because people are capable of doing terrible things to each other. I steadily carry on with my work and I am helped by Isiaiel*. Then several wood splinters are removed from Rose's back. They are energetic residues from the time she was tied down and abused. Now they work as implants and disturb her energy fields, causing Rose's back pain.

We go to the seventh layer and work on her uterus. All these rejections have made her very insecure, so the relevant theme is 'being and feeling like a woman'. What Rose heals now has an intergalactic impact, so it's a good thing. But the choices of others can also affect you on an intergalactic level, which can really floor you. My spirit guide Itmam tells her to keep her spirits up and a week later angel Ruhiel* disconnects the soul paths of Don and Rose once and for all. Now that Don has decided he does not want a relationship with her, the two of them have to be disconnected.

We work in layers 13 and 17 and, of course, it is about letting go of the sadness regarding Don. Angel Jofiel* will keep Rose company during the following days. Angel Israfel* assists me during the treatment and invites Rose to write down everything that bothers her, because putting her grief into words can help her heal.

Don's deceased ex-wife Melanie joins us and feels very different, now. The earthly tyrant is gone and she has a serene energy. I have to admit that I check this three times with my own spirit guides to be absolutely sure there is nothing fishy about it, because I notice myself thinking, *It won't be long before she starts pushing again.* But no, she really did go to the Light and now she is Melanie of the Light, a beautiful purified soul. It turns out that in a previous life she was Rose's grandmother and she will guide her from now on. 'The security Rose is longing for will come,' she says as she rocks her like a fetus.

This bond explains the intense shock reaction Rose had when Melanie died. She and Don had an agreement, but Rose and Melanie had also been connected for ages. Her death was the beginning of a new phase and paved the way for Don and Rose to continue their lives together in love. This 'together' will not become a reality. 'In love' surely will.

Don's and Rose's case shows that beautiful and good soul agreements might be made, but as a human being, you have Free Will. Personally, I found it difficult to remain neutral in this situation, because as a human being I think people should stick to the agreements they have made and it was painful for me to watch the consequences of exercising that Free Will. The angels and spirit guides also did their best to encourage Don to make his choices according to the soul agreement, because apparently, this would have been good for everybody involved. So I am inclined to have an opinion about Don's actions.

However, I would not do him any justice with my opinions. Just like everybody else, he is a soul on an earthly journey, making the choices he is allowed to make. It is the soul who chooses for itself which experiences it wants to go through, whether there is a master plan or not, and who decides for itself who it wants to share those experiences with.

The only thing I am allowed to conclude since my experience with Rose and Don is that soul paths and agreements are not all fixed before you are born. There is always plan A, but plans B, C, D, E and F could also be under construction. If someone decides to deviate from the plan, or when an accident happens and someone dies prematurely, replacement plans can be devised and agreed upon during someone's life. My experience so far has been that this usually takes place when people are asleep, and that this process takes place through the fourth, astral aura layer, the layer in which you can travel without your physical body.

Viewed in that way, it is hard on Rose and Don, because it was a great opportunity for them. On the other hand, it's not something insurmountable. In most cases, there will be new opportunities to experience specific things, only in a different way to what was originally planned.

Aura Layer 18: Field of Unity – Dealing with Inner Contradictions and Contradictions between You and Others

Nowhere can duality be experienced as on planet Earth, and nowhere is contrast as great as on our planet. Duality is the collective term for contradictions or discrepancies. It is these contradictions that make it possible for us to really experience the things we go through and to experience different emotions. Without sadness, you can never learn the value of true happiness; without hatred, you cannot experience love; without white, you don't know what black is; without small, large has no meaning; without hot, you have no idea what cold is; and without darkness, you cannot experience light. Everything has its opposite, and learning how to deal with these strengthens the energy in your eighteenth aura layer.

More specifically, it is about contradictions within yourself (I would like to lie down on the couch, but I would also like to have a healthy body, so I should really go to the gym now), or between you and someone else (I am white and she is black, or I am a man and she is a woman, I love classical music and he likes tearjerkers). If you are unaware of it, contrast and contradictions cause you to form opinions and judgments, which often lead to prejudice. When you judge someone or something, you disconnect, and that is exactly what layer 18 is about.

The Field of Unity and Oneness is the field attached to that layer. Of course, everybody experiences things that can increase their eighteenth layer energy, but if you have come to this life with something specific that you want to learn, you can be sure there is work for you in layer 18. The simplest rule of thumb for dealing with duality is: is this a choice out of love or a choice out of fear? With love or without love? If you always choose *with love*, you will most easily resolve apparent dilemmas of contrast.

The apparent duality between people who are 'enlightened' and people who are not, the conscious and so-called unconscious, can be found in aura layer 18. If everything is 'I' and 'I' am not different from 'you', we are all the same; or 'in Lack'ech', as the Mayans put it so beautifully, then thinking in terms of separation does not work. Each and every one of us is a human being. We are all essentially the same. And if someone else does not live with much awareness (assuming this can be accurately perceived and is true), that will also affect me, because we are all connected to each other and we all form a larger whole through this aura layer.

Aura layer 18 also works on an intergalactic level. Everything cleared up here contributes to the larger whole. The more neutral you try to be in your dealing with contradictions and conflicts, the more easily you can allow others to have their own opinions or ways of doing things and the more you contribute to a better universe.

Jasper has had a burnout, which I helped him recover from. He's doing fine now, but there are still two things that bother him. He feels so much inside his body that it scares him a little. He is afraid of the supernatural, of the paranormal and, as a result, of feeling. It triggers the fear that's bothering him anyway; he is afraid he won't be able to deal with what life has in store for him. In layer 18, I come across this issue and I am going to clear it up. I tell him he can deal with anything that crosses his path, otherwise he would not attract it.

You are always strong enough for any experience, even though temporarily you might think differently. This is one of the basic principles underlying your soul's incarnations. There are no impossible tasks; there are only easy to very difficult tasks. And if you aren't feeling well, that will be the case for a limited period of time and you should not stay in it. And if you feel fine, that will also be for a limited period of time and you should not get attached to that either. Just experience the moment, because that is what it's all about.

Jasper solves his inner dilemmas and can move on. He can get back to work.

I am in the hospital with Jessica, waiting for the doctors to collect her for her operation. Jessica is a sturdy woman who has difficulty walking because she is suffering from hammertoes and she is about to undergo an operation on her left foot. To make sure things go as smoothly as possible, she has asked me to treat her before, during and after the operation. So fifteen minutes before the operation, I open the aura layers around her left foot so they cannot be cut through and are not affected too much. It looks like Moses and the Red Sea: the layers neatly spread apart and I make sure her entire body knows what is going to happen.

During the operation, I am in the waiting room in a kind of trance. To an outsider, it looks as if I am reading a magazine, but I'm not turning the pages. I am present, but in a way I'm not, and I can feel that my energy is used elsewhere by Jessica's attendants so they can help her the best they can. I write down the times at which I feel specific dips and almost tip over. When I go through the status report later, these turn out to be the exact moments when the anesthetics start working and the first cut is made in her foot. I also experience her coming round again and I am told everything is taking place in the eighteenth layer, the Field of Oneness. Jessica is healing contradictory issues within herself: work or having another child, losing weight or getting pregnant first, being on Earth as a grounded human being or floating slightly above and having contact with the hereafter.

When Jessica is back in her hospital room, I ask the nurse if she would mind me working on the patient for a while. She does not mind. In fact, she is very interested and stays for a while to watch me. First I apply Humpty Dumpty* to her aura and remove the traumas that were created today by the cutting. In layer 5, I adjust her blueprint to the new angle of her toes, so her bones will not be able to grow back to their previous state. Finally, in layer 14, I see how Jessica has lived her life up until now. It is about her worldview and thoughts that are determined by her feet, which cause her to create in a more limited way than otherwise possible for her. Her life could be much richer, if only she believed it herself.

This issue is linked to experiencing the Divine connection in layer 18 in the form of unity. The moment you leave this serene oneness, you have temporarily left the earthly duality, the struggling and the squabbling, behind. To apply this to Jessica's situation, she has come to believe in the earthly contradictions so strongly that she no longer trusts that our planet is just the decor of her self-written play, and that all she has to do is attune to the Source within herself or in others in order to know what can really be created in her life.

Then something funny happens: in aura layer 15, the spiritual layer of humanity and the layer of healing on a group level, I come across two past lives in China, both as a geisha-like concubine, and both with bound feet. Geisha feet and hammertoes, the same unnatural angle, and I never thought something like that could be the cause!

In the sixteenth layer, it becomes clear that Jessica has come to bring Light and help lift the Earth and its inhabitants to a higher level. We have an agreement that I will support her with it by treating her now, because when she is able to stand with both feet flat on the earth, she will be able to ground herself better and let energy drain away and, consequently, she will be able to handle difficult energies more easily.

When Jessica is back home, I give her an after-treatment. Again, it is about the unity within herself in layer 18. We witness how the negativity toward herself and others goes away, which allows her to view life in a different way.

Stefan is the manager who cheated on his wife in the chapter about aura layer 7. But this happened for a reason, because the person he cheats with is Josephine. He has a soul agreement with her, which contains this extramarital affair. This explains the incredibly strong attraction they have for each other. From the soul perspective, they almost have to conduct the affair. What exactly is going on?

Both of them have taken upon themselves several tasks and have decided to learn several things. And in case they can't do this on their own, they make the soul agreement to help each other as a friendly favor, because they have known each other for several lives. If they meet each other and have already succeeded in learning those lessons without each other's help, it is very unlikely something will happen between them, because the goal of their relationship is to have a certain learning experience. But if they need a push in the right direction, there is an enormous attraction. So soul agreements are very ingenious.

In layer 13, I come across a shared past life. It takes place in the early nineteenth century and they live as a farmer and his wife in Groningen in the Netherlands. Josephine does not want to talk about her feelings, which is also the case in her current life. She is mostly concerned with the world around her and coming across as a nice person. According to Stefan, she is insincere. Nevertheless, he is very attracted to her. In this life, Stefan's energy asks her to be pure and lay off her artificiality. Josephine invites him to have the courage to feel his emotions and express these. This is very convenient, because in this marriage he sometimes feels inferior. His wife Lisa is good with words and can express her emotions very well. Next to her, he sometimes feels like a clumsy boy trudging behind his wife.

In layer 15 we can find the Spiritual Field of Humanity and things are healed on the group level. In Stefan's layer 15, his knees are locked. He is unable to take a single step. His four spirit guides appear and his main guide turns out to be a woman called Maike. She sounds German. I get to see a life in Spain, in 1648. Stefan is a warlord who crosses the river with his troops. Many of his men are killed. 'Stefan' is also killed because he has made the wrong decision. He thinks that at certain spots, the river is shallow enough, but this is not the case and they drown. Consequently, in his current life he is afraid to make choices. He is afraid he will do the wrong thing again and ruin other people's lives. For this reason, he initially cannot cope with no longer seeing his ex-lover; he has finished with her, but he's afraid he has made the wrong choice again.

Next, there is a life in 1710 in which he is a nun, a Mother Superior to be exact. In this life, he also sees the consequences of leading others and determining what they can and cannot do. He experiences this as affecting other people's lives in a negative way, so now he is afraid to undertake anything that has certain consequences for others, no matter who they are.

During the next session, we work on guilt, fear and concern, in layer 18. It's about having the courage to be honest with his children about him cheating on his wife, the contrast between wanting to be honest and giving a child too much information. In his seventeenth layer, I see that his aura does not have a protective layer, and how hard his experiences are for him as a result. By choosing a life without a protective layer, he has forced himself to learn to deal with things. There is nothing he can do to escape this.

That is very convenient, because in layer 18 we meet Stefan again, this time together with his current wife Lisa. They live in East Germany and they are sisters. It is the year 1824 and they are left behind after a big fire that kills both their parents. Lisa is the eldest of the two and takes command of the situation. She is going to take care of her sister. She is a bit of a know-it-all. We are in layer 18 and the two of them have regular disagreements, so it's about duality. Lisa is the eldest now and, one way or another, the Lisa-knows-best pattern repeats itself automatically, because Stefan has a nice, wise wife in his present life, so listening to her almost comes naturally. Removing the old construction hurts in his pelvic area, so he will not fall in the same trap again and will be able to stand on his own feet.

Two weeks later we work on inequality, the almost mother-child relationship they have with regard to making choices. Stefan wants the two of them to be equal. In order to achieve this, we start in his seventh aura layer, the layer of the life plan. He makes the new decision to commit to his choices in the future. So he wants to show his true colors, not just to Lisa but to himself. It is related to his root chakra.

Finally, in layer 17, we come across a terrible choice. This life takes place in World War I in northern France and it pulls on his stomach chakra. It makes him sick with fear, which I can feel as well. He is a woman who is forced to choose between losing her own family and betraying someone who is hiding. So: either someone else dies or her entire family is killed. It's impossible for her to make the right choice. There will always be losers; people will die. Of course, she chooses the safety of her own family. As a result, she feels guilty for the rest of her life with respect to the person who is killed. This feeling of guilt is part of his present family theme and keeps him from expressing his preferences and what he really wants. I get the impression this is the final big issue in relation to making and expressing choices and I round off the session.

Culinary journalist Bea writes cookery books and has undergone several types of therapy, when she asks me for help. She has had a very unpleasant childhood and very painful experiences. In a way, she has coped with all that, but now she is stuck. She doesn't know what to do anymore and asks me for advice. While I am talking to her on the phone, I notice she has done quite a lot, but there are still a few issues in her higher aura layers. The rest sits very well in place, but her personal thinking and emotions, which can be found in layers 3 and 2, are negatively affected by blockages in layers 15 and 18. Just up my alley.

When she comes to my practice, I meet a nice woman who talks as if she is Eeyore, the depressed donkey from the Winnie the Pooh stories: loads of misery, but she talks about it with self-mockery and humor so she can cope better. Her third eye is pulling tremendously and her crown chakra is almost closed off. So she is disconnected from her 'GPS' and makes all decisions based on her thinking capacity. The back of the head (the brainstem, to be exact, where large nerve bundles run from her head to the rest of her body) is overstimulated and stings. She also has a complex family, which proved too much for her mother, so she developed depression. Bea's father is utterly indifferent. When we talk about her parents, this affects her third eye and the sinuses in her forehead start to hurt.

Bea has had quite an eventful life. She used to be a hash dealer, has stolen things, has sprayed graffiti and in no way could she restrain herself regarding the things she did. She still struggles with alcohol. Unfortunately, she sometimes hears people who have died and she is frequently bothered by entities who say all kinds of negative things to her. This makes the back of her head hurt very much and when she is bothered by them, she washes it away with alcohol.

The first part is in layer 12 and is related to family karma. Her grandmother has a secret during the war. We are not told what it is, because this would not benefit Bea and there is obviously a reason it has been a lifelong secret. All I know is it has something to do with betrayal. Because it is blocking Bea, I remove the core of the problem and we move on to layer 15. There I see Bea in Russia. She is a woman who practices black magic. She vows to use her powers in an improper way, for her own gain; it does not contribute to healing on a group level and it therefore blocks layer

15, preventing her from making a connection to the Spiritual Field of Humanity.

When this connection is restored, we go to aura layer 18. Again, there is a past life. She is on a boat bound for Australia, where she is a woman living with her husband and they are starting a new life Down Under. Full of hope, they embark on the tough sea journey. It's not long before her hope is replaced by horror when her husband suddenly dies. Grief-stricken, she arrives in a new country all by herself and she is on her own from that moment on. She is very lonely and has a very tough life. This rough life helps her experience contrasts and provides her with the opportunity to learn from them and deal with them in a neutral way. She cannot do it all by herself. She is too frustrated. She feels robbed and there is no one she can open her heart to. She is all alone. Given the fact that in that life she never found inner peace, she carries the accumulated anger over to her next life, which is the next opportunity to deal with it. From saving comes having.

Her life plan can be found in layer 7. Unfortunately, I find a large lump in it. I remove the lump so she can move on to the next phase. This is the phase she chose and created before she was born. In layer 12, I stumble upon the residues of her drug abuse, which is a reaction to her family karma. I remove numerous strains of vermicelli-like muck from her aura. It is an excessive quantity. She hasn't used drugs for a long time, but she takes large quantities at a time. If people knew how long and severely this affects their aura, perhaps they would reconsider. But when it's in your life plan, you will take the drugs, just like Bea did.

When I connect her third eye to her knees, I work my way further down from there. Everything that is coming in and is too much for her I let drain way into the earth and through her body. I teach her the best way to do it. In this way, she can do it herself if necessary. Afterwards, Bea feels nauseated and she is very obstinate. She wants to visit her father, who lives in my neighborhood. I advise her not to do that today. I have just cleared up issues related to family karma and I explain to her that she risks taking new issues from him. She just needs to rest after the treatment, but she thinks differently. She protests a bit and after telling her any decision is fine, I wish her goodnight.

She leaves my practice grumbling, but the next day she calls me and tells me I gave her the right advice. She doesn't need to tell me that, but it is always nice to hear. She admits she was very angry at me, but that it was a good thing I said it and let her do what she wanted to do. Some things she does too mindlessly, almost as a habit, like visiting her father simply because she happens to be in the neighborhood. She doesn't ask herself if it would make *her* feel good.

A few weeks later, I get some more feedback from Bea. She still doesn't understand how it works, but everything is going more smoothly. She has met a new love, but she doesn't think she is ready for a relationship. Nevertheless, she enters one and of course there are some things she has to heal, but the age-old issue she was carrying along is over and done with.

During the following months, the love she found develops into a serious and profound relationship the likes of which Bea has never experienced before. I am grateful I have been allowed to remove residual energies after she did so much herself. And I am happy for her, because she is now able to open herself up to the great love she has found.

In aura layer 18, people are confronted with the contrast between what they experience and how they would like to feel. This contrast and the subsequent friction cause people to work on themselves and to be on their way to unity. Unity is first experienced through inner peace. And when you feel your inner peace, it can eventually lead to an experience of total connectedness with All That Is, no matter what situation you are in. Then you are able to experience total Divine Oneness.

Aura Layer 19: Gateway to All Other Dimensions

In layer 19, we find the connection between the different dimensions – 3D, 4D, 5D and higher. Everything is possible in aura layer 19. For instance, you can go to your past-present-future and you can move between these three in this aura layer. It is quite complicated to imagine this. Therefore, I will give you a three-dimensional example (which is not really possible, of course, because you cannot explain four- or five-dimensional concepts in a three-dimensional world). You could look at it like this: try to see the soul as a small ball travelling through all its lives, on its way to being Highly Conscious, toward Light, with the Source as its final destination. It travels from left (the past) to right (the future) and is constantly in a particular place (the present, the now).

This ball is the only continuing connective factor and the rest is a kind of matrix surrounding that soul point. So, the soul is surrounded by a three-dimensional cobweb that enables you to visit past lives (for example, to the left of the ball) or future incarnations (to the right of the ball). But you can also go to parallel incarnations (in front of and behind the ball) or to other dimensions, for example, parallel incarnations in earlier times (the web to the left of the ball, which runs in front of and behind the trajectory of the ball). You can even go to other dimensions, such as the underworld and the planes between lives.

The difference between aura layer 19 (where the gateway is, the passage, the access to all possibilities) and aura layer 10 (which you use to create your future) is that in layer 10 we find the blueprint. Layer 10 contains the request song and the plan for the way you would like things to be, the image of it. See it as a picture in the travel guide for your next holiday destination. In layer 19, you can find the connection to that dimension where that image is reality, i.e. the holiday destination itself. It already exists there; you just haven't got there yet.

Layer 19 is the one you can use to write history, both backwards and forwards. This is where you can find the connection between past, present and future and certain types of entanglements between different dimensions and lives. Going to these dimensional fields uses up a lot of energy, because it requires you to change your frequency. You have to adapt the frequency of your body's molecules. Raising your frequency causes you to be icy cold and very tired.

Lowering your frequency also makes you very tired, because your energy goes to the dimension that vibrates at a lower frequency, as is the case with an Earth ray or negatively charged field or person. In short, working in these fields takes a lot and you cannot do this twenty-four hours a day without getting exhausted.

My neck hurts when I welcome thirty-five-year-old Michelle for her first session. It turns out to be her neck pain; I already sensed her before she came in, when I tuned myself to her – a good start.

Michelle believes in the supernatural, but at the same time she is very skeptical. In itself, this is a good thing, because you should never believe anything just because someone else says it's true. When someone makes cynical remarks, however, things get a bit more difficult, because it affects energy fields and makes perception more difficult. Fortunately, Michelle is not cynical, but she is critical – *very* critical.

She suffers from several things. She has problems with her mother regarding her disabled brother; her father passed away twenty-five years ago and she misses him a lot; and, finally, she is stressed out, partly due to legal proceedings instituted against her husband. As mentioned before, her neck hurts, she suffers from lower back pain and her throat chakra is blocked.

I ask her to give me the benefit of the doubt and I start in aura layer 6, where traumas from earlier times can be found. I see an entity there. It's a farmer who is fifty-nine years old when he dies in 1895. This gentleman has worked much too hard all his life and he is the father of a mentally handicapped son. His field is attached to Michelle's lower back, right where Michelle feels pain. The farmer thinks very negatively. He is disappointed in life and struggles with the fact that he has to leave his mentally handicapped son behind when he dies. He is stuck in his negativity and that is the reason he did not go to the Light when he died.

Michelle, in turn, is struggling with the fact that she lives on the other side of the country, that her family and job put a lot of stress on her, and that she cannot visit her brother every week. To be honest, she would rather not see him, because he is so disabled that she can't get through to him and therefore does not enjoy those visits. So the entity is attached to her trauma of having a severely handicapped brother. Saint Germaine* helps me remove this negativity and we take the man to the Light.

Now that Michelle is in a better mood, we can move on to aura layer 9, the layer of group agreements. I come across an agreement between her mother, brother and herself and she has to let go of the old way she dealt with that agreement. I read that her mother is quite rule-abiding. She likes to decide what happens and how things are supposed to be done. She also thinks Michelle doesn't visit her enough and she often vents her opinion without people asking her for it. Michelle has worked through that issue and she can now start working on deciding how to go about her agreement with her brother. In this way, she works out what being a sister means to her.

Then, in Aura layer 14, I suddenly feel her father standing next to me. The question is: will she believe me? I tell her that I think the man standing next to me is her father. I can even describe his outward appearance. Her reaction, as can be expected, is quite critical and I hear myself ask a question I have never asked a client before: 'What kind of work did your father do?'

'Estate agent. My father was an estate agent,' Michelle promptly replies.

'Oh,' I say, somewhat bewildered. 'That's strange, because he says *architectural draughtsman.*'

Michelle bursts out laughing and cries out, 'Yes, that's right! Originally, he was, and later he became an estate agent! He's really here, that's great!' She is moved by this 'reunion' twenty-five years after he died. So am I, and I continue talking to him.

Her father has come to help her with an issue that I summarize under the heading 'people cannot be trusted'. At the time, he had unpleasant experiences and Michelle expressed her solidarity with him when she was three years old by withdrawing, just like he did. She learned how to distance herself from others, which she is still very good at and she does it all the time. But she is unaware of this because she thinks she's always right. After all, she does not trust people and she can always find a reason why this or that person cannot be trusted. So she always sees evidence for her prejudice and this is exactly how it works. Her father sees that this no longer benefits his daughter and he has come to help her. Her thinking is affected by other people's thoughts telling her that people cannot be trusted. This prevents her from attracting the positive things that would fit in her life. We reorganize the field and clear it up. After this, we round off the session. Michelle is still on her guard, but she is also convinced.

A month later, we start again in aura layer 12, the layer with past lives that are further worked through in the form of family karma. It is about her connection with her brother Ronald. I see a past life as husband and wife. In this case, he is the woman and she is the man. Michelle promises him: *I will always take care of you.* She still does this now, by partly carrying his karmic burden and by overcompensating. She forces herself to achieve and do a lot in her life. After all, she is living for two people. I neutralize that promise, because it was meant for that past life only, and I cleanse the rest of the layer. Her father re-joins us and tells her that she 'cannot achieve everything by fighting for it'. She understands what he means, because she fights through every difficult situation and often starts unnecessary battles.

This is also related to two lives in layer 17, the layer in which soul races work and heal together. In the first life that emerges, it is the year 1617 and she is a man, a knight. The theme is 'dishonesty'. There is an unfair battle and she gets hurt in her lower back (vertebrae L2-L3) and her right shoulder. The other past life takes place even earlier: 1510-1511. Righteousness is important in that life, in which she is an eight-year-old girl who has to perform oral sex on a bishop. Then there are two more lives in which she is abused by clergymen as a boy. These issues are not easy to look at or carry along. The injustice has caused her to revolt again and again in similarly inappropriate situations in her current life. It could also give her very unpleasant feelings when the media report sexual abuse by clergymen, or make her react more strongly in unfair situations, such as the lawsuit against her husband.

Finally, we go to aura layer 19. I can see there is something wrong in the area surrounding her uterus and first chakra. I see a strange scar in her intestines. She got it when her daughter was born. One of her child's feet penetrated Michelle's intestinal wall and she nearly died. In layer 19, I correct the event. I am allowed to do this in such a way that it seems it never happened. This enables Michelle to decide whether she wants a second child. I thank her father and Michelle and wish her good luck with her decision.

Marie is on my treatment table and says in astonishment that she only has one sister, and that her mother never had a miscarriage. I am equally astonished because next to me is the soul who insists he is her brother. So I asked Marie, 'Could it be possible that your mother had a miscarriage?' We are confused until I notice in which layer I am. It is layer 19, the layer of other dimensions, including things that are not yet there or could have been there.

I ask the boy if he really is her brother and he says, 'Yes, her unborn brother who was not allowed to come.' I ask his spirit guides if his mother was actually pregnant with him, which was not the case. Then I suddenly understand the whole picture. Marie explains that her mother would have liked a third child, but did not trust the situation with her husband anymore because they were having too many problems and she didn't want to be left alone with three children. Now I am able to interpret the situation.

It is about a family issue of a brother who was never born because his future mother, whom he had an agreement to be born to, changed her mind. After all, Free Will goes before everything. She decided she didn't want a third child and took steps to ensure she would not get pregnant again. As a result, the brother could not take his karma to Earth and resolve it. He 'grew up' in the spirit world. But because he would have also worked on family karma, Marie has carried the weight of this karma with male issues. So Marie put on a brave face and took on all kinds of family-related tasks that were not part of her life path.

I am allowed to repair this in layer 19 in a fan around her head. I explain to her brother that she can no longer bear this burden for him and her family. I request that he ask his guides if a different incarnation can be arranged for him, so he can go do what he would like to do. He will have to do it in a different family, because his original mother is sixty years old and unable to have children. He thinks this is a good idea and, when I sense that everybody is calm again, I round off the session. All in all, it has been a very peculiar experience.

Martha is someone who wants to help people deal with difficult life experiences. So far, she hasn't been very successful, because she can only do it if she has the courage to open herself to the whole person, to their pleasant and less pleasant qualities. You cannot say, 'I only work with your pleasant side.' In order to make clear to her how this works, I open my heart to her and tell her I am doing it. She experiences what it feels like. Then I close it off a bit and have her experience what that feels like. Yes, it's not nearly as pleasant. I open up again and get to work in layer 19.

This is where her mindset is stuck in her bones. There are all kinds of thoughts, conclusions and assumptions that are not very pure and have rigidified in her skeleton, so they are very persistent. I see fluorescent, light-emitting bones. They become lighter and lighter and the more bone mass, the more light I perceive. And I can read the different frequencies from the colors. It is a beautiful spectacle and I can see her bones becoming lighter and lighter while I am filtering out the blue muck. Next, this muck is purified with the help of Ezekiel and a wise old man, one of Martha's spirit guides, and I send the purified energy back to her bones for her next life. Martha no longer has to carry the burden of false assumptions.

She says she doesn't have any real problems, but she comes for a session anyway: Gabrielle, who is thirty-three years old with a young daughter. She made the appointment because she is always attracted to the wrong men and she is fed up with that. She's ready for a nice one!

During the anamnesis interview, my vision gets worse. This is not strange, because Gabrielle normally wears glasses but she currently has them off. One of the temples is broken and she has temporarily repaired it with adhesive tape. When she puts them on, it's like I have put in my contact lenses and I can see clearly again. In a figurative sense, there is also something she does not see: she gives men too much space and she is too easy on other people. She is also very sensitive to masculine beauty and vulnerable to sexual manipulation. She *needs* sex. Men can sense that and sometimes take advantage of it. I can see that she disconnects and withdraws when things get difficult. There is an issue attached to her liver relating to her father. He has other women outside his marriage to Gabrielle's mother, but her mother turns a blind eye to it.

Gabrielle was a women trader in a past life and, as it later turns out, that life is essential. In her current life, she encounters different women that she traded and did not treat very nicely, but this time the tables are turned. Now she is the one who constantly gets the short end of the stick. Two of these people have a great impact on her. Her ex-husband criticizes her a lot and her present boyfriend likes power games. She takes her ex-husband Julio from a poor tropical island to the Netherlands. He is ten years younger than her, makes her pay for everything, and while she realizes she is being used, he is such a sweet thing that she goes along with it. 'Looks are so important,' says Gaby. Once in the Netherlands, a child and a residence permit later, the fat is in the fire and they split up. In layer 9, the group agreement layer, I come across the issue with Julio. The agreement between him, their future child and Gabrielle was so strong that she went along with it against her better judgment and played her part in the play they had agreed upon.

We remove the residual energy of Julio and go to James, her present boyfriend. She describes him as 'a looker and a horny man'. He has an attachment in layer 8, the layer of soul agreements between two souls. James and Gabrielle play power games: not telling each other that they love each other, withholding sex from each other, not seeing each other on their birthdays to make the other person feel unimportant. No relationship can withstand such things, and they can never bring about anything positive.

What I see is quite clear: James doesn't see her most beautiful side. He doesn't see who she really is and only uses her as practice material for himself. He also has to heal that power issue, which is the reason they met each other. His cutting remarks are like pricking a fat, lazy, red cat enjoying a bit of sleep. She only wants to be left alone and the whole thing makes her very tired. The message is: 'You decide when you want to fight'. In that sense, James is also practice material for Gabrielle. She needs to decide for herself what she wants to go along with. She is going to learn to set boundaries.

Her spirit guide Perpetuü appears and says, 'Fear is ungrounded.' I suspect a small language barrier and say, 'You probably mean fear is *unfounded.*' But I am sharply corrected. The spirit guide tells me he has said it exactly the way he means and I heard it correctly the first time. The way he says this makes me feel put in my place and I repeat everything to Gabrielle.

Then I realize the cleverness of Perpetuü's remark: it's kind of a pun. On the one hand, her fear is unfounded; there is no reason for it because it has no foundation. On the other hand, fear can only get to you when you are not grounded. When you are not grounded, you can't get rid of tension, and when you accumulate too much tension, fear can get the better of you. Perpetuü compliments me for my insight and I report everything to Gabrielle. So the message is: make sure you stay grounded so your fears don't get the better of you – and there is no reason for you to be afraid. I wonder why this has to be said in such a complicated way sometimes.... During the next session, we will work on another issue.

Meanwhile, in aura layer 10, I come across a past life in which Gabrielle is a female witch and witnesses another witch being burned at the stake. It is the year 1836. Suddenly her throat is pierced by a kind of spear, a pointed branch. She is recognized and unmasked as a witch. She dies. I am allowed to clear up this part, so she can apply her esoteric gifts again and make use of her female intuition. This is necessary, because there is also a life before it, which takes place in the seventeenth century and during which 'Jesus-like' behavior is strictly forbidden. That is the description I hear and I conclude that this refers to things like hands-on healing.

'All hands on deck,' Perpetuü says cleverly. Take on more, use your hands to heal and play with words more. Sometimes it's enough just to touch someone, instead of using a lot of words. If the person agrees to it, touching can bypass the brain and people can also feel what you mean. When their heads come in between, there are all kinds of interpretations, thoughts and views that can interfere with the purity of the message. The same words can have deeper meanings, so play with them, says Perpetuü. They touch upon deeper layers.

'Oh,' I reply, 'just like when I give someone a cordial welcome when it really comes from the heart?'

'Right,' Perpetuü says contentedly. 'Intention and choice of words determine everything.'

Then we go to layer 19 and see Gabrielle living as a monk in Bavaria, Germany, in 1583. She is the eldest son of the family and therefore has to enter a monastery. Things don't go very smoothly, because when he is around twenty-two years old, the monk wants to discover women. He wonders about the differences between men and women and looks at the meaning of those words: man and woman. What does it mean to be a man and what does it mean to be a woman? His 'fieldwork' causes him to be excommunicated and consequently banned by his family. He is a disgrace. He himself does not mind, because he lives according to his own values and standards, and he spends the rest of his earthly days with his sweet wife in a small village.

This life has left Gabrielle with two limiting assumptions in layer 19: 'I cannot pour out my heart' and 'opening my mouth costs me too much'. We rewrite them as: 'it is safe to express my opinion and say what I think and want'. The difference with rewriting limiting conclusions in earlier layers is that in those layers, I rewrite the final conclusion after the person has died, whereas here we are allowed to rewrite his limiting thoughts during his past life. It's as if I have gone back in time and am part of it. Eventually the monk dies of heart failure, as was foreseen in his life plan.

A few weeks later, I receive an e-mail from Gaby: 'I'm doing well, I'm very busy, I have a lot to do and I feel fine. I'm sure our session contributed to this.' I don't know exactly how she is doing with all the nice men of this world, but I trust she is doing fine in that area as well.

Sometimes choices and events from the past have a limiting effect on your future. This is the case when they have caused a blockage in the gateway to your field of possibilities. If, for example, you can only use one of two gateways, only part of your original arsenal and options is accessible to you. And because of these limited options, you can also make use of part of your original creation possibilities in aura layer 10, because you can only create what you can connect yourself with.

It's like a travel agency website. You can look at the specifics of a limited number of holidays, but there is no link showing you the contents of the entire site, so you can only see part of it. The problem is that you don't know which part you're missing, because you *are* getting information. You even get specific travel options. However, this can give you the idea that the country and holiday destination are right, but that you would rather book a different hotel, although you are unsure which one. Aura layer 19 is the layer in which you can heal problems like these.

The scar of Michelle's first delivery caused her to risk not having a second child. The scar, which was her blockage in the gateway to her possible future, is healed and now the road is clear. Some people have physical blockages, while others struggle with blockages that are more energetic in nature.

Aura Layer 20: Knowledge of the Light and Anti-Light

Good and 'evil', pure and impure, Light and anti-light. In a nutshell, these are the keywords of aura layer 20. This layer is about being pure, recognizing purity and living a pure life. If you know the biblical story of Adam and Eve and the apple, in this layer it's about whether or not you let yourself be tempted to take a bite, even though you know very well that you are doing the wrong thing. People who work with themes in layer 20 are making choices in their lives relating to: 'Which path do I choose? The easier one (which often contains less light) or the right one (which often has the highest light content)?'

To give you an idea of what this might look like, I will give you a few examples:

- Do I take that parking spot from under someone else's nose because it will save time (somewhat darker option) or do I wait until another one is available (lighter choice)?

- Do I visit my mother because I'm supposed to (gives less light to both you and your mother) or do I not call on her because I don't feel like it (from an earthly point of view, not very nice perhaps, but it is the lighter choice)?

- Do I kiss another man when my boyfriend hasn't given me much attention for a while, so I can feel like a woman again (darker choice) or do I tell my partner how I'm feeling about it (lightest choice)?

These can be big and small things, difficult and easy things, but when something is going on in this layer, it almost always has serious consequences.

The difference between layer 20 and layer 18 is that in aura layer 18, you learn to deal with contrasts and consequently learn to have fewer outspoken preferences and aversions. You become more neutral and balanced: whatever is going on in your life, you respond in a stable way. Layer 20 is about fundamental choices for the good in your life and, therefore, the good in other people's lives.

The purest choice is always the best one for all involved and always contributes to the highest good. You are the only one who can determine what is right in your situation. You are the only one who has your particular package of soul agreements and personal learning goals, so you are the only one who can feel and know what is right for you. And when every step is pure, the end result will be the highest achievable. That is what is strived for in this aura layer.

Tyler is a seventy-year-old man who had intestinal cancer four years ago, as well as a prostate operation. As a result, he has a stoma (an artificial opening to the outside of the body) and he has become more or less incontinent. He has little control over his bladder and has to urinate every two or three hours. This means he finds it difficult to sleep through the night, which makes him more tired than he would like. We set to work in the hope that he will gain more control over his bladder and get more sleep.

I have six sessions with him. All of them start with a choice in aura layer 7, the layer of his life path, and on every occasion he chooses to enter a new phase. In layer 10, his creation layer, I come across thoughts of his own and remarks of other people and doctors about what is and is not possible after the operation. For example, I find the thought, *My nerve has been cut, so it does not work anymore.* In my experience, this is not always true, so it can be helpful to neutralize this assumption. After that, we work in different layers. One time, I work together with the angel Isiaiel* on his penis and nervous system. In fact, I perform a kind of percutaneous angioplasty on him and flush everything out through his legs and feet. This will have a lot of impact.

During another session, I cleanse layer 12, the layer of family karma, the field relating to his intestinal cancer. He is now able to hold his urine for an extra hour and the involuntary urine leakage has also improved. Also in layer 12, I come across two past lives. The first is linked to his bladder. Tyler is a Native American who makes medicines and drums from the bladders of his enemies. This life is followed by a life as a Native American boy who is afraid of the drumming of the enemy. He hears it as they surround his village, just before they approach to initiate the battle.

Meanwhile, during the night Tyler only has to get out of bed once to go to the bathroom. He can hold his urine for five hours now and it is his stoma, not his bladder, that wakes him up. Also, over the past few weeks he has become a lot calmer, but also more tired. I see a past life in the family karma layer. This life is about family energy. I see that Tyler's life is finished when he is very ill. He is allowed to go, he can pass on, but he does not want to leave his wife and (small) children behind. So he chooses to continue his life because of her and the children. By making this choice, he takes upon himself a karmic load for his family, but this comes at a price because he doesn't feel well and has lost part of his dignity as a man.

Right from the start of our series of sessions, Tyler gets calmer and more cheerful. He regains the old twinkling in his eye and makes jokes the way he used to. His wife tells me he is back to the old Tyler. She is very happy with it. But without being aware of it, Tyler is very angry. This anger is also in his twelfth family karma layer. He has difficulty coping with his physical condition and, fortunately, I am allowed to clear that part up. Next, I come across a kind of energetic myoma in layer 20, which is related to his penis and runs from layer 16 up to and including layer 20. It is on his right side and has to do with what he thinks is possible with regard to his recovery. Will everything function again the way he wants it to? Light and anti-light. What is pure and what is not? What is right and what is not? He is trying to find out for himself and his family what is right for him, and he tries to live accordingly. In this way, he heals himself in layer 20.

Next, I work on the stoma exit, because it irritates him. Meanwhile, Tyler has indicated that he is stable; he isn't improving, but he certainly isn't doing worse. Nevertheless, he has even more control over his urinating than before. To be honest, I am quite happy that his nervous system has recovered to the extent it has, four years after the operation, but sadly the problem cannot be solved entirely. He is right about that. I work two more times on anger and obstinacy issues in layers 12 and 19 and my spirit guides tell me I have done everything I can for him.

We round off the treatments with mixed feelings of considerable progression in relation to the urination intervals and his improved mood, but also disappointment because he did not heal in all respects.

Diana is a woman who already has two daughters but would like to have two more children. The strange thing is that several psychics have been predicting for years that she actually will get two more children and most of them think they will be twins, a boy and a girl. Furthermore, people often think she is pregnant, but she has not been for five years. I have also noticed the presence of two souls around Diana. I have even communicated with one of them, the girl. Diana herself thinks the other soul, the boy, will be mentally handicapped. She doesn't care; she just wants to have all her children around her.

Today, Diana is suffering from a migraine behind her right eye. On a rational level, she is unhappy about her life and has come in for a session. As is so often the case, her two future children hang around her and, in layer 20, her son comes in and what he says is quite shocking to his mother.

I start in layer 20 by opening her uterus and pelvic area and I perform a spiritual operation there. Everything is rigid and covered with a kind of cobweb blocking the energy. Consequently, her throat chakra is closed off. This makes it more difficult for her to speak and emotions are in the way. Her future son emerges. He calls himself Casper and says he does not want to be born again. He is too afraid. He gives two reasons for wanting to stay in the spirit world. He confirms that he would be mentally handicapped and, when he thinks about it, it seems like a difficult life. He knows the outlines of his life, so he is aware of the consequences of his handicap. He doesn't like it and it scares him off. In the spirit world, he can do anything and he can communicate without difficulty. Once he is incarnated, that would be a greater challenge and he doesn't know if he's up to it.

But there is another reason why he has decided not to incarnate: his mother gave up her job for her first two children, but a year or so ago she started working again and she wants to continue working, even if she gets more children. Her future children will have to spend a lot of time in childcare. He does not want to be handicapped and go to childcare as well. That will be too difficult for him; he just wants to stay with his mother. He has a lot of fear and I remove it via his mother. And although I understand where Casper is coming from, I think he has made his decision out of fear, so he has not chosen the lightest option. Now he reconsiders the soul agreement with his future mother, which causes a blockage in aura layer 20. What is pure and what is not?

I conclude that plan B has replaced the original design. Meanwhile, I continue working on his mother's throat chakra and third eye. Diana's world view has been affected and distorted over the past few months as a result of her grief and the absence of her two unborn children. It is her greatest heart's desire and every month, when she starts to menstruate, she is overcome by her emotions. It is very frustrating for her that she does not get what she wants, while for others, everything seems to fall into their laps. She has difficulty coping with it and it has made her harsher and sharper in the way she expresses herself. I notice this in her throat chakra. Lady Portia* comes to help her become non-judgmental and neutral again, which she needs in her job. I remove the issue, starting at her feet and moving right through her body and crown, and slowly but surely her headache subsides.

Marian is a thirty-seven-year-old dark beauty from the Randstad (an urban agglomeration of Western Holland) who, as she describes it herself, seeks help with her 'oceans of sadness'. I can sense my head searching, because something peculiar is going on in her head, so tuning in to her is somewhat difficult. But it doesn't take long for me to notice what she is doing: she sometimes dissociates. When she has difficulty in dealing with things and when her emotions get the better of her, she becomes verbally sharp and starts focusing on others. And when for one reason or another she does not succeed, she pulls out and is literally gone for a while. She steps out of her body and just isn't home. So she either takes it out on other people or she goes within and gets stuck – not an easy thing to keep balanced.

The largest and most acute problem that we will work on during the first session is letting go of her ex-husband Bertram, with whom she would really like to renew their relationship. On a physical level, this has already happened; her ex-husband has become her lover. They have been divorced for two years and have two children together. The tricky thing about the whole situation is that they see and speak to each other quite a lot, partly because of the children, and Marian is very jealous of his new girlfriend. She throws an awful scene and thinks she has a right to do so. After all, Bertram still sleeps with her because physically they have always gotten along very well. But sleeping with each other is not the same as having a relationship and when he wants to have a relationship, she doesn't, and vice versa. They don't have a real relationship and their mutual expectations aren't very clear. As a result, Marian does not have the 'right' to be jealous, if such a right even exists.

Apart from that, Marian hates sleeping alone, which makes her vulnerable to Bertram's charms, and she is inclined to step into a situation that isn't good for her anymore. Furthermore, someone once predicted that she would only have two great loves in her life and Bertram is already number two. I do not like psychics who say such things, because once you have heard these things, you can't forget them. The only thing you can do is try to ignore the fearful voice in your head that keeps reminding you of how insecure you are feeling. In other words, it's difficult to make your own choices when you think you have just wasted your last chance and you don't want to be alone for the rest of your life.

Marian swears to me that she wants Bertram back and that she is prepared to do anything to get him, but I doubt it. There is so much drama and so many emotions attached to the whole situation that it does not seem entirely pure to me and I see age-old connections between the two that could affect the whole thing.

We start in aura layer 9, where her group agreements with other souls can be found. I come across four circles of connections with other souls, which give her a safe foundation for her current process and life goal. These agreements help her enter into her processes. They are her social safety net. Then we go to aura layer 18, the field of dealing with contrasts and contradictions (dealing with disappointment is also part of this) inside yourself and between you and others. In this layer, we work on getting clarity about her relationship with Bertram.

I instantly see a past life in France. 'Marian' is a woman who wears a chastity belt. It is a large metal suit, tightly secured and hidden. She has promised herself to Bertram 'forever' and the promise still stands. For that reason, she also thinks she can never respond to another man or fall in love with another man, let alone feel sexually excited about another man. I rewrite the promise, making it temporary, which means it is only valid for that past life, because that was what she meant at the time.

Then I see a kind of old tree rising from her heart chakra, which consists of old and dead connections. It makes me think of the Giant Fig Tree* I once saw in Australia, with its giant roots sprouting from it like big snakes. These grey-brown arms the size of trees are connections from past lives. They still exist and have not been detached. They use up a lot of energy, just like myomas. So Marian is still energetically connected to various main characters from past lives in an unhealthy way. Energy is still flowing from her to them and vice versa. These are lifelong connections that take a lot out of her and block and limit her current energy and love flow. So I start trimming. I carefully remove the superfluous connections, I cauterize the ends (both in Marian and the other party), I trim the rest and I remove the remaining dead branches and trimmings. When I have finished this part of the session, her heart chakra is open and clean.

This is all preparation for getting to work on the next relevant life with Bertram in layer 20. 'Marian' lives in a harem. It is Bertram's harem and he is clearly the boss; he is a very manly man. 'Marian' is just one of many women and does not have a strong position. She loves him very much, but he does not love her. He only loves her body, because she is a beautiful woman. She gives birth to three of his sons and her love for him, which at the time is still unconditional and profound, is too confronting for him. He avoids and ignores her. She becomes a mere shadow of her former self; she is put away and degraded to the lower hierarchical regions of the harem community. She suffers greatly from this because her most beautiful gift – her pure love – and she herself are not seen or appreciated.

This is one of the reasons why, in her current life, Marian has a tendency to seek attention and confirmation from others regarding her outward appearance. She is a good-looking woman, so she gets the confirmation and appreciation most of the time, but that doesn't solve the underlying problem. I remove the sting of the problem from aura layer 20, because it has caused her compass to wobble. She knew what pure love was and what it feels like when things are right, but in later life she started to behave in improper ways because of disappointment felt in previous lives. She no longer had the courage to trust the good.

The rest of this session is described in the chapter about aura layer 21.

Choosing what is good is the theme in aura layer 20 and we as human beings are not always able to assess what is pure. It is easier to do this for yourself, provided you are honest. But for other people, it is much more difficult. Can you appreciate a soul when it does not want to be born because it is afraid of a life as a handicapped boy? And is it possible that its birth is still the most elevating route?

And what if you are pregnant with a severely handicapped child and within the first three months of the pregnancy, you are told your child will have such a difficult life? Should you opt for an abortion or leave it to nature? Do you go along with the other things that cross your path? Which path contains the most light? Are you in favor of euthanasia in certain situations, in order to prevent unnecessary suffering? Or do you think the soul will leave its body when it is ready? How black-and-white is life? And can life be predicted?

The really big choices people can be confronted with, which are connected to aura layer 20, can never really be made unequivocally. Every human being and every soul is different, and what's good for one person or soul is not necessarily good for another. It's up to every individual soul to determine what is the most loving and light-filled choice. Letting go of your judgment about these matters is a very loving thing to do, because there is not a single human being on the planet who can really know what someone else should do.

Aura Layer 21: Knowledge of the Divine Origin of All Creatures

Knowing you are one with the Source, and that all creatures are of Divine origin and therefore have a pure essence, no matter how they behave, is the central theme in aura layer 21. It is about propagating the essence of life, the love in every human being and the love of the Universe, God or the Source, or whatever you want to call it, which is there for every human being. When you are working on issues in layer 21, you are acknowledging your true essence and you are trying to see it in others. You see that every human being is a Divine Soul wearing a human cloak and you experience love for All That Is – exactly as it is.

Josie is thirty-five and thinks she is on the verge of having a breakdown. When I tune myself to her, I notice her fear is justified. She is so tense that she is literally stiff all over, because she does not relax between her daily tasks. When she comes home, she has to run a busy household. I get a headache above my right eye and on the side of my head. It extends to my neck, and then I do something I'm not supposed to be able to do. I squint. It gives me a headache and I can feel this is caused by her brow chakra, her third eye, which is spinning sideways.

We start at the beginning and I tell Josie that she needs to release her accumulated tension between tasks, because otherwise her body will stay in hyper mode and the hormones responsible for releasing stress will not work as well as when she only releases her tension at the end of the day. I teach her a couple of exercises. We start with a muscle relaxation exercise**, so she can experience what her body feels like when it's relaxed. This enables her to notice when she is accumulating tension and find out what causes it. That way, she can learn to release the tension before getting into trouble. I also teach her my chakra cleansing exercise**, so she also notices energetically where something is blocked and she can remove the blockage herself, without relying on me.

Next, I go to aura layer 21 and I see that she saw a ghost at the age of seven, which scared the living daylights out of her. The ghost was very negative and she was terrified. Since that experience, she has kept her sixth chakra closed off, because that prevents her from seeing anything. Whether she needs to or not, she closes it off just to be sure. Josie has two New Age children and is frequently confronted with their energies. One way or another, this has caused her sixth chakra to open up again, which causes the friction in her head. There is a conflict between the reopening of the chakra and her trying to keep it closed off. This causes her headaches, which she swallows away with aspirin.

The blockage is in layer 21, because all creatures are of the same origin, including the entities she is afraid of. When you start to sense that on a deep level and start to live accordingly, you can make contact with every creature and see the Divine in them. Of course, it is advisable to be aware of the fact that there are malevolent creatures – but even they are of Divine origin, and when you can really feel that, you will soften your outlook, judgment and opinion.

I go to her thirteenth layer, where I come across an egg-shaped blob that extends from her forehead to her navel. It is related to her panic and her reaction to seeing ghosts, but not all of it is entirely hers. In the thirteenth layer, your brain impulses are affected by the way other people think and that is what bothers her most. There is a lot of thinking and judging going on around the world regarding ghosts and this disturbs her. It does so literally, because it affects her bodily functions. I clear up the field and disconnect her from the way the masses think about this subject.

Entities are not scary; you just have to know what you can and cannot do. Josie indicates being interested in helping people go to the Light. I explain to her how this works and how you can set boundaries when doing it, because otherwise it can occupy you for days and she doesn't have time for that. This greatly reduces her fear of seeing entities again and she goes back home reassured and relaxed...with homework, because she is going to relax her body and cleanse her chakras every day.

A bit more about Marian from the chapter about aura layer 20, the woman who had difficulty letting go of her ex-husband. In aura layer 19, I come across a past life in Ireland. She is Gaelic and is living in a castle. This is where the dissociating originated. She experiences very unpleasant things and teaches herself to float just above her body when life gets too tough. Bertram, her ex-husband in her current life, is a woman who helps her and tends to her wounds. This creates a strong bond and deep trust between the two of them. I leave their bond intact, but I neutralize part of their history in layer 19, so she will stop dissociating. This will make it easier for her to consciously experience new things.

Next, I see a beautiful image in layer 21: I see a water treatment plant, which I can use to remove the muck from several lives. She can return to the Source and make contact again with the Divine in every being. All her negative experiences have caused her to forget how to do this. It is quite difficult, if not impossible, for most people to see someone who has done all kinds of terrible things to them as a Divine being and learning soul. I am allowed to remove all negative thoughts and feelings caused by her negative experiences.

Then, I work on a difficult issue in layer 21. I detach three very nasty entities and guide them to the energetic gateway in the garden. That gateway is the entrance to other light levels and I am sure there is a good reason why it's in my garden. I see it as a 'Stars in Their Eyes door', from the TV show in which contestants walked through a special door and came out the other way having undergone a total transformation to impersonate showbiz stars. Similarly, our planet has places where energy can be more easily transformed, and I can help entities go to different places that are more appropriate for them. I am told they are not allowed to go straight to the Light – they first have to acquire more experience – but they can go to the gateway and make a step in the right direction to a more positive in-between plane.

The entities talk to Marian when she is asleep, which affects her in a negative way. They feed her with impure thoughts that lead to impure choices. That's why they are in layer 21. When they have been removed, she will go back to her pure essence and know the essence of life.

After the session, Marian feels strangely calm. All the drama has gone and she is quiet. A few days later, she tells me Bertram has lost his attraction for her. I explain to her that he might still be attracted to her, because he is still carrying with him those past lives, and that it would not surprise me if he tried to run after her a bit faster; but that she has also gained a lot, because she can feel again what she does and does not want. This is much easier for her now and, after a couple weeks, she tells him she can no longer go along with the casual way he treats her. She loves him very much and wants either a real relationship or none at all. A purely physical relationship is out of the question. Given the fact that he has indicated he does not want to commit, she decides she only wants to have a loving friendship with him, which is possible because the old fig tree has been trimmed.

Millie is a twenty-five year-old teacher who seems to suffer from Chronic Fatigue Syndrome (CFS). She is constantly exhausted, has migraines, her muscles ache and teaching has become very difficult for her. Her back is also bothering her; there are days when she is not even able to get out of bed. When she loses her job because of budget cuts, she takes it personally and thinks she has failed in her work. That makes her so insecure that she is thinking about quitting the profession and re-educating herself for a different type of work. Her spleen, where her life energy is formed, is stinging, and although her health has failed her for years, I feel it won't be long before she feels better.

In aura layer 12, in which past lives are worked through in the form of family karma, I come across a sexual assault in Amsterdam, when she was sixteen years old. This is the reason why initially she does not have the courage to make an appointment with me. She doesn't want to talk about this trauma and, fortunately for her, she does not have to; I can see it without talking about it and I am allowed to remove it. But if she does not want to talk about it, I can't explain to her that it is related to her family karma.

Next, in layer 14, I see the consequences other people's thoughts have for Millie's life. When she is nineteen, she suffers severe brain damage due to a car accident and she is in a coma for several weeks. She survives, but there is some residual damage and she has to learn almost everything anew. This process is influenced by the Mental Field of Humanity, which contains the thoughts about what is possible and reasonable after brain damage. There is an energetic scar running from the left side of her crown to her nerve bundle.

It turns out this was not the first time she suffered brain damage: in a life in 1631 in Nicaragua she is a young man of sixteen who is hurt by an earthquake. He cannot move any more, he cannot control his muscles, because that part of his brain no longer works. Something fell on his head. 'Millie' is afraid he will let his mother down if he dies, because his father is already dead and there is only the two of them. In her current life, this fear of dying expresses itself in the exact opposite way, namely in the form of separation anxiety, the fear of being abandoned by others. Her fear is rooted in her heart. I neutralize it, so her muscles and brain function again and there will not be any echoes from past.

Next, in layer 21, I heal the field that affects layers 14 and 12. She knows again who she really is, and that others are also souls on their way home. She takes along that knowledge to the other layers, causing the final sharp edges to disappear, and then we have finished for the day.

She calls me one week later. Millie can hardly believe how well she feels. She is a lot fitter, has no muscle and back pain anymore and she has found a new job out of the blue. She is teaching again.

Joseph is an intelligent, boisterous seven-year-old boy when he visits my practice for the first time. He immediately starts asking questions about how everything I do works and wants to know if he can take apart the anatomy model I have in my practice. I tell him he can, and I also let him take apart the head with brain parts. He is astonishingly good at reassembling it; he is even better at it than I am.

Joseph is officially diagnosed with ADHD and Asperger's syndrome, a form of autism. He also has nettle rash and is bullied at school. He doesn't have any friends and he feels lonely. He has built up quite a lot of anger and frustration and has mentioned several times that he wants to die. That is why his parents have asked me for help, to see if something can be improved so that Joseph can start enjoying life more.

The first thing that strikes me is that Joseph does not look me straight in the eyes. He feels overstimulated, which makes him very fussy. His crown chakra is far too open, which allows the subtle world to come in too easily. Both his spirit guides and nasty entities are constantly bombarding him. This is bothering Joseph. In a way, he hasn't really arrived on Earth and he has no idea what he has come here to do. He still has to learn how to handle the impulses fired at him and his chakras are unbalanced: his sixth and seventh chakras are too open, so he receives too much input there, while his first chakra is closed off, so he is not grounded and therefore can't let go of all the extra tension caused by the extra input of the sixth and seventh chakra.

I feel a large lump of anger and there is a lot of tension around his stomach; he is resisting physically. I indicate that the doctor's diagnosis could have been worded somewhat more carefully, because I can clearly see the Asperger problem and I can do something about it. I can alleviate the stress in his head and release the pressure, to a certain extent, but he will always carry it with him, because he has signed up for it for this life. It is his specific degree of difficulty.

But the ADHD is a different story. I even wonder if it really is ADHD. I would like to tell him that, from my perspective, the diagnosis is a bit too easy. I think the 'ADHD' has more to do with the fact that he is highly sensitive and he tries to release the overstimulation by being hyperactive, which is also a way to release tension. However, for now, he will continue taking his medication and we will not do anything without consulting his doctor.

In aura layer 6, his personal traumas of his current and previous lives, I come across two past lives. In the first, he is a five-year-old Native American girl and her tribe is wiped out. She dies angry, actually very angry, because she doesn't get her way. She can't do what she planned on doing at the soul level, because she dies too soon; she takes this frustration to her current life.

Next, there is a life in the Philippines. He is a six-year-old boy who suffers from malaria. He dies, so again he cannot do what he came to do. As a result, he has nettle rash on his head and the themes from his past life are 'I want to finish what I have come to do' and 'impatience'. There is still so much he wants to accomplish. I remove the irritation and we round off the session. I see the relaxation and softness in his eyes and bring this to his mother's attention. This allows her to see which way the wind is blowing.

As mentioned, Joseph is highly sensitive, so I am extra careful about how much I remove per session. His mother calls me three days later and tells me that the first day after the session he was quite unmanageable, but things have improved since that day.

Three weeks later, Joseph comes in for his second session. His eyes are beaming, he makes eye contact and he instantly begins to talk. Among other things, he tells a story about how dirty he is. To be honest, I have no idea what he's talking about. All I see is a normal, clean boy. Of course, all my anatomy models have to be taken apart and reassembled again. While he is doing this, I am trying to find out what he meant by 'dirty', but I still don't notice anything strange about him. It turns out to be an old issue that is emerging now.

Today we work in layer 12 and will keep doing that during the following sessions: healing past lives in the form of family karma. He is confronted with all these issues so he can heal them with the help of his family, especially his mother. The first time, it is a past life in which he is a thirty-two-year-old woman. She has 'scabies'. In fact, it is psoriasis, but because she looks so 'dirty' and the man she falls in love with doesn't want to have anything to do with her, she commits suicide. She does not belong and is aggressive and angry. This is the life where Joseph's idea that he is dirty originates. An old thought that can be removed now.

During the following session, I come across two past lives: one as a boy who is enormously aggressive due to the fact that he is discriminated against. He dies when he is five years old. In the other life, he is a girl who dies angry at the age of six after being beaten with a stick by her tribal chief. Angry, angrier, angriest.

The beautiful thing is that Joseph is becoming calmer and calmer, and that when he is taking a bath at home and his mother tells him to sit down, he does so instantly. They are both astonished about the fact that he is actually listening to her.

Then there is another life in layer 12, as a woman in Russia. She is torn apart by rules and is very angry because people have abandoned her and don't come to rescue her.

During the following session, there is a very tough issue in layer 13, including several entities. We remove them and clear up the area they can attach to. And Joseph keeps improving. I give him some protective flower remedies and, a few weeks later, we start in layer 7: his life plan can be readjusted. The evil can be removed, because he has been trying to deal with it long enough. With this, we can finish off his anger issue and move on to other themes.

After he has given me a drawing he made himself, depicting fresh flowers, we go to layer 12, the family karma layer, and we come across a life in ancient China. He is a man and he draws Chinese symbols. He's a real bantam. Part of him is stuck in that life and doesn't know he is living his current life, so we perform a soul retrieval to get that part back to the 'here and now'. (Only now his mother tells me he frequently jumps around the room making kung fu movements. And he only wants to eat Chinese food with chopsticks. The chopsticks are still there.)

Then there is a life as a doctor. His pancreas gets overstimulated by substances injected into him in a German concentration camp during World War II. I think it is insulin and it's about the way it affects his brain and bodily functions. But there are also images of a similar experiment somewhere else and that one is about hormones, the thyroid gland and leukemia.

Then there is a life in 1968. He used drugs and there are still energetic residues in his seventh layer, obstructing his life plan. It takes me more than ten minutes to remove this old field. Next, through layer 8 (a personal soul agreement with his mother) he can finally come down to earth, and his throat chakra is cleansed because he has said so many unkind things to her.

Meanwhile, Joseph has a real girlfriend, they are 'going steady', and the school is questioning the ADHD diagnosis. His behavior has changed so much lately that they have doubts about labelling him that way.

The following session takes place several months later. His eyes are soft and straight almost the entire time and he makes direct eye contact more often. But Joseph has a headache. Something is wrong with his right eye and throat. The day before, he changed his medication. It doesn't feel right at all and I attune the new medication to his third layer, his thinking capacity. It does him a lot of good. Then I remove the energetic cord* of one of his friends, which goes to the back of his stomach chakra and extends to his sixth chakra (third eye) at the front. Joseph is finished for the day.

Five months later, he visits me again. He still looks fine and it is clear to me that he is enjoying the visit. This time he says he hears entities and although sometimes he invents the strangest things, he is not inventing this. He can see them and describes one that he sees with his eyes closed, with his third eye. He can even draw the entity. I can sense he is absolutely right. I see entities differently, with my eyes open, but in the end we read the same energy cloud and we just do it in our own way. It is one of his spirit guides and when he tells me it's a blue girl, something comes to my mind. Itmam, my blue Muppet eagle from the Pleiades, is also blue. So I ask Itmam if the blue girl is from the same area as he. This is indeed the case.

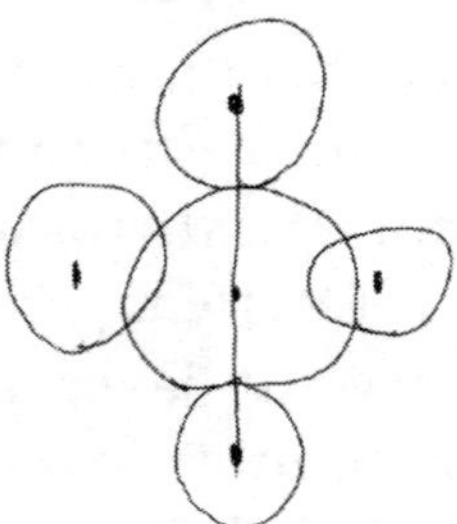

Figure 10: The picture Joseph drew to show how he perceives his guides

I explain to Joseph that the blue spirit guide can be trusted, but that unfortunately this is not the case with most entities, because they have not first gone through the car wash and to the Light. So for the time being, he should send them away.

Otherwise, they could make him do all kinds of weird things. At best, they will start with positive things so you are blinded to their dubious nature, but eventually things go wrong, because they are not focused on your highest good. I do an aura protection exercise** with him and his mother, and we agree that he will call me if he is afflicted by anything he can't get rid of. At the moment, he is going through energetic growing pains, and in a few months he will be ready for understanding and dealing with the next issue.

Finally that afternoon, we work in aura layer 21. A life emerges in which Joseph is a girl who dies at the age of nine. She has always lived an honest and pure life, a child of God, typically layer 21 and very pure. Nevertheless, it hasn't done her much good. She lives in a ghetto, she is penniless and, although she does not do anything wrong, she is killed after a fight between vying gangs. She has doubts when she dies. Would she have survived if she had been tougher? As a result, Joseph can be more sensitive in terms of listening to negative entities in his current life. The treatment allows him to go back to the Source, from which he is otherwise secretly lured away.

When I look at how much happier Joseph has become since we first started, I am happy and grateful that I have been allowed to help this boy really start living on Earth. He has a much easier life now.

I will end this chapter with another of those grateful meetings. My client is Jeremy and his good friend Viktor died a few months earlier in a skiing accident. A few days after the accident, Jeremy called me to ask if I could contact Viktor, but it was too soon. Viktor needed some time to go through his transition and deal with his life experiences and unexpected death. Now he has done so and thinks it's great that his friend wants to visit him like this. When I ask him to come, he does so immediately.

Viktor feels like a bouncing ball, one big heap of energy – someone who enjoys life, I can sense that immediately. And he feels so alive that I can hardly believe he has no physical body anymore. His energy is so strong that I think of something. I ask Jeremy to open the palm of his left hand and I ask Viktor if he can tickle it. I hear 'no problem' and Jeremy looks at me somewhat dumbfounded. He can feel Viktor tickling him. I enjoy witnessing it.

Then I tune to Viktor and he has a lot to say. He is sharp, funny and very straightforward. When I tell him that, he replies, 'Look who's talking!' and he is absolutely right. He makes me laugh and I translate everything I hear for Jeremy.

Viktor shows me a lot of images. First, there is a lot of white. It's the snow of the avalanche that swallowed him up. I see the images from the sky, as if I'm a bird that hangs above it and watches what happens. He shows me a snow scooter and how he is transported. I get a terrible headache, so I think he must have sustained brain damage. The strange thing is that I see it all through Viktor's eyes. He shows me what he saw, but something is wrong. I see it from above and I don't understand why. Suddenly I realize what it means and ask him if I am right. 'Yes,' he says. 'I had already left my body before I was officially pronounced dead. Immediately after the hit and before the snow scooter came. I was hanging there and I watched. The whole time.'

He continues: 'I launched out of my body at an enormous speed. Cool!' I can see it happen, as if he is being launched from an F-16 in an ejection seat. He is only connected to his physical body by a silver cord.

I repeat his words to Jeremy and tell him I am under the impression that he is quite a speed merchant. Jeremy chuckles and fully endorses this.

Viktor goes on and says he did not have any pain. Not even when he was transported to the hospital. He waited until his brother was there and then left his body. He did not feel anything; he did not have any physical pain and he was not in his physical body anymore. I see that Jeremy is reassured, but Viktor continues his story.

He has a message for his friend: 'When it is your time, do not resist.'

I add: 'If you say to yourself in advance, *When it's my time, it's alright and I will cooperate,* this will help you and your death will not be such a struggle.'

But Jeremy says you can never know if it's really your time, because perhaps you are supposed to learn how to fight for your life and he plans on doing exactly that. He is afraid of dying, so I explain to him that you can program yourself by saying that when it really is your time – and only your soul knows when that is – you can feel it and the best thing you can do is allow it to happen and not swim upstream. But for the moment, this falls on deaf ears.

Next, Viktor talks about Jeremy's sister. She died when she was still a child, when she was run over by a car. Jeremy hasn't fully come to terms with it yet. Viktor takes away part of the pain with his words. He shows me images of the accident and says she also left her body immediately after the hit. The thing is that Jeremy has lived with the pain of knowing that his sister screamed with pain before she finally died. I ask Viktor how this is possible. Can a body still function when the soul has left it? Viktor says this sometimes happens. The body can still show a physical reaction, for example, in the form of a sound or involuntary movements, but the essence, the soul, does not feel anything at that stage. The soul has already left the body, but it is still connected to it through a silver cord. When the cord is gone, human beings die instantly. But sometimes someone is hanging above his or her body, so he or she has time to realize that (s)he is dying. And sometimes this takes place in front of bystanders or surviving relatives. It gives them just a little more time to realize what's going on.

I want to be absolutely sure and ask again, 'She had no pain at all when she was lying there? She didn't feel anything?'

'No,' Viktor says, 'just like me, she had already gone before she could feel anything. Her crying could be seen as a physical reflex. Believe me, it was over in the second.'

I don't know what to say and I set to work. In layer 21, I remove a large lump related to Jeremy's fear of dying. In this twenty-first aura layer, people work on themselves by connecting to the fact that they, too, are of Divine origin. This often happens by initially thinking the opposite and therefore experiencing the opposite. They feel too small or too unimportant and apparently aren't worth so much light and love. Jeremy did not trust his own Divine origin. This prevented him from seeing that he, too, is essentially light and love, and this is what caused his fear. He knew he wanted to go to the Light after his death, but he doubted if he belonged and would be welcome there.

When I finish working on this issue, I notice something is bothering Viktor. Just before he died, he was double-crossed by a friend of his and that is what I am feeling. So I ask him if I am able and allowed to clear that up for him and, fortunately, this is the case. I do it and thank him for his explanation and help for Jeremy. He replies by saying he will come and tickle him once in a while. When Jeremy works too hard or takes things too seriously, Viktor will come and interfere, just like in the old days. But he says it in such a playful manner that I am sure it will only do Jeremy good. He can feel him and he can still enjoy their friendship, only in a different form.

And if he is capable of doing that now, I'm sure that when it's Jeremy's time to leave his body and make the great crossing, Viktor will be waiting for him, to guide him so it will go as smoothly as possible. A wonderful thought.

The Light within you and others and focusing on it is the key to healing any pain points in your twenty-first aura layer. It's about having the courage to trust the fact that you yourself are also a point of Light and, therefore, can be a point of Light for others. Light is contagious. One spark can be enough to breathe new life into the extinguishing Light of others. Do not hide your Light under a bushel, but let it spread out.

Marianne Williamson described it the best way I have ever heard:

'Our deepest fear is not that we are inadequate.
Our deepest fear is that we are powerful beyond measure.
It is our light, not our darkness, that most frightens us.
We ask ourselves,
Who am I to be brilliant, gorgeous, talented, fabulous?
Actually, who are you not to be?
You are a child of God.
Your playing small does not serve the world.
There's nothing enlightened about shrinking so that other people won't feel insecure around you.
We are all meant to shine, as children do.
We were born to make manifest the glory of God that is within us.
It's not just in some of us, it's in everyone.
And as we let our own light shine, we unconsciously give other people permission to do the same.
As we're liberated from our own fear, our presence automatically liberates others.

Epilogue

Epilogue

As you will have noticed, this book contains channeled information. This information was given to me by deceased people, spirit guides, angels and other Light Beings. Part of the information can be checked, but a large part cannot.

I needed the information in order to sketch a broader perspective, a new perspective from which to look at one's daily reality and the situations I describe. ADHD, fear of the paranormal, obstinacy, depression, (un)faithfulness, sprained body parts, abuse, alcoholism, autism, insomnia, addiction, dismissals, choice of partner, neck complaints – almost everything people go through looks very different when viewed from the perspective that a soul is simply collecting experiences. Sometimes this makes it easier to deal with the situation and prevents you from judging too quickly, and sometimes it does not. I hope I have given you an impression of the diversity of ways in which those learning experiences can express themselves. And as you know, there are as many ways to gain experiences as there are souls.

Unfortunately, the type of learning theme does not always make clear in which aura layer there is a blockage and to which development it contributes. For example, you can have a blockage in aura layer 6 in the form of being abandoned by your loved one that only bothers you, and you can grow if you deal with the situation. But if the blockage is in layer 8, it is part of the soul agreement between you and your ex-lover. Then both of you will learn from the experience.

If the blockage is in layer 9, it is part of a group agreement. Then it's possible that one person has to be 'abandoned' in order for another person to enter into a relationship with someone else. If the blockage is in aura layer 12, your family energy will benefit from your experience and you will heal an issue that positively affects the energy fields of your relatives. If the blockage emerges in layer 18, it's about practicing how to deal with contrast. Then it's about things not going your way and how you deal with that. If the challenge is found in aura layer 21, it is about learning to see the person who has left you alone as the Divine being he or she essentially is. In short: the learning theme does not necessarily say anything about its possible goal. In order to find out the goal, you have to be able to read auras.

Fortunately, you don't have to be able to read or heal auras when you are going through your experiences, because although reading all this might give you the impression that people always need the help of a (paranormal) therapist or psychic, this is not the case for most (learning) experiences. Most of it you do on your own, usually without even being aware of it. Sometimes, however, it all becomes a bit too much or it takes too long, which makes it more difficult to deal with and let go of the things you have experienced. They can get stuck and form a blockage in your aura. In such cases, it is helpful to call in the help of someone who can assist you with that.

And when you are looking for someone to help you, birds of a feather flock together. Like attracts like, which also goes for energy. It applies to relationships and every other type of contact, so it also applies to the people who come to my practice. So I will mostly attract people who feel a resonance with who I am and how I work. Others will not even know I exist, which is fine, because that mechanism also enables me to focus on what I can do best. In that way, I can support the right people. I mostly work with complex problems related to the functioning of the brain, the nervous system, the hormonal system, themes of sexual abuse and other types of violence, and with life purposes and life goals. In most cases, my clients don't know beforehand where their problem resides, which is not necessary. Their problems are often related to the higher aura layers, which I think is very interesting, because it has allowed me to discover a new area of healing where I feel at home.

However, 'higher aura layers' are not better than 'lower' aura layers. The only thing it says is that when you have a problem in aura layer 10, it's not much use to work only in aura layer 3 because this will not result in a structural solution. Conversely, if you have a problem in layer 3, clearing up layer 10 won't do any good. It's always about knowing what you are doing.

Sometimes something higher and more expensive does say something about its quality – but what good are gold bars to you, which are seemingly more valuable, if you are hungry and there is not a slice of dry bread around? Everything has its value and, depending on the context, this value becomes clear. The environment determines what this value is according to earthly standards. It is totally subjective.

And just as the value of something is determined by its environment, the client describes his relationship with his parents and other people in the subjective biased way he sees things. And sometimes I take over the client's choice of words, but this doesn't mean I see people the same way the client does. However, it can be helpful, because the choice of words tells me where I can find a problem. This, in turn, gives me clues for my next question, leading to the lighting up of the auric problem area. And when that field is activated, I can work in a more goal-oriented way. It's that simple.

When I am working, I have no judgment or preference and I do not see the qualities of people they are struggling with as *problems*. I see all sensitivities and characteristics as opportunities for personal growth. Since my own illness, I have thought: people have their characteristics and qualities for a reason and they make you who you are. Why would an aptitude for mathematics be more valuable than dyslexia or diabetes? They are only characteristics to be dealt with. What's more important is what you do with them, how you use them for your self-development. That is part of the game we are playing together here. And it goes without saying that I also struggle with my characteristics once in a while. After all, I am a human being, just like everybody else.

However, opportunities for self-development or not, I deal with a lot of distress in my practice. I sometimes wonder why things have to be so difficult and painful, particularly in relationships. Then I look outside and I see my neighbors slowly walking by. They are real gems. He is seventy-three and she is a few years older. They have been together for fifty-seven years. And she still occasionally touches his arm when I'm talking to them and he still helps her get in the car and I still see them walking hand-in-hand. Their love for each other is radiant, and although I know their life paths have not been strewn with roses, I enjoy watching them and I am nourished by their warmth. It shows me it is possible to live in love with yourself and each other.

People sometimes ask me if pleasurable past lives can also be read; after all, something always seems to have gone wrong. The answer is simple. Of course there are happy or fulfilling lives. In fact, there are many more than the negative lives I come across. But you don't have to focus on them, because they do not affect you negatively in your current life. Apart from that, I work with people's traumas and blockages, which means I am focused on them, so it would be a waste of time and energy to read five positive lives first, which we don't have to do anything with. I am quite goal-oriented. It is always my aim to do what is necessary for the client I am working with. And as I said before, I do not make it up myself; I tune into their soul.

With all this goal-orientation and the aura layer theory, and quite a number of cases with positive end results, it seems life might be just as 'makeable' as I used to think. However, reality is different. And I certainly don't want to give you the impression that from a human point of view I always succeed in helping people solve their problems. When people ask me why most of the time I do succeed but sometimes I do not, I can't explain it to them. I don't know. I can usually sense when I can help someone and I am often told what the result will be. Sometimes the end result differs from the information I have been given beforehand, which leaves me sort of empty-handed.

Part of the game is that souls determine what they have come to do on Earth and which choices they make. You as a human being, the earthly expression of your soul, determine a lot of the details by making daily choices and by deciding how you deal with everything you experience. But there are also things that are beyond your control. You don't exactly understand why or how, but you have to deal with them. That's life. In the end, it's not in your or my hands. Everything is written in God's hands and all you can do is surrender to that great mystic power giving direction to our lives.

That's the way I see it, so I am not afraid of death. At least, that's how I feel right now. I am very curious about what else is there. Sometimes I am allowed a glimpse of it, but I'm aware that it is only a fraction of what there is. It is always limited to what I can understand with my human brain. So I am intrigued by what will happen when my soul is not wrapped up in my body anymore and it's my time to make the big crossing –

and really go on a journey of discovery.

Acknowledgements

Acknowledgements

I would like to thank the people and (Light) Beings who have enabled me to write this book, both directly and indirectly and both recently and during the course of the years. Of course, everybody I have met has influenced me and therefore helped shape who I am, one way or another. It all depended on what I did with it myself.

First of all, I thank my clients for the trust they have put in me. Thanks to you, I have been able to accumulate the material for this book.

My special thanks go out to:

Wim Vaags, my professor and thesis supervisor at the TU (University of Technology in Eindhoven) who, as I thought at the time, died prematurely during my final graduation project. You were the first one who really saw me as I am and who had more faith in me that I had myself.

Jan Barends, the first soul I consciously recognized. By standing by me and not letting yourself be put off (too often), you have helped me with your warmth and humor to face my demons and tackle them so they are now a thing of the past. You have no idea how grateful I am for that.

My mother, Ria Grandiek, and loving stepfather, Piet Meij, for your unconditional love and support and your willingness to be open to my somewhat peculiar personal path.

Erna Peters, dear friend and colleague with whom I can share so much in good times and bad, I also thank you for working with me on Rose's case.

Joyce Heijnen, for your enormous power and love. Courageous, sweet friend, your so-called black-and-white view of things helps me tremendously!

Annelies Wagemakers, you seem to be even more differentiating and non-judgmental than I am, and yet so human. You are very dear to me.

Daan Fousert, for an unasked-for life lesson. You made clear to me that working in the service of others is only possible if you respect your own boundaries.

Arrie van der Lecq, for your purity and tremendous devotion with which you stood by me and helped me grow during my illness.

Margreet de Klerk, because your passing put things in an even broader perspective. Thank you for your willingness to 'speak from the other side'.

Carlina Douw, dear sister, your illness was the basis for my explorations. Your way of looking at and dealing with things has put me on my personal path, because it is so different from mine and gave me food for thought.

Sjoerd Roorda, because you taught me what enjoyment is and what loving someone really is about.

Senna Douw, my sweet dog, who time and time again brings me back to the 'here and now'. You are pure love and teach me that I deserve it too.

My children, who have not taken on an earthly form, yet have told and taught me so much.

My spirit guides Beatrice, Itmam and Mutawi, doctor Shalazar and Harakin (I promise I will never call you HaraKiri again) and all the others who support me so often and unselfishly during my treatments and contemplations.

Mechthild de Leijer, for your faith and trust in me. God needs human hands to do his work and you are a wonderful set of hands.

My Dutch publisher, Jitske Kingma from Elikser Publishing Company, for your humor, your allergy to patronisation and the fact that you recognized my manuscript as being valuable. I am very grateful to you that, with your help, I could publish it.

Lisette Janssens, for your support and friendship (and taking care of Senna) during the – oftentimes laborious – process of getting this book published in English.

Carla de Hoog, Marja Bogaard and Myriam Reulen for your efforts helping me during my search for an English publisher, and Ione Steinhäusler, Lynn Serafinn, Nancy Goodyear and Vrinda Pendred for your expertise and advice in relation to the publication of this book and all activities that were involved in this. I learned a lot from you!

Peter Nugteren, for bringing back a smile in my eyes and capturing it in the book's beautiful cover picture.

And, finally, thank *you* for reading my book and enabling me to share my experiences with you.

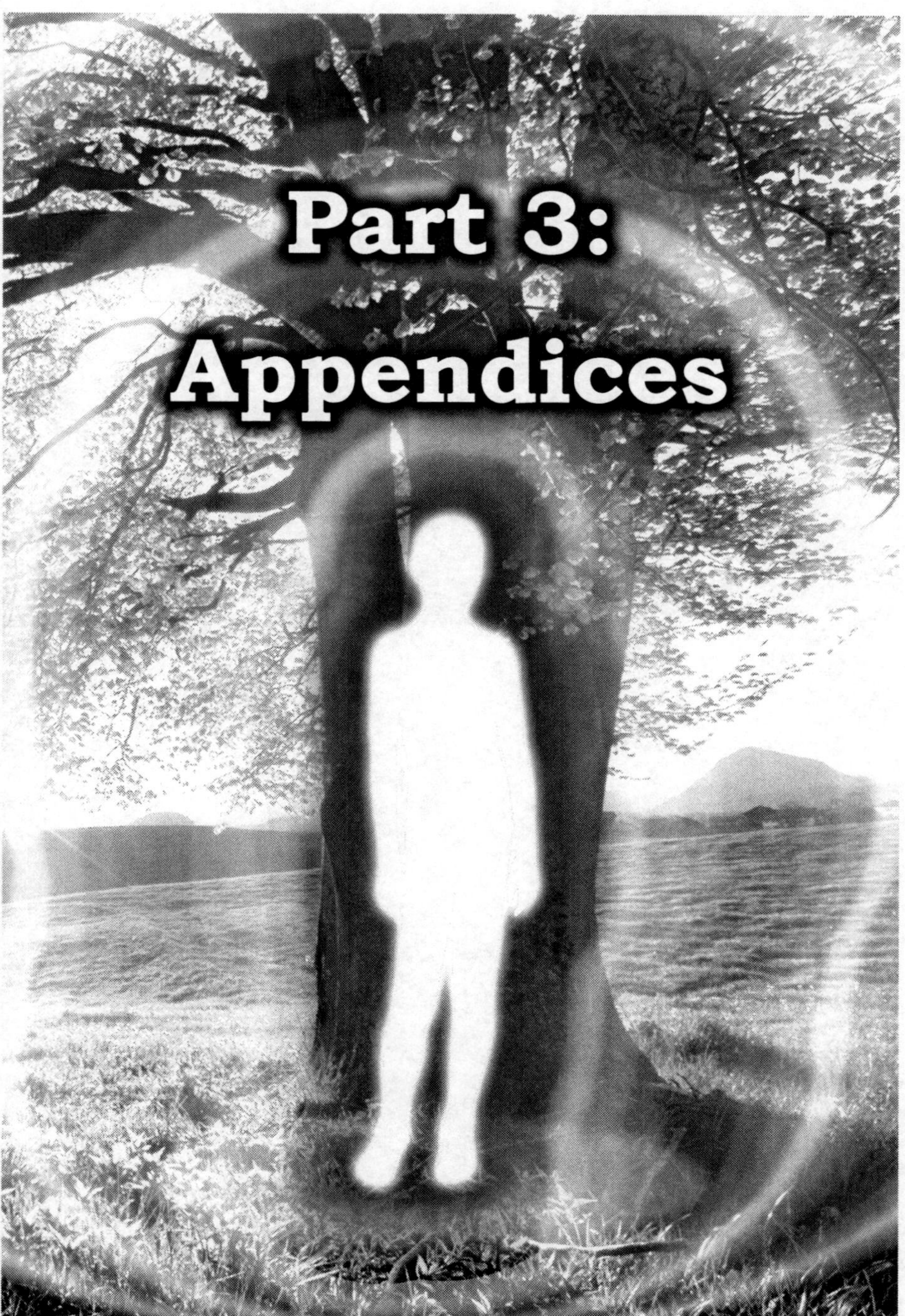
Part 3:
Appendices

Glossary

ADD: Attention Deficit Disorder. A disorder that causes the neurotransmitters in the brain to work differently to the average person. Inattention, limited attention for the environment and concentration problems are the most important symptoms.

ADHD: Attention Deficit Hyperactivity Disorder. A disorder that causes the neurotransmitters in the brain to work differently to the average person. The symptoms are lack of concentration, limited attention for the environment and hyperactivity.

Affirmation: a positively formulated phrase you repeat to yourself in order to program yourself and your body in the right way.

Angelica: angel of purity and the completion of old phases.

Angels: Light Beings of the highest level who reside in the spirit world. They usually do not incarnate as human beings, but are always ready to help people with their loving energy if people ask for it.

Archetypical field: a field in which all the experiences relating to a certain archetype/theme are connected and, together, form a field. For example, the archetype of the Mother, the Lover, the Don Juan or the Hermit.

Ascended Master: a soul that has incarnated and reached such a high level of consciousness and enlightenment that it belongs to specific group. Just like angels, an Ascended Master can be called in for help for good causes and has his own specific themes and qualities.

Ascension: awakening, enlightenment.

Atlantis: a civilization with a high level of psychological and spiritual knowledge and powers, which disappeared around 9500 B.C.

Aura: the personal energy field in and around your body.

Bioenergetics: a form of bodywork centering around muscle tension in the body. By performing exercises with the tensed part of your body, the accumulated tension will be released, together with the accompanying emotions and the stories behind them. This creates insight.

Blockage: a stagnation of energy.

Bodywork: a collective term for a number of therapeutic techniques that work with the physical body in order to resolve blockages in the functioning of a person, which is often linked to having the courage to feel emotions.

Candida albicans: a type of fungal infection.

Chakra: an energy distribution point in the body. For their position and specific function, see appendix 'Chakras and Their Functions'.

Cord: an energetic connection between two people, an energetic line you build up, which allows you to exchange energy with other people, even from a distance.

Consciousness: spiritual insight.

Deva: a spirit that belongs to the plant world, the spirit guide of a tree or plant.

Dopamine: a hormone that functions as a neurotransmitter in the brain and affects the experience of pleasure, happiness and wellbeing.

Earth ray: an energetic crack in the earth that absorbs the (positive) energy.

Emmanuel: guardian angel.

Emotional: relating to feelings.

Endocrine system: glands in the body that produce hormones.

Entity: a deceased soul that did not go to the Light, but stayed on Earth and is unable to go to the Light on its own.

Etheric pocket rescue (also called Humpty Dumpty): a liquid product from Aurasoma that repairs your aura after a physical mishap. This causes your body to go back to the situation before the mishap took place, instead of reacting to the injury.

Ezekiel: angel, prophet and priest.

Flower remedy: a naturopathic homoeopathic plant-based dilution. Used to be made by putting pieces of a plant in water in order to let the active qualities give off an energetic imprint and charge to the water molecules. Nowadays, more durable techniques are used to extract the active energies of plants, which leave plants intact and alive.

Foot reflex: reactivating the self-healing ability of the body through (reflex) points on the feet corresponding with organs and other parts of the body.

Gabriel: one of the archangels; the messenger from God of new hope and new ambitions and goals. Brings strength.

Giant Fig Tree: a very large hollow fig tree that can easily hold several adults.

Grounding: making contact with the ground through your feet to enable a surplus of tension to leave the body through the feet. Comparable to an earth wire.

Hilarion: Ascended Master who helps you let go of inaccurate or unnecessary self-images and who gives you direction and space to find yourself.

Implant: an artificially inserted energetic object that disturbs the energy and functioning of the aura and therefore of the body.

Isiaiel: angel of a more harmonious future.

Israfel: angel of poetry and the poetry of life processes.

Ithuriel: angel who helps you to live according to your true self.

Jofiel: angel who helps you find the right role or job in life.

Karma: the universal law of cause-and-effect. Everything has consequences, which are sometimes big and sometimes small. Sometimes you experience those consequences immediately and sometimes one or more lives later.

Kuthumi: Ascended Master who supports you with finding and taking your personal space on Earth. This strengthens the connection between the realms of the angels, human beings and Devas.

Lady Portia: Ascended Master who supports you with looking at yourself and others without judgment, with forgiving yourself and others, and with finding your inner balance.

Lemuria: name of the continent and civilization that existed on Earth about 75,000 years ago.

Life plan: the plan which, as a Soul, you agree to experience during your incarnation as a human being.

Light Worker: a medium who helps people with the development of their consciousness and growth in relation to the energetic transition of the Earth and its inhabitants in the years around 2012 and after.

Lyme disease: an infectious disease caused by the *Borrelia burgdorferi* bacterium. This bacterium is usually transmitted through tick bites.

Maha Chohan: Ascended Master who supports you with speaking from your heart.

Meditation: experiencing your inner self through inner peace and introspection.

Medium: someone who can communicate with souls who no longer have a physical body. For example, people who are deceased, spirit guides, angels or Light Beings of a different origin. A medium can read their energy and translate it into language. This is how he or she communicates with them.

Mental layer: layer 3; the layer where rational thoughts and thinking patterns are located.

Meridians: energy channels that are also used in acupuncture. They are a kind of transport channel that brings energy to and from an organ. This happens through your aura layers and nervous system and back again.

Metatron: archangel who connects you to your Divine origin and therefore helps you understand and accept your shadows.

Michael: archangel of truth and justice. Supports you with speaking your own truth and living according to it.

Morphogenetic field: a concept introduced by biologist Rupert Sheldrake; invisible energy field with a certain charge or frequency.

NEI: Neuro-Emotional Integration, therapy developed by Roy Martina, M.D. aimed at letting go of (hidden) emotions from the past.

Neuro: concerning the nervous system.

New Age children: children who are more sensitive than the average child and have the light body and nervous system belonging to the people who inhabit the earth and its energy field after the consciousness leap of 2012.

Orion: angel of new beginnings and a clean slate.

Orthomolecular therapist: therapist who uses orthomolecular food supplements. These body-friendly supplements contain the right (ortho) concentration of nutrients on a molecular level and support the body's self-healing powers.

Osteopath: specialist physical therapist who works with the loco motor apparatus/muscles and bones or organs.

Past life: expression for a previous life, a life which, chronologically, you lived before your current life, in a different physical body.

Pavlov: scientist who developed the stimulus response theory. Pavlov constructed the stimulus response theory. Every time he was going to feed a piece of sausage to a dog, he rang a little bell. Soon the dog learned to associate the two ideas – the sound of the bell and the sausages – and it started salivating when it heard the bell, even without being given any sausage. People can be conditioned into responding the same way, e.g. thinking you know what another person is going to say, or how something is going to work out, and acting on that beforehand. This is called a Pavlovian reaction. When you habitually respond to something that has not yet happened (and might never happen) you are less capable of determining your own behavior.

Physical: concerning the body.

Pleiades: a star cluster also known as the Seven Sisters or Seven Stars.

Pleiadic Light Worker: a medium who helps people with the development of their consciousness and growth during the energetic transition of the Earth and its inhabitants in the years around 2012 and is assisted by spirit guides of Pleiadic origin, called the Pleiadians.

Psychometrics: sensing what is going on in someone's physical body and aura.

Quintessence: a liquid Aurasoma product that connects you to a certain master energy and helps you develop your own master qualities.

Rachmiel: angel of consolation and compassion.

Raphael: archangel of healing and harmony; the bringer of Light.

Reincarnation: the process of rebirth. *Re* = again and *incarnation* = becoming flesh. This is the continuous process of the soul that chooses to be born into a human body, lives, dies and chooses to be born again, etc.

Ruhiel: angel of change and a new beginning.

Saint Germaine: Ascended Master who helps with the transmutation of negativity and offers protection against negative forces.

Shaman: natural healer of indigenous people and tribes who also communicates with the spirit world; similar to a Native American medicine man.

Soul: indestructible, eternal, Divine Essence of every living being.

Soul agreements: agreements between two or more souls to share certain experiences.

Spirit guides: Light Beings that form your personal team of assistants in the spirit world. Most people have three and they mostly stay with you during your entire life. In contrast with the angels, spirit guides have lived as human beings themselves and gained a lot of experience as a result. Using that experience and their larger view of your life plan, they give you advice about the things you encounter in your life.

Spiritual: concerning the meaning of life.

Trance medium: a medium who goes into a trance and lets (Light) Beings use his or her body to communicate with people. This being temporarily controls the medium's speaking functions, which enables him or her to communicate with people.

Transmutation: breaking off and processing toxins in your body.

Uriel: archangel who helps you with transformational processes; the transmutation of difficult energies and with creation.

Water vein: underground water stream that can cause disturbances and energy depletion aboveground.

The Chakras and Their Positions

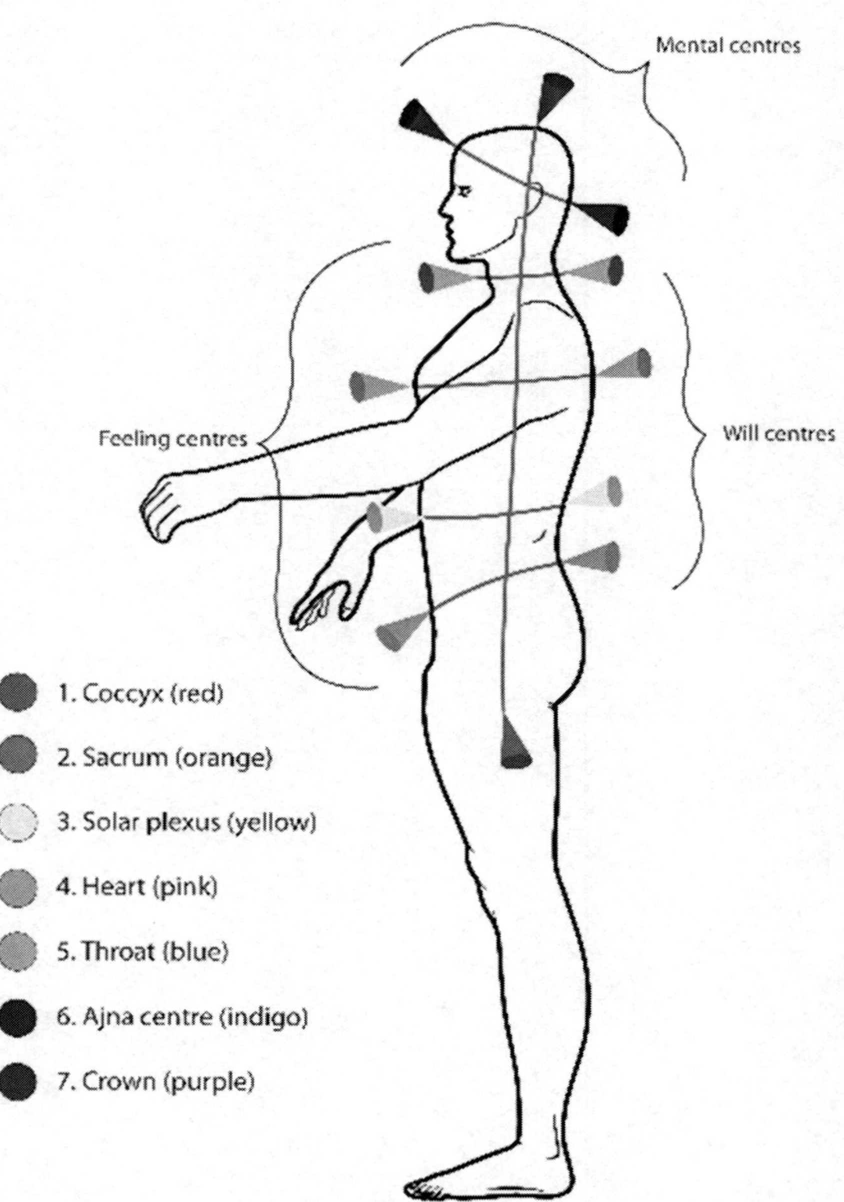

The Chakras and Their Functions

MAJOR CHAKRA	FUNCTION	LOCATION	HOW IT EXPRESSES ITSELF
1. ROOT	Vitality Physical and sensual desires Basis of the ego Materialisation of creation	1. Root	Will to live Quality of physical energy
2. SACRAL	Emotions Creational power Sexuality	2a. Sex chakra (front, 1 inch above pubic bone)	Quality of love for the partner Giving and receiving mental, physical and spiritual pleasure
		2b. Sacrum	Quality of sexual energy
3. SOLAR PLEXUS	Related to second chakra Connects willpower to the ego When functioning well, sublimation of first and second chakras Receiving station of other people's energy Sensing situations and people	3a. Front of sternum at stomach level 3b. Diaphragm at the back	Pleasure and expansiveness Spiritual wisdom and awareness of your own place and task in life and within the universe Healing Attitude toward own health

MAJOR CHAKRA	FUNCTION	LOCATION	HOW IT EXPRESSES ITSELF
4. HEART	Inner life, growth of desire to spiritual growth	4a. Heart centre	Feeling of love for and friendship with others
			Being open to life
		4b. Between shoulder blades	Your own will
			Will of ego, as opposed to the outside world
5. THROAT	Communication, connection with yourself and others, relations. Expressing yourself	5a. Throat	Receiving and assimilating
			Expressing who you really are
		5b. Lower cervical vertebra	Sense of self-worth within society or work
6. AJNA CENTRE (THIRD EYE)	Sense of reality, seeing clearly, transcending the material world, insight into the purpose of your life. Receiving station of the mental energy of others	6a. Forehead, between eyebrows	Ability to visualise and conceptual insight
		6b. Lower back of the head	Practical intelligence
			Ability to execute ideas in a practical way
			Ability to pick up other people's thoughts and ideas without using words

MAJOR CHAKRA	FUNCTION	LOCATION	HOW IT EXPRESSES ITSELF
7. CROWN	Contact with your higher self and the larger whole. Seeing and experiencing the creational power within yourself and around you, clairsentience	7. Crown	Integration of total personality in life and the spiritual aspects of humanity

Muscle Relaxation Exercise

Close your eyes. Breathe slowly. Follow your breath inside. Feel how you are breathing and do not change anything consciously. Feel how you are sitting on your chair, where your feet touch the ground, where and how you are sitting on the chair, and how the chair and the Earth support you.

Focus your attention on your right foot and contract all the muscles in your right foot. Keep them contracted as long as possible and then suddenly let go.

Turn your right ankle a few times in both directions and focus your attention on your right lower leg. Contract all the muscles in your lower right leg as long as possible. Let go.

Then contract the muscles in your right upper leg. Hold on, and when it's almost too much, let go.

Now go to your left leg. Focus your attention on your left foot and contract all the muscles in that foot. Hold on as long as possible and then suddenly let go.

Turn your left ankle a few times in both directions and go to your lower left leg. Contract all the muscles in your lower left leg and hold on as long as possible. Let go. Contract all the muscles in your left upper leg. Hold on and then suddenly let go.

Go to your pelvic area. Contract all the muscles in your pelvic area and buttocks and hold on as long as possible. Then let go.

Go to your lower abdomen. Contract all the abdominal muscles you know you have, and all the muscles you did not know you had, and hold on as long as possible. Let go.

Focus your attention on your chest. Take a deep breath and tighten your entire chest (if you wish, you can pull your arms to the back). Hold on. Just a little longer. Then let go.

Now go to your right shoulder. Lift it as high as possible and keep it tight. Then let go. Then go to your left shoulder and lift it as high as possible. Let go.

Go to your lower back and contract the muscles there, for example, by bending over. Hold on. And let go.

Then your upper back. For example, push your shoulders forward and arch your back. Hold on and let go.

Your right arm: make a fist and hold it for a few seconds. Let go. Move your right wrist and contract the muscles in your lower arm. Let go. Then your upper right arm. You can push it against your body, hold on and let go.

Left arm: make a fist and hold it for a few seconds. Let go. Move your left wrist and contract the muscles in your lower arm. Let go. Then your upper left arm. Brush it tightly against your body, hold on and let go.

Back to your shoulders: pull them up and pull your head down in between them at the same time. Let go.

Then your neck: pull your head slowly to the left. Slowly let go. Then pull your head to the right and let go. Push your chin against your chest and contract your muscles. Let go. Let your head fall backwards and let go.

Then pinch your hair to massage the skin of your head (if you don't have any hair, massage the skin of your head directly!).

Finally: make some funny faces using as many muscles as possible. Hold on as long as possible! And let go.

Massage your ears for a minute, get up and move a little. Then sit down quietly and notice what your body feels like.

Grounding Exercise

Sit quietly on a chair with your legs next to each other and your feet flat on the ground. Rest your arms in your lap or in a meditation posture, but don't cross them.

Close your eyes and take a few slow breaths. Relax. Keep breathing and follow the breath going in. Feel how you breathe and don't change anything about it. And while you are breathing like this, try to feel where in your body there is still some tension. When you feel it, just observe it; you don't have to do anything about it. Everything is as it is.

While you are sitting quietly, feel how you sit on your chair and where your feet touch the ground. You can feel where you make contact with the ground and chair, how you are sitting on your chair and how the chair and the Earth support you. If any thoughts come into your head, just observe them and don't do anything with them. You could see them as clouds floating by. Sometimes they float by and they always go away again.

Then focus your attention on your feet. Go into the soles of your feet and imagine them being glued to the earth. Next, imagine that roots begin to grow out of your soles into the earth. Right through your shoes, through the floor, through the cement, through different earth layers, deeper and deeper. You grow further and further and your roots become stronger and stronger, until you are securely anchored in the earth.

Imagine sucking energy from the Earth through your roots and your feet as if you were sucking a drinking straw. Every time you breathe in, you fill yourself with energy. You fill yourself with Earth energy through your feet and legs. It might be helpful to give the energy a color so you can better 'see' where the energy goes.

Next, while your body continues to fill itself with energy through your feet, focus your attention on your coccyx. Let a golden cord, drainpipe or tail extend from your coccyx into the earth. Through the chair, through the floor, through the cement, through the various earth layers, deeper and deeper. Further and further and stronger and stronger, until you feel strongly connected to the earth. And when your tail/cord/drainpipe is securely anchored, imagine that the tension still stuck in your body or swirling around in it goes into the earth through your coccyx. Every time you breathe out, you send what is still there but is of no use to you into the earth. And while you are doing that, you keep filling yourself with Earth energy. So when you breathe in, you fill yourself through your feet, and you release tension through your coccyx when you breathe out.

Then you go to your crown. Imagine a small sun above your head, and that you have a small slide in your crown that you can open a little. Feel how the sunlight fills you. Every time you breathe out, you fill yourself with the light, with the energy from the universe, and you release tension through your coccyx. And every time you breathe in, you fill yourself with Earth energy.

Do this exercise until you feel energized and calm.

Chakra Cleansing Exercise

Sit quietly and make sure you are grounded. In this exercise, you make use of the seven main chakras and a few other chakras that regularly do not function properly. For the position of the main chakras, see appendix: 'Chakras and Their Position'. For the functions, see appendix: 'Chakras and Their Functions'.

Close your eyes and ask for guidance from the Light. Put your hands on top of each other (for women, mostly left on right; for men, the other way around, so right on left).

Begin by going to your first chakra, your root chakra, which is situated at groin level. Put your hands on it and feel how the warmth of your hands slowly extends through your body. Imagine your hands giving light or being small heaters, and that your hands are the conduit providing you with purifying lights and healing energy from the universe. Imagine filling this chakra with all the energy you need (if you find this difficult, just focus on the warmth radiating from your hands and extending through your body) and release all the energetic waste and tension through this chakra and the drainpipe attached to it. You may want to yawn when you release the tension and your mind may calm down when this chakra has been cleansed.

When you have done enough, continue with your second chakra: lay your hands on top of each other on your lower abdomen, just above your pubic bone, and do the same there.

Next, go to your stomach and cleanse this chakra.

Then go to your heart chakra. In men, this is situated between the nipples, and in women, where the band of the bra crosses the sternum. Lay your hands on it, breathe slowly until everything that may be released is drained away and the space that has become available is filled with new clean energy.

Next, go to your thymus chakra. This is a minor chakra relating to growth. It is situated on your chest between your heart chakra and your throat. Relax it and cleanse it. Then go to your spleen, which is situated on your left side, right in the middle at about stomach level. Let go of the residual energy and fill it with new light.

Then go to your liver, which is right across your spleen on your right side, slightly more to the front. Do the same as you did with your spleen: replace the old energy with pure new energy.

Next, go to your throat. A lot can be released here and when you are working on your other chakras, your throat can feel a bit constricted because you are shifting the 'muck' toward the exit (via your throat to your mouth). Take your time to cleanse it and keep breathing. If you have to cough, don't put your hand in front of your mouth, because then you will put anything coming out back in again.

Your forehead (third eye) is next.

After that, go to your crown. Lay your hands on it and let the energy stream. Next, starting from your crown, fill your entire body with new, clear, pure light of exactly the right color. Leave it to your soul to determine the color.

Note 1: The filling and releasing can take 1 minute per chakra, or it could take 15 minutes. Just take the time needed and you will notice that when you do this exercise on a regular basis, you will get better at it and it will take less time. In most cases, it will take increasingly less time unless you are going through rough times. The chakra that takes longer to cleanse will give you clues as to what you have clogged up.

Note 2: You can also perform the exercise as above, but instead of lifting your hands from your body when moving to the next chakra, keep touching your body and take along everything between chakras. This is similar to squeezing a tube of toothpaste and pushing everything up to the throat so it can be released.

Note 3: When you are very restless, you can first work from top to bottom to ground yourself and then cleanse your chakras from bottom to top.

Meditation Exercise

Adapted from an original exercise by Gerard Brekelmans, the late Director of Academie voor Natuurgeneeskunde Zuid-Nederland.

Close your eyes and look inside cross-eyed. With your eyes closed, try to look at a point behind your eyes in the center of your head (your eye muscles make a small knot). Imagine a small round bullet on that focal point. Imagine your head is just the skin, only an outside layer, and let the bullet follow the skin starting at the front, going up between your eyebrows, in a straight line to the back, all the time making contact with the inside of your skin. The bullet takes along all the tension you come across on the way and it rolls to your crown, then to your neck, and then it goes to your coccyx via your vertebrae. Next, you pull a drainpipe from your coccyx into the earth and all the tension flows into it. This type of meditation also allows you to stay centered (in your own energy).

Aura Protection Exercise

Written in collaboration with paranormal therapist Anton Loos.

Imagine a balloon around your aura, the nozzle facing upwards. In the nozzle, there is a filter you can control. This allows you to let energy out or in.

Your aura is not too tight around you, but not too loose either. You give the balloon a positive color, today's color. This can be the same color as yesterday's, but it doesn't have to be. It is the color you need today and it doesn't have to be tomorrow's color either.

There is a golden sun above your head, shining its golden rays on and around you. Breathe in this golden energy through your crown chakra and send the energy through your entire body, all the way down to your toes. When you breathe in, you send the golden positive energy through your solar plexus (stomach chakra) into the balloon. Fill the balloon around your aura until it feels just right. Next, turn the nozzle toward the earth. Look at the energy inside the balloon. Is it the same all over or does it contain a different (contaminated) color? Breathe this contaminated color out of the balloon and replace it with today's color.

Now experiment with different materials the balloon is made of:

- Make it a brick balloon. How does that feel? Perhaps you want to make a window in it? Or would you like to be totally protected?
- Make it a wooden balloon.
- Make it a glass balloon.
- Make it a diamond balloon.
- Try what Perspex feels like.

- See what thick rubber feels like and then make your aura bigger, big enough for you to have enough space when somebody pushes against it and big enough so no one can cross your boundaries. You are the one who decides how far someone else can dent the rubber. If you wish, you can make it stiffer! Also experiment with the color of the rubber and see what happens.
- Make your aura wall out of cotton wads.
- Or make it into a waterfall that continuously cleanses you.
- Rub green soap on your aura and see how everything and everybody who wants to grab it cannot get hold of you.

Adjust the size of the balloon when, for example, you are in a crowd (party, shopping center). Release just enough energy from the balloon so you decrease its size and don't bump into other energies around you as much. Make it a little bit bigger when you are alone or when there is a lot of space around you. In this way, the balloon protects you against energetic attacks and allows you to stay centered.

If you aura is too wide, you may want to pull it in a bit. You can use the image of a lamp for this. Imagine your aura as the radiation of a lamp. Imagine that this lamp can radiate a certain amount of light. When it does this within a radius of ten yards, the light will be less intense than when it does it within a radius of one yard. Just look and see how far your aura radiates. Make the circle of light surrounding you smaller, increasing the intensity of the light; the light becomes brighter.

You can use your mind to pull your aura closer to you and tighter around you. This reduces its size, causing it to bump into other energies less frequently. Furthermore, it makes your aura more compact and more difficult to be penetrated by other energies. This gives you more inner strength and it keeps you centered.

If you know your basic attitude is quite open, you may want to focus on this on a regular basis when pulling your aura in.

Index of Client Issues

ISSUE	CLIENT	LAYER
BACK PROBLEMS	Michelle	19
BLADDER	Hank	4
BREAST CANCER	Mariah	15
BRUISES	Senna	1
BURNOUT	Jasper	18
CANDIDA INFECTION	Egbert	16
CHILDLESSNESS, DIFFICULTY CONCEIVING	Diana Eva Janet	20 16 8
CHRONIC FATIGUE SYNDROME	Millie	21
COLON CANCER	Tyler	20
COMMUNICATING AS NEW AGE CHILD	Norbert	17
COMMUNICATION WITH A CHILD WHO HAS DOWN'S SYNDROME	Sarah	12
COMMUNICATION WITH DOWN'S SYNDROME	Ben	12
COMMUNICATION	Bert Danielle	8 16
CONFIRMATION, SEEKING	Josh Mike	2 15

ISSUE	CLIENT	LAYER
EMOTIONS, DEALING WITH	Francis Jake Matt	15 15 7
EMOTIONS, LEARNING HOW TO FEEL	Charles	7
ENCEPHALITIS	François	13
ENERGY, GIVING AWAY	Mariah	15
EXCLUSION, FEELING OF	Dorothea	9
EXTRAMARITAL CHILD	Stefan	7
EXTRAMARITAL RELATIONSHIP	Stefan	18 7
FAITHFUL, BEING	Daphne	9
FAMILY KARMA AND ANGER	Tyler	20
FAMILY KARMA	Marie Susan	19 17
FATIGUE/TIREDNESS	Sandra	5
FEET, CROOKED	Jessica	18
FINANCIAL MANIFESTATION	Jim	11
FINANCIAL PROBLEMS	John	6
FOOD ALLERGY	Nate	6

ISSUE	CLIENT	LAYER
MAKING CHOICES	Raul	14
MISCARRIAGE	Marie	19
MONOGAMY	Daphne	9
NECK PROBLEMS	Mark	5
	Michelle	19
NERVOUS SYSTEM	Finn	5
NEW AGE CHILD	David	15
	Debbie	11
	Neil	12
	Norbert	17
OBSTINACY	Nate	6
ONE-NIGHT STAND	Joe	10
OVERBURDENED, BEING	Michelle	19
OVERBURDENED, MENTALLY	Jude	3
OVERSTIMULATED CHILD	Amber	13
OVERSTRAINED, BEING	Claire	14
	Emma	10
PARANORMAL CHILD, BEING	Dennis	13
PARANORMAL ADULT, BEING	Emma	10
	Jasper	18
	Margaret	16
	Nate	8
	Seb	10

ISSUE	CLIENT	LAYER
SEX ADDICTION	Charles	7
SEXUAL ABUSE	Millie	21
	Derek	14
	Elizabeth	8
	Jake	15
	Janet	8
	Marjorie	16
SEXUALITY	Annabel	16
SHOCK	Maria	11
SHOULDER PROBLEMS	Mark	5
SLEEPLESSNESS	Claire	14
	Tim	17
SLEEPWALKING	Leah	13
SADO-MASOCHISM (S & M)	Caroline	16
SELF-DEPRECATION	Ilse	10
SOUL AGREEMENTS	Don and Rose	Interlude
SPEAKING UP, FEAR OF	Joy	6
	Mariela	10
	Stefan	7
'SPRING CLEANING'	Margaret	16
STRESSED OUT	Josie	21
SUICIDE (GRANDFATHER)	Amber	13

About the Author

ANNEMIEK DOUW, MSc is a management coach, energetic therapist, light-worker, medium, trainer and author. Coming from an unlikely background in engineering, Annemiek has always been interested in how people think and grow at a physical, mental, emotional and spiritual level. In her work within the government and business sectors, she began to see how illness comes into people's lives, often making it unpredictable and seemingly out of control. This influenced her to start exploring bioenergetics and other alternative therapies, eventually leading her to complete a 3-year course at the Natural Medicine Academy South-Netherlands to become a paranormal therapist. In 1998 she dedicated herself to this work full-time.

She later fell ill herself for an extended period of time, which allowed her to gain first-hand insight into the human experience of illness, and to learn how the soul is an internal compass that continuously guides. Probing more deeply into how this compass works, Annemiek discovered 21 layers of the soul that influence our ability to grow and to heal in our bodies, minds and relationships. This discovery became the foundation of her unique healing style, and today Annemiek helps clients heal at many levels, and teaches them how to read this compass for themselves. In 2011 she shared her unprecedented work in the Dutch language book *De ziel in het licht van haar hogere auralagen*, followed in 2013 by its English language version, *21 Layers of the Soul*. In 2014 she will release a sequel to *21 Layers of the Soul* in Dutch, soon to be followed by an English version under the working title *More Layers of the Soul.*

Connect with Annemiek

Main website:
www.annemiekdouw.nl

English language website:
www.annemiekdouw.com

Blog (in English):
www.annemiekdouw.nl/blog

Twitter:
@AnnemiekDouw

Facebook:
www.facebook.com/Annemiek.Douw
www.facebook.com/AnnemiekDouwAuthorHealer

Receive a Free Gift from Annemiek Douw

Annemiek has prepared a handy, one-of-a-kind "21 Layers of the Soul Poster" for you, clearly showing all the aura layers, so you can hang it on your wall and identify the auras any time you wish. This is an excellent tool for anyone who works as a healer, is working with a healer, or is using the book for self-healing. The poster is downloadable as a high-resolution file, which you can print out and frame.

To download your aura poster, go to
www.annemiekdouw.nl/blog/21LayerPoster
Enter you name, email and the coupon code: **SENNA**